DELEUZIAN CONCEPTS

Cultural Memory

in

the

Present

Mieke Bal and Hent de Vries, Editors

DELEUZIAN CONCEPTS

Philosophy, Colonization, Politics

Paul Patton

STANFORD UNIVERSITY PRESS

STANFORD, CALIFORNIA

Stanford University Press
Stanford, California

Printed in the United States of America on acid-free, archival-quality paper

Library of Congress Cataloging-in-Publication Data

Patton, Paul.
   Deleuzian concepts : philosophy, colonization, politics / Paul Patton.
     p. cm.
   Includes bibliographical references and index.
   ISBN 978-0-8047-6877-1 (cloth : alk. paper) — ISBN 978-0-8047-6878-8
(pbk. : alk. paper)
   1. Deleuze, Gilles, 1925–1995—Political and social views. 2. Political science—
Philosophy—History—20th century. I. Title.
   B2430.D454P37 2010
   194—dc22

                      2009038159

Typeset by Thompson Type in 11/13.5 Adobe Garamond

To Moira

Contents

Acknowledgments

This book draws on essays previously published, although not always in the form in which they appear here. I am grateful to the publishers for permission to reprint material from the following articles and chapters:

"Mobile Concepts, Metaphor and The Problem of Referentiality in Deleuze and Guattari," in Maria Margaroni and Effie Yiannopoulou, eds., *Metaphoricity and the Politics of Mobility*. Amsterdam and New York: Rodopi, 2006, 27–46. With the permission of Editions Rodopi.

"Future Politics," in Paul Patton and John Protevi, eds., *Between Deleuze and Derrida*. London and New York: Continuum, 2003, 15–29. By kind permission of Continuum Publishing.

"Concept and Politics in Derrida and Deleuze." *Critical Horizons*, 4:2, October 2003, 157–175. With permission of Brill Publishing.

"Redescriptive Philosophy: Deleuze and Guattari's Critical Pragmatism," in Patricia Pisters, ed., *Micropolitics of Media Culture: Reading the Rhizomes of Deleuze and Guattari*, 29–42. Amsterdam: Amsterdam University Press, 2001. Extracts reproduced with permission of Amsterdam University Press.

"Events, Becoming, and History," in Jeffrey Bell and Claire Colebrook, eds., *Deleuze and History*, 33–53. Edinburgh, UK: Edinburgh University Press, 2009. Reproduced with the permission of Edinburgh University Press.

"The Event of Colonisation," in Ian Buchanan and Adrian Parr, eds., *Deleuze and the Contemporary World*, 195–220. Edinburgh, UK: Edinburgh

University Press, 2006. Reproduced with the permission of Edinburgh University Press.

"Becoming-Animal and Pure Life in Coetzee's *Disgrace.*" *ARIEL: a review of international english literature*, Special Issue: Law, Literature, Postcoloniality, 35:1–2 Spring 2006, 101–119. Reproduced with the permission of the Board of Governors, University of Calgary, AB.

"Deleuze's Practical Philosophy," in *Symposium: Canadian Journal of Continental Philosophy*, 10:1, Spring 2006, 285–303. Extracts reproduced with the permission of the editor.

"Deleuze and Democracy." *Contemporary Political Theory*, 4:4, December 2005, 400–413. Reproduced with the Permission of Palgrave Macmillan.

"Deleuze and Democratic Politics," in Lars Tønder and Lasse Thomassen, eds., *Radical Democracy: Politics between Abundance and Lack*, 50–67. Manchester, UK, and New York: Manchester University Press, 2005. Extracts reproduced with the permission of Manchester University Press.

"Becoming-democratic," in Ian Buchanan and Nicholas Thoburn, eds., *Deleuze and Politics*, 178–195. Edinburgh, UK: Edinburgh University Press, 2008. Extracts reproduced with the permission of Edinburgh University Press.

"Order, Exteriority and Flat Multiplicities in the Social," in Martin Fuglsang and Bent Meier Sørensen, eds., *Deleuze and the Social*, 21–38. Edinburgh, UK: Edinburgh University Press, 2006. Extracts reproduced with the permission of Edinburgh University Press.

"Utopian Political Philosophy: Deleuze and Rawls." *Deleuze Studies*, 1:1, 2007, 41–59. Extracts reproduced with the permission of Edinburgh University Press.

I am grateful to Hent de Vries for encouraging me to submit my book to this series. Many people have commented on earlier versions of the essays collected here, some in response to papers presented at conferences and seminars and some in response to written drafts. Among those who have provided me with helpful feedback and suggestions I would especially like to thank: Manola Antonioli, Miriam Bankovsky, Jane Bennett, Constantin Boundas, Sean Bowden, Rosi Braidotti, Ian Buchanan, Claire Colebrook, William Connolly, Simon Critchley, Chris Danta, Rosalyn Diprose, Simon Duffy, Bela Egyed, Martin Fuglsang, Moira Gatens, Gary Genosko, Eugene Holland, Duncan Ivison, Anthony Laden, Gregg Lambert, Craig Lundy, Catherine Malabou, Maria Margaroni, Paola Marrati, Todd May, Philippe Mengue, Dirk Moses, Adrian Parr, Patricia Pisters, John Protevi, Marc Rölli, Linnell Secomb, Daniel W. Smith, Bent Meier Sørensen, Charles J. Stivale, Kenneth J. Surin, Nicholas Thoburn, Lasse Thomassen, Lars Tønder, Simon Tormey, James Williams, and Effie Yiannopoulou.

Research for this book was supported under Australian Research Council's *Discovery Projects* funding scheme DP0772933.

Abbreviations

References in the text are, first, to the original French, then to the English translation. Where translations given in the text depart from the published editions, these are my own versions of the original French.

Deleuze

NP   *Nietzsche et la philosophie,* Paris: PUF, 1962; *Nietzsche and Philosophy*, translated by Hugh Tomlinson. Minneapolis: University of Minnesota Press, 1983.

DR   *Différence et répétition*, Paris: PUF, 1968; *Difference and Repetition*, translated by Paul Patton. New York: Columbia University Press, 1994.

LS   *Logique du sens*, Paris: Minuit, 1969; *The Logic of Sense*, translated by Mark Lester with Charles Stivale. New York: Columbia University Press, 1990.

F   *Foucault*, Paris: Minuit, 1986; *Foucault*, translated by Seán Hand. Minneapolis: University of Minnesota Press, 1988.

LP   *Le Pli: Leibniz et le Baroque*, Paris: Minuit, 1988; *The Fold: Leibniz and the Baroque*, translated by Tom Conley. Minneapolis: University of Minnesota Press, 1993.

P   *Pourparlers*, Paris: Minuit, 1990; *Negotiations, 1972–1990*. Translated by Martin Joughin. New York: Columbia University Press, 1995.

CC   *Critique et clinique* Paris: Minuit, 1993; *Essays Critical and Clinical*, translated by Daniel W. Smith and Michael A. Greco. Minneapolis: University of Minnesota Press, 1997.

ABC   *L'Abécédaire de Gilles Deleuze, avec Claire Parnet*. Paris: DVD Editions Montparnasse, (1996) 2004. (References by letter.)

ID   *l'Île Désert et Autres Textes, Textes et Entretiens 1953–1974*. Edited by David Lapoujade, Paris: Minuit, 2002; *Desert Islands and Other Texts 1953–1974*, edited by David Lapoujade and translated by Michael Taormina, New York: Semiotext(e), 2004.

DRF   *Deux Régimes de Fous. Textes et Entretiens 1975–1995*. Edited by David Lapoujade, Paris: Minuit, 2003; *Two Regimes of Madness: Texts and Interviews 1975–1995*, translated by Ames Hodges and Mike Taormina, New York: Semiotext(e), 2007.

Deleuze and Guattari

AO   *L'Anti-Oedipe*, Paris: Minuit, 1972; *Anti-Oedipus*, translated by Robert Hurley, Mark Seem, and Helen R. Lane. New York: Viking, 1977; reprinted by Continuum, 2004. Page references to the latter edition.

K   *Kafka: pour une littérature mineure*, Paris: Minuit, 1975; *Kafka: For a Minor Literature*, translated by Dana Polan. Minnesota: University of Minnesota Press, 1986.

R   *Rhizome* Paris: Minuit, 1976; "Rhizome," translated by Paul Foss and Paul Patton, *Ideology & Consciousness*, 8, Spring 1981, 49–71.

MP   *Mille Plateaux*, Paris: Minuit, 1980; *A Thousand Plateaus*, translated by Brian Massumi. Minneapolis: University of Minnesota Press, 1987.

QP   *Qu'est-ce que la philosophie?* Paris: Minuit, 1991; *What Is Philosophy?* translated by Hugh Tomlinson and Graham Burchell. New York: Columbia University Press, 1994.

Deleuze and Parnet

D   *Dialogues* (with Claire Parnet), Paris: Flammarion, new edition, Collection Champs 1996; *Dialogues II*, translated by Hugh Tomlinson and Barbara Habberjam, London: Athlone Press, 2002.

DELEUZIAN CONCEPTS

Introduction

The essays assembled here are the result of an ongoing effort to delineate and develop some of the lines of force within Gilles Deleuze's political philosophy. They focus on three main issues: first, the conception of philosophy as the creation of concepts worked out in collaboration with Félix Guattari and then set down in explicit form in *What Is Philosophy?* (1991, 1994); second, Deleuze's recurrent attempts to understand the nature of events by distinguishing between a virtual and an actual dimension or between pure and incarnate events; third, the sense in which this conception of philosophy was political from start to finish. With each of these issues, my aim has been not merely to identify and describe significant developments within Deleuze's later philosophy but to push them further by bringing them into contact with other problems and other philosophers.

The other philosophers include French contemporaries, such as Jacques Derrida and Michel Foucault, whose own work is reflected in greater or lesser degree in that of Deleuze, but also contemporaries within the Anglophone world with whom he did not engage, such as Richard Rorty and John Rawls. For a long time, there was a reluctance to compare Deleuze's thought with that of others who worked with different philosophical vocabularies, perhaps because it was believed that he was a sui generis thinker. This was especially surprising in relation to Derrida because, in France, they were often lumped together as philosophers of difference.[1] Since Deleuze's death and Derrida's acknowledgment that they shared a number of theses, the reluctance among Anglophone commentators to compare them has begun to fade (Derrida 2001d).[2] There are now an increasing number of comparative studies of their work, although there is no agreement on the extent to which they can rightfully be regarded as fellow travelers.[3] While comparisons with Derrida are relatively easy, given the family resemblances among the different traditions and vocabularies of postwar French philosophy, comparisons with Anglo-American philosophers are more challenging. These are also more important because they contribute to the larger project of bringing Deleuze and other French philosophers into conversation with the very different idioms and traditions of English-language philosophy. To that end, in Chapter 3, I draw an explicit comparison with some of Rorty's views that points to the ways in which Deleuze's philosophy can properly be regarded as pragmatist. In Chapter 9, I compare Deleuze's utopianism with the "realistic utopianism" of Rawls's political liberalism.

As well as bringing Deleuze into contact with other philosophers, I bring his philosophy to bear on questions and problems that were only marginally present in his own writings, such as the nature of history, the event of colonization, and the institutions and political norms of contemporary liberal democracy. I address these questions on the basis of what Deleuze actually said, however limited this may have been in relation to some of these issues. For example, he wrote very little about history, and much of what he did write was disparaging, even though his work with Guattari drew extensively on the work of historians. He made only occasional passing remarks about colonization, even though his work has since become an inspiration and a resource for many postcolonial artists and theorists.[4] He wrote relatively little about democracy and only one sentence in *What Is Philosophy?* evokes "becoming-democratic" as a form of resistance to present-day liberal capitalist democracies. This underdeveloped concept of "becoming-democratic" provides the basis for much of my argument in Chapters 7 and 8 about the normative turn in Deleuze's later political philosophy. Contrary to the widespread view that Deleuze's political thought is antithetical to liberal democratic politics, I argue that "becoming-democratic," along with other concepts such as the "micropolitics" described in *A Thousand Plateaus* (1980, 1987), enlarges our understanding of democracy. In Chapter 9 I argue that this concept provides the key to understanding both the critical function and the immanent utopianism of Deleuzian political philosophy.

If the outcome of all these encounters is a more liberal and democratic Deleuze, scarcely recognizable to many of his readers, so much the better. I can hardly be criticized for having undertaken the same kind of reading that allowed him to produce a transcendentalized Hume, a

Bergsonian Nietzsche, and a self-deconstructing Kant—the kind of reading that he suggested could present us with a philosophically bearded Hegel or a clean-shaven Marx (DR 4, xxi). However, the interest of reading this self-proclaimed Marxist alongside egalitarian liberals such as Rawls and Rorty is not simply to present a domesticated Deleuze all dressed up in coat and tie with his fingernails neatly trimmed. On the contrary, I believe that these encounters are a way of demonstrating that his philosophy has something to contribute to contemporary political philosophy more widely construed. They enable us to see that there is life in his philosophy or rather that there is *a life* in the sense that he argues that a virtual, generative power lies behind any enduring individual. The abstract nonorganic life at the heart of Deleuze's philosophy implies the possibility of a series of approaches to domains and problems other than the ones about which he actually wrote. In this manner, for example, we might suppose that there are resources in his philosophical concept of events yet to be exploited in relation to our understanding of history or that the normativity inherent in Deleuzian concepts has something to offer political philosophical reflection about the norms of contemporary liberal capitalist societies. My aim throughout these essays has been to explore the transformative effects that Deleuze's philosophy might have in relation to other domains such as historiography, postcolonial theory, or normative political philosophy. In this respect, I sympathize with Alexander Lefebvre's desire for a different tone and a different use of Deleuze, one that might acknowledge that he provides "underexplored resources" to think about "a broader range of social, political, and legal thought and practice." Lefebvre's use of Deleuzian concepts to deepen our understanding of legal judgment is strong evidence that a "sober, more mundane use of Deleuze might prove rewarding" (Lefebvre 2008, xiv).

I Philosophy, Concepts, and Language

Deleuze's commitment to movement in thought is one of the most remarkable but also most puzzling features of his way of doing philosophy. It is clear that he means more by this than just the fact that philosophical thought evolves in response to changing circumstances or that it develops in response to external as well as internal problems. Already, in *Difference and Repetition* (1968a, 1994), he had made clear his affinity for those philosophers such as Kierkegaard and Nietzsche who sought to "put metaphysics in motion" (DR 16, 8). In *A Thousand Plateaus* he and Guattari sought to give concrete expression to the idea that philosophical concepts could be mobile, both in themselves and in their relations with other concepts. This "rhizome-book" represents Deleuze's most sustained effort to produce mobile philosophical concepts. The text is an assemblage of plateaus rather than chapters, and there is no overall argumentative or narrative structure that links these in any particular order. The concepts created undergo continuous variation as components are modified in the passage from one plateau to the next. The book ends without a conclusion but instead with a set of definitions and rules for the construction of concepts. Clearly, the "system" of concepts laid out in the course of the book could be continued in any number of directions. *What Is Philosophy?* makes it apparent that these are philosophical concepts and that they are constructed differently to the concepts with which we are familiar from science or everyday life.

Chapter 1, "Mobile Concepts, Metaphor, and the Problem of Referentiality," examines the nature of these "mobile concepts" with reference to some case studies from *A Thousand Plateaus*. It shows why it is essential to take Deleuze at his word when he says that philosophy is the creation of concepts and explores some of the consequences of his conception of philosophical concepts as a certain kind of ideational multiplicity. How should this experimental work be read? To what do these concepts refer? What is the status of the vast amounts of apparently empirical material presented in the course of this book? In particular, it asks why Deleuze and Guattari so vehemently reject the suggestion that they produce metaphors and insist on the "literality" of their use of language. It turns out that Deleuze's reasons for resisting the concept of metaphor overlap with Derrida's reasons for arguing that concepts in the ordinary sense of the word should be understood to be derived from a primary domain of metaphoricity. In "White Mythology" Derrida argues that the very concept of metaphor is irreducibly "metaphorical" and that a more encompassing concept of metaphoricity provides a better way to understand the relation of language to nonlinguistic reality (Derrida 1982, 207–272). Deleuze rejects the concept of metaphor and the importance attributed to metaphor in philosophy, but his own conception of the mobility of philosophical concepts resonates at several levels with Derrida's account of generalized metaphoricity and his views about the essential iterability of concepts.

Chapter 2, "Deleuze, Derrida, and the Political Function of Philosophy," compares their respective conceptions of the manner in which philosophy serves a political function. Without wishing to deny the real differences of style and philosophical vocabulary that separate them, I point to certain similarities between the conceptual strategies employed by Deleuze and Derrida in relation to the political function of philosophy. Chief among these are a shared commitment to an open future and the manner in which they make use of a distinction between conditioned and unconditioned forms of particular concepts.

Deleuze and Derrida also share a pragmatic conception of the value of philosophy, in the sense that they see it as a certain kind of intervention in the world. As Deleuze asks, following Nietzsche, What would be the point of a philosophy that harms no one (DR 177, 135–136)? The pragmatism of Deleuze's later work extends to what John Protevi refers to as its "toolbox" element, that is, its aspiration "to be useful in relation to particular thinkers, particular activities or particular problems" (Protevi 2007, 8). The explicit comparison with Richard Rorty's pragmatism undertaken in Chapter 3, "Redescriptive Philosophy: Deleuze and Rorty," helps to bring into focus some of the ways in which not only certain theses but also certain features of his way of doing philosophy can properly be regarded as pragmatic. As in the comparison with Derrrida, this requires the kind of conceptual translation that establishes correspondences between otherwise disparate philosophical vocabularies. Once again, to suggest that Deleuze and Rorty converge on a number of issues is not to deny that there remain important differences between them. Rorty shared Derrida's skepticism about the thesis that philosophy creates concepts, but he was also critical of the idea that there were such things as pure events, let alone the idea that these could be expressed by philosophical concepts. I pursue the question of the usefulness of this way of thinking about philosophy in Part II.

II Colonization and Decolonization in History and Literature

In a conversation with Raymond Bellour and François Ewald published in 1988, Deleuze suggested that his work had always been concerned with the nature of events: "I've tried in all my books to discover the nature of events: it is a philosophical concept, the only one capable of ousting the verb 'to be' and its attributes" (P 194, 141). While this concern with the nature of events is more pronounced in some of his books than in others, it remains a prominent theme from *The Logic of Sense* (1969, 1990a) until *What Is Philosophy?* It led him into a series of engagements with earlier metaphysical theories of events, especially that of the Stoics but also those of Leibniz, Whitehead, and Bergson. However, we should not rush to conclude that Deleuze produced a coherent metaphysical theory or concept of the event. His claim in the interview with Bellour and Ewald is more modest, namely that he has repeatedly tried to discover the nature of events. He does not say that he has succeeded or that he has arrived at a final theory of the nature of events.

Nevertheless, certain theses about the nature of events do recur throughout his later work. Chief among these are the related distinctions he draws between pure events and their incarnation in bodies and states of affairs, between a virtual realm of becoming and an actual realm of embodied historical events, and between philosophy and history. Chapter 4, "History, Becoming, and Events," examines this network of concepts, in part by retracing some of Deleuze's attempts to discover the nature of events that draw on elements from the philosophy of the Stoics, Nietzsche, Charles Péguy, and Foucault. It focuses on the differences between Deleuze's philosophical approach to events and that of the historian or genealogist. It attempts to spell out what it means to claim that philosophical concepts provide knowledge of pure events and why the distinction between history and becoming is so important for Deleuze.

Chapter 5, "The Event of Colonization," pursues further these questions by asking whether this way of thinking is helpful in relation to already known types of historical event. Unlike the pure events expressed in Deleuze and Guattari's newly created concepts (to become, to deterritorialize, to capture, and so on), colonization provides a relatively familiar event and a relatively concrete set of problems with which to explore some of his more puzzling theses about events. How do pure events relate to ordinary events, and how is this a useful way to think about historical events? The focus of this case study is the legal event of colonization, as this was carried out under British law in certain parts of the New World, especially Australia and Canada. The aim is to show how the Deleuzian concept of the pure event enables us to understand the history of countries formed by colonization and how this concept helps to rethink present relations between colonizers and colonized. I argue that a Deleuzean concept of the pure event of colonization has something to offer the ongoing project of decolonization.

Chapter 6, "Becoming-Animal and Pure Life in Coetzee's *Disgrace*," undertakes a Deleuzian reading of J. M. Coetzee's novel *Disgrace*, in which the internal decolonization of South Africa provides the background for the lives of the characters. Although he wrote very little about colonization, Deleuze wrote a great deal about literature or "writing." On his view, genuine literature is produced by those for whom writing, like philosophy, went beyond lived or even livable experience to engage with pure life or becoming (CC 11, 1). This chapter argues that Coetzee's novel is genuine literature in Deleuze's sense of the term. It retraces Coetzee's approach to the event of decolonization from the inside, as it were, by way of the becoming-animal that is manifest in the life of the central character. It explores the personal and political dimensions of Deleuze and Guattari's concept of becoming-animal and shows how *Disgrace* presents this form of minoritarian becoming as a path for individual and social change in the aftermath of colonization. Finally, it demonstrates and explores the affinity between Deleuze's concept of an immanent life expressed in singular form and Coetzee's conception of "the only life there is," shared by individual humans and animals alike (Coetzee 1999, 74).

III Normative Political Philosophy

The commitment to movement in Deleuze's thought is nowhere more apparent than in his engagement with political philosophy, where new orientations and new concepts continued to emerge right up until his very last texts. For example, in interviews toward the end of his life he began to insist on the importance of jurisprudence and law and to draw attention to the philosophical functions of shame and a sense of the intolerable. He defended becoming-revolutionary and becoming-democratic as among the primary means of resistance to the present and outlined a concept of societies of control as opposed to discipline or capture.[5] There is an extensive literature on societies of control, and his remarks about jurisprudence and law have recently been taken up in the context of efforts to develop a Deleuzian philosophy of law.[6] However, there has been little discussion of the ways in which some of these new concepts in Deleuze's later political philosophy signal an engagement with normative political issues that was largely absent from his earlier writings with Guattari. This development in Deleuze's political philosophy is the focus of the final three chapters.

Chapter 7, "Philosophy, Politics, and Political Normativity," builds on the account of Deleuze's conception of philosophy developed in Part I to analyze the normative dimension of the concepts developed with Guattari. Against the tendency to treat these concepts as a form of empirical social analysis, I draw attention to the ways in which they are better understood as ethical concepts or concepts of practical reason. I outline the kind of normativity implicit in key concepts from *A Thousand Plateaus* and examine some of the paradoxical injunctions that follow from these concepts: how to make a body without organs, how to pursue lines of flight while avoiding their dangers, and so on. A central claim of this chapter is that the normativity inherent in these Deleuzian concepts remains formal in relation to the explicitly political norms that are supposed to govern the institutions of liberal democratic societies. In relation to these norms, the axioms of de- and reterritorialization are like the rules of an uninterpreted formal language. By contrast, Deleuze's comments during the 1980s and early 1990s about law, human rights, and democracy provide the occasion and the rationale for showing how these rules might be brought to bear on liberal democratic norms. I pursue this engagement further by pointing to the resources in his earlier collaborative work for developing a more robust concept of "becoming-democratic" and by arguing that the need for such a concept is an overlooked consequence of the sense in which his later philosophy is both political and critical. The concept of becoming-democratic expresses the immanent utopianism of Deleuze's later political philosophy. Drawing attention to the connection between becoming-democratic and the utopianism of the conception of philosophy outlined in *What Is Philosophy?* prepares the ground for the comparison with Rawls in Chapter 9.

Chapter 8, "Deleuze and Democracy," addresses the widespread view that Deleuze's political thought is antithetical to liberal democratic politics, either because it does not engage with the same concepts and problems as liberal democratic political theorists or, as Philippe Mengue and others have argued, because it is positively hostile to the majoritarian concerns of democratic public reason (Mengue 2003; Thoburn 2003). Following Rorty's argument against Foucault and Derrida, we might say that in common with these other "postmodern" thinkers, Deleuze offers at most new resources for the private ironist but nothing for the public political sphere (Rorty 1989). In contrast, I argue that critics and sympathetic commentators alike confuse Deleuze and Guattari's hostility toward the present state of liberal democracies with hostility toward democracy as such. Far from proposing an alternative to democratic politics, their concept of micropolitics enriches our understanding of the democratic political process. Their concept of opinion as the enemy of philosophy further clarifies the sense in which philosophy as they understand it is political.

Following on from the argument in Chapter 7 that there is a normative turn in Deleuze's late political philosophy, Chapter 9, "Utopian Political Philosophy: Deleuze and Rawls," seeks to further narrow the distance that separates him from normative political philosophy by comparing his utopian conception of philosophy with the "realistic utopianism" of Rawls's political liberalism. Considered from the perspective of their implicit or explicit normative commitments and the manner in which each understands the relationship between philosophy and opinion, the distance between Deleuze's late political philosophy and Rawls's liberalism is considerably less than we might have thought. This comparison serves several purposes in relation to Deleuze's political philosophy. It helps to identify the normative principles implicit in Deleuze and Guattari's criticism of existing liberal democracies and to show why the further development of this kind of criticism requires attention to normative questions, thereby further narrowing the gap that separates Deleuze from liberal normative political philosophy. At the same time, it allows us to see how Deleuze's conception of philosophical concepts might provide a useful way to understand Rawls's conception of a just and fair society. The final section of this chapter picks up elements of the discussion of mobile concepts in Chapter 1 and argues that understanding philosophical concepts as open systems shows how we might develop a detailed conception of society as a fair system of cooperation while remaining open to forms of justice or democracy to come.

How to Read Deleuze

The essays that I have assembled here criss-cross each of the various problematic fields—philosophy, concepts, language, history, colonization, political normativity, utopianism, and so on—from different angles. They often return to the same issues but from a different direction and with different aims. Above all, they do not constitute an attempt to see Deleuze's thought as a whole or to discern what drives it from one subject matter to another in the way that he sought to uncover the implicit logic of Foucault's thought (Deleuze 1986a, 1988a). This is a question not just of modesty but also of conviction. I agree with François Zourabichvili that nobody really knows nor can claim to say what is "Deleuze's philosophy" (Zourabichvili 2004b, 12). It is not just that we have not read him, literally, as the inventor of concepts that remain to be explored.[7] I am skeptical of the idea that there is such a thing as Deleuze's definitive philosophy. I am equally skeptical of claims that his work turns around a single fundamental idea, such as Peter Hallward's recent suggestion that all of Deleuze involves variations on the theme "that if being is creativity, it can only fully *become* so through the tendential evacuation of all actual or creaturely mediation" (Hallward 2006, 2).

It is not only that Deleuze is sometimes an elusive thinker but, more importantly, that he is an experimental thinker committed to a conception of movement in thought. He once declared his belief in philosophy as a system only to add that, for him, "the system must not only be in perpetual heterogeneity, it must also be a *heterogenesis*, which as far as I can tell, has never been tried" (DRF 339, 365). It is tempting to see Deleuze's work as a whole, and not only particular experiments such as *A Thousand Plateaus*, as a heterogenetic system. However, this would be to grant it more continuity and consistency than it in fact possesses. His philosophical works do not form a single continuous text. His practice of philosophy is more problematic or problem driven than this way of reading it would allow. There is always movement and discontinuity in his thinking from one problem or series of problems to the next. Discontinuities are especially apparent between his early sole-authored works and those he wrote later in collaboration with Guattari and with Parnet. However, even the early works were exercises in collaborative thinking. They form a succession of attempts to think with and through Hume (1953), Nietzsche (1962), Kant (1963), Bergson (1966), and Spinoza (1968b). He returned to this style of thinking in his books on Foucault (1986a) and Leibniz (1988b). If, as I argue in Chapter 1, we should take seriously his commitment to movement in thought, how then should we read these repeated efforts to think through and with others?

There is no doubt that he learned much from other philosophers, but always for particular purposes and always in relation to a specific project. In his extended *Abécédaire* interview with Claire Parnet, he denies that he is an intellectual or a "cultivated" thinker in the sense of one who possesses a stock or reserve of knowledge (Deleuze 1996). With obvious allusion to Descartes' suggestion in his *Discourse on Method* that the philosopher embarking on a project should first lay in provisions, like a mariner setting out on a long voyage, he insists that:

I have no reserves. I have no provisions, no provisional knowledge. And everything that I learn, I learn for a particular task, and once it's done, I immediately forget it, so that if ten years later . . . I have to get involved with . . . the same subject, I would have to start again from zero. (ABC, *C comme culture*)[8]

Over and above the denial—no doubt exaggerated—that he has accumulated any intellectual reserves, this remark implies that he is not someone who seeks to elaborate a systematic body of thought or "a philosophy." Even when he returns to the same thinker, the same problem, or the same concept, this is only to begin again so that we are confronted each time with a different thinker, a different problem, or a different concept. It is not difficult to find examples of this procedure in Deleuze's work.

Consider the differences between the Nietzsche presented in *Nietzsche and Philosophy* (1962) and the Nietzsche presented in "Nomad Thought" delivered at the 1972 "Nietzsche aujourd'hui" conference at Cérisy-la-Salle (ID 351–364, 252–261) and *A Thousand Plateaus* (1980, 1987). The first is a rigorous and systematic thinker who constructed a philosophy of nature around the complex concept of will to power. For this Nietzsche, philosophy is an art of interpretation, where this implies discovering the forces that determine the nature of a given object or event. The concept of force expresses the pluralistic character of this philosophy of nature because forces are plural by nature: "It would be absolutely absurd to think about force in the singular" (NP 7, 6). Any force is essentially related to other forces from which it differs in quality and quantity. The will to power is then defined as the differential and genealogical element that *produces* the differences in quantity and quality between any two or more forces in relation to one another (NP 59, 52–53). On this basis, Deleuze reconstructs the rest of Nietzsche's philosophy, presenting him as a critical philosopher who transforms the character of Kantian critique, who remains resolutely antidialectical while nevertheless offering an account of the mechanism by which human nature is transformed over time. Nietzsche's concept of eternal return is presented as expressing the principle of differentiation at the heart of this metaphysical system: It is not self-identity but rather the diversity and multiplicity of being that returns eternally (NP 55, 48). To this extent, the reconstruction of a systematic Nietzschean philosophy already involves an idea of heterogenesis similar to that mentioned above.

By contrast, the second Nietzsche hardly belongs in philosophy at all. He is rather the inventor of a new kind of discourse, a counter-philosophy that is defined by its essential relation to the outside, to intensity and to laughter (ID 355–362, 255–260). The difference between these two Nietzsches corresponds to the distinction drawn by Blanchot between a unitary, coherent, and continuous speech and a "fragmentary" speech, both of which may be heard in Nietzsche's writings (Blanchot 1992, 151–170). Far from proposing a philosophy of nature, the second Nietzsche is an aphoristic thinker whose texts are no longer the expression of an interiority (soul, consciousness, essence, or concept) but rather stand in immediate relation with outside forces. For this reason, Deleuze says in, "Nomad Thought" that reading Nietzsche is not a question of interpretation but of connection with forces external to the text. The connections to particular outside forces determine the meaning of an aphorism in a particular place and time. One force's interpretation will be another's misinterpretation. This is the essential ambiguity or plurality of thought as a war machine, the idea of which is related to Deleuze's long-standing interest in alternatives to the representational image of thought. Nietzsche was always an essential point of reference for this project. In *A Thousand Plateaus*, the project of making thought a war machine in immediate relation with the forces of the outside is described as "a strange undertaking whose precise procedures can be studied in Nietzsche" (MP 467, 377). In the history of Deleuze's repeated attempts to describe such a thought, the path from the systematic to the fragmentary Nietzsche passes through the social, political, and intellectual upheaval of 1968. It is also worthwhile to note how difficult it is to reconcile his 1972 comments about the aphoristic and revolutionary Nietzsche with Hallward's account of his philosophy as essentially extraworldly and preoccupied with lines of flight that lead beyond the everyday material and social world.

Deleuze's successive treatments of Nietzsche present us with a different thinker on each occasion. For an example of returning to the same problem but with a different focus and within a different network of concepts, consider the problem of the nature of events and their relationship with language. In *The Logic of Sense*, Deleuze relies on the Stoic distinction between a material or physical realm of bodies and states of affairs and a nonphysical realm of incorporeal entities that included time, place, and the sense or "what is expressed" of statements. Following the Stoics, he takes the sense of a statement to be identical with the event expressed in it: "The Stoics discovered it along with the event: Sense, *the expressed of the proposition*, is an incorporeal, complex and irreducible entity, at the surface of things, a pure event which inheres or subsists in the proposition" (LS 30, 19). This Stoic metaphysics implies that events stand in an essential relationship both to bodies and states of affairs on the one hand and to language on the other. In *A Thousand Plateaus*, this intimate relationship between events and the forms of their linguistic expression reappears in the "Postulates of Linguistics" plateau in the form of a relationship between the "incorporeal transformations" current in a given society at a given time and the collective assemblage of enunciation that determines what can be said. Incorporeal transformations are events, such as the transformation of the accused into a convict that may occur at the conclusion of a criminal trial. The attribution of events or incorporeal transformations to bodies in turn brings about changes in the properties of the bodies concerned, as a result of changes of status or changes in their relations to other bodies. The relationship between such events and the collective assemblage of enunciation is the basis for Deleuze and Guattari's argument that the use of language is a key component of the effectuation of these "incorporeal transformations" current in a given society at a given time. More generally, it is the basis for their suggestion that a political analysis of language should focus on this pragmatic, "order-word" function.

The passage from *The Logic of Sense* to the "Postulates of Linguistics" plateau shows that the movement in Deleuze's thought does not imply that there are no enduring problems. On the contrary, as he suggested in the conversation with Bellour and Ewald cited above, he had always been concerned with the nature of events. His recurrent theses about the nature of events do involve returning to the same concepts and the same distinctions between pure events and their incarnation in bodies and states of affairs, between a virtual realm of becoming and an actual realm of embodied events and between philosophy and history. However, as this example also demonstrates, changing the problems on which these concepts are brought to bear, or changing the network of other concepts within which they appear, has consequences for the concepts themselves. Deleuze makes this point in commenting on the differences between *Difference and Repetition* and *The Logic of Sense*:

The novelty for me lay in the act of learning something about surfaces. The concepts remained the same: "multiplicities," "singularities," "intensities," "events," "infinities," "problems," "paradoxes," and "propositions"—but reorganized according to this dimension. The concepts changed and so did the method, a type of serial method, peculiar to surfaces; and the language changed . . . (DRF 59–60, 65).

Similar points could be made about many other concepts that reappear in different contexts, different relations to other concepts and different problems: for example, his different uses of Freud and Lacan; his different accounts of Spinoza's immanent causality and the relation between substance, its attributes, and modes; or his different versions of Nietzsche's "untimely" and its relation to history.[9] In Chapter 4 note 16 I comment briefly on the differences between his analysis of F. Scott Fitzgerald's "The Crack-Up" in *The Logic of Sense* and the analyses of the same text in *A Thousand Plateaus*. Deleuze's response to suggestions that he is no longer consistent with his earlier thinking is sometimes completely unapologetic. For example, in the discussion following the presentation of "Nomad Thought" to the conference at Cérisy-la-Salle in 1972, he was asked whether his remarks about irony and humor meant that he no longer drew the same distinction between them that he did in *The Logic of Sense*. He replied: "I've changed. The surface-depth opposition no longer concerns me. What interests me now is the relationships between a full body, a body without organs, and flows that migrate" (ID 364, 261).

If it is true that Deleuze's thought is problematic and problem driven in the manner that I have suggested, then this must have implications for how we should approach his books. At the very least, we need to be sensitive to the movements that occur in his thinking from one text to another. In this manner, against those whom he describes as "the promoters of a generalised Deleuzianism," Réda Bensmaïa asks whether it is not "a misrepresentation of his thought simply to assume that the Deleuze we are dealing with in *A Thousand Plateaus* is the same Deleuze of *The Logic of Sense?*" (Bensmaïa 2010, 121). Bensmaïa insists on the transformations that have marked the evolution of Deleuze's thought, even to the point of suggesting that we should consider "Deleuze" as a multiple philosophical persona with many names. He outlines a conception of Deleuze-philosopher as a mediator, "dark precursor," or differentiator, always in movement between two series and always displaced in relation to itself: "It will always be necessary, in this sense, to recognise that there is a *virtual and/or undifferentiated* (name of) Deleuze which remains always to be discovered *despite all its actualisations*, and that his readers reinvent him as 'himself' but always 'other' each time that an affect or a percept drawn from one of the concepts of his work speaks to them" (Bensmaïa 2010, 133).

This kind of historical sensitivity need not deny the existence of "local" continuities within some of Deleuze's works. For example, Vincent Descombes writes that Deleuze "is above all a post-Kantian. His thought is subsequent to Kant's Transcendental Dialectic, in which the ideas of the soul, of the world and of God are criticized" (Descombes 1980, 152). There is some truth to this claim if we restrict its scope to the works to which he refers, namely *Nietzsche and Philosophy* and *Difference and Repetition*, with occasional references to *The Logic of Sense*, *Bergsonism*, and to *Kant's Critical Philosophy*. All of these works were published between 1962 and 1968. By contrast, it is less defensible to place the unworldly aspects of his early work or the aristocratic elements of *Nietzsche and Philosophy* on the same textual plane as the minoritarian becomings of *A Thousand Plateaus* to theorize a uniform position that amounts to "Deleuze's politics" (Mengue 2003, Hallward 2006, Boundas 2007). His way of doing philosophy does not lend itself to the kinds of summary formula that pronounce him to be a philosopher of immanence, of creativity, of the extraworldly, or that describe him as an essentially aristocratic and antidemocratic thinker. His commitment to movement in thought raises a question mark over all claims to have discovered the essence of his philosophy.

These essays make no claim to identify the essence of Deleuze's philosophy. They do not pretend to have identified the definitive name of his philosophical persona but only to have added some additional names to the list. By isolating some elements of his later philosophy, extending these, and bringing them to bear on other thinkers, other activities, and other problems, they try to read Deleuze in the spirit of his own experimental approach to philosophy.

PART I   PHILOSOPHY, CONCEPTS, AND LANGUAGE

Mobile Concepts, Metaphor, and
the Problem of Referentiality

Deleuze and Guattari's distinctive version of poststructuralist theory relies on a metaphysics of process as opposed to product, becoming as opposed to being, and lines of flight or deterritorialization as opposed to the capture of primary flows. This metaphysics affects their conception of thought as well as its objects. They undertake a rhizomatic or nomadic practice of thought in which concepts are not built in orderly fashion on secure foundations but constructed, as it were, on the run, in the course of an open-ended series of encounters with diverse empirical contents. This philosophical practice is not well understood by critics, who often take them to be employing metaphors rather than constructing concepts. Thus, they are often read as proposing metaphors of multiplicity by analogy with botanical rhizomes or as proposing metaphors of movement or deterritorialization by analogy with real nomads, and so on. In turn, this reading leaves them open to criticism directed at both the reliability and the ethics of the referential claims imputed to them. For example, Christopher L. Miller argues that their reliance on anthropological sources in the discussion of nomadism commits them to an "anthropological referentiality" that is inaccurate as well as complicit with colonial discourse (Miller 1998, 181 and 196). While he recognizes that Deleuze and Guattari's project is not straightforwardly representational, Miller supposes that it must rely either on direct representation or on metaphor (indirect representation).

By contrast, Caren Kaplan criticizes them not so much for their supposed referential claims but for their participation in a modernist European imaginary construction of colonized peoples. She argues that the "metaphors of explanation" used by Deleuze and Guattari and other poststructuralist critics "reinforce and depend upon specifically modernist versions of colonial discourse" (Kaplan 1996, 85–86). In particular, she argues that their privileging of the "nomadic" and related processes of becoming-minor and deterritorialization amounts to a "metaphorical mapping of space" that reproduces the modern Eurocentric valorization of distance and displacement (Kaplan 1996, 88):

> Deleuze and Guattari appropriate a number of *metaphors* to produce sites of displacement in their theory. The botanical metaphor of the rootlike "rhizome," for example, enacts the subjectivities of deterritorialization: burrowing through substance, fragmenting into simultaneous sprouts, moving with a certain stealth, powerful in its dispersion. Rejecting the classic Western humanist *metaphors* of family trees and genealogies, the rhizome destabilizes the conventions of origins and endings . . . As a *metaphor* for politics, then, the rhizome constitutes an anarchic relation to space and subjectivity, resistant to and undermining the nation-state apparatus. (Kaplan 1996, 87, *emphasis added*)[1]

Such a reading flies in the face of Deleuze and Guattari's repeated denials that their novel use of words involves the use of metaphor. At the outset of their discussion of machinic social organization in *Anti-Oedipus*, they cite Lewis Mumford referring to Franz Reuleaux's "classic definition" of a machine before insisting that the social machine "is literally a machine, irrespective of any metaphor" (AO 165–166, 155). Later they insist that societies may be regarded as machines "in the strict sense, without metaphor" (AO 299, 272). In *A Thousand Plateaus*, in the course of describing the physical, organic, and semiotic stratification of an unstratified, deterritorialized plane of consistency on which the most disparate kinds of things and signs freely circulate and collide, they insist that this metaphysics does not rely on a metaphorical use of words: "There is no 'like' here, we are not saying 'like an electron,' 'like an interaction,' etc. The plane of consistency is the abolition of all metaphor" (MP 89, 69). Later they insist that, when they characterize capital as an "axiomatic," they are using the word in a literal rather than a metaphoric sense (MP 568, 455).

Similarly, in conversation with Claire Parnet, Deleuze is unequivocal in his rejection of metaphor: "There are no proper words [*mots propres*], neither are there metaphors (all metaphors are sullied words [*mots sales*], or else make them so). There are only inexact words to designate something exactly" (D 9, 3). This comment plays on the ambiguity of *propre*, which can mean both "proper" and "clean." Later in *Dialogues*, he comments with reference to the concept of faciality that he and Guattari put forward on the basis of an extension and combination of the concepts of white wall, black hole, and a particular social machine of overcoding the human body:

Here is a multiplicity with at least three dimensions, astronomical, aesthetic, political. In none of the cases are we making metaphorical use: we don't say that it is "like" black holes in astronomy, that it is "like" a white canvas in painting. We are using deterritorialized terms, that is, terms that are torn from their domain in order to reterriorialize another notion: the "face" or "faciality" as a social function. (D 25, 18)

Finally, with reference to their conception of language as a combination of fluxes of expression and content in immanent variation, he and/or Parnet write that when a word "assumes a different meaning, or even enters into a different syntax, we can be sure that it has encountered another flux or that it has been introduced into a different regime of signs. . . . It is never a matter of metaphor; there are no metaphors only conjugations" (D 140, 117).

What are we to make of this persistent refusal of the status of metaphor for such an apparently idiosyncratic vocabulary? Moreover, supposing we do take at face value Deleuze and Guattari's claim to write literally rather than metaphorically, what does this imply with regard to the referential status of their philosophical concepts? What does it imply for those critical readings that do not take seriously their refusal of metaphor? My goal in this chapter is, firstly, to examine what is at stake in this hostility toward metaphor and, secondly, to ask what relationship this has to their conception of philosophy as the creation of "mobile" concepts. Finally, I will suggest that the critics who see no alternative apart from empirical social science or metaphors miss an important dimension of their novel practice of philosophy. To this extent, their criticisms fall short of their intended target.

Antirepresentationalism and Mobile Concepts

Deleuze's renunciation of metaphor flows from some of the most fundamental commitments upheld throughout his philosophy: his rejection of the representational image of thought, his pragmatism, and his long-standing interest in the mobility of philosophical concepts. In *Difference and Repetition*, he offers a characterization and criticism of what he calls the "dogmatic" image of thought. This is the dominant conception of thought in the history of philosophy, modeled on the act of recognition and thereby supposing a fundamentally passive relation to the world. Against the philosophical tradition that supposes that the world is already named and that the task of thinking is to discover the names of things, he advocates an image of thought as engagement with problems. He abandons the idea that human thought has a natural affinity with the truth in favor of the idea that truth is a function of the sense or meaning of what we say. He replaces the dogmatic image with an image modeled on the involuntary response of an apprentice struggling to come to terms with a new craft, recalcitrant material, and unfamiliar tools (DR 213–215, 164–165). An apprentice is someone who learns how to identify particular problems and how to approach them in a way that leads toward their solution. A variation of this image of the philosopher as craftsperson reappears at the beginning of *What Is Philosophy?*, where it introduces the definition of philosophy as the creation of concepts. The philosopher is a friend of concepts in the sense that a carpenter or a joiner is a friend of wood (QP 9, 3). The apprentice and the craftsperson are not simply metaphorical representations of the philosopher but variant forms of the conceptual persona that is the real subject of Deleuze's pragmatic conception of philosophy.

A Thousand Plateaus outlines an explicitly pragmatic conception of thought and language as means of intervention in, rather than representation of, the world. Deleuze and Guattari reject the representational idea of the book as image of the world in favor of a conception of the book as interacting with the world. In their view, "the book assures the deterrritorialization of the world, but the world effects a reterritorialization of the book, which in turn deterritorializes itself in the world (if it is capable . . . " (MP 18, 11). The concept of the order-word or slogan (*mot d'ordre*) outlined in Plateau 4, "November 20, 1923—Postulates of Linguistics," best exemplifies this conception (see below, pp. 28–32). A slogan is not something that is evaluated for its accuracy or truth-value but for its effectiveness. *What Is Philosophy?* proposes a no less pragmatic conception in suggesting that philosophy "does not consist in knowing and is not inspired by truth. Rather, it is categories like Interesting, Remarkable or Important that determine success or failure" (QP 80, 82). The point is not to reduce philosophical concepts to mere slogans but to suggest that, like slogans, philosophical descriptions should be evaluated in terms of their usefulness rather than their truthfulness. Of course, to be effective, philosophical concepts must in some way "map" the world. However, "mapping" has to do with performance rather than representation and should not be understood as a matter of naming, copying, or tracing the preexisting articulations of the world. What distinguishes mapping from "imitation" or tracing is that "it is entirely oriented toward an experimentation in contact with the real" (MP 20, 12).

A third distinctive feature of Deleuze's antirepresentational image of thought is his long-standing interest in producing mobile philosophical concepts. On more than one occasion he expresses his admiration for those philosophers, such as Nietzsche, Kierkegaard, and Bergson, who aspired to put concepts in motion. In *Difference and Repetition*, he explains the interest in theater shared by Nietzsche and Kierkegaard with reference to their common desire "to put metaphysics in motion" (DR 16, 8). In an interview in *Negotiations* he suggests that, just as the invention of cinema brought motion into images, so Bergson provides us with one of the first cases of self-moving thought (P 166–167, 122). He makes no secret of his antipathy toward ways of thinking that serve to block movement, such as the appeal to eternal values: "These days it's the rights of man that provide our eternal values. It's the constitutional state and other notions everyone recognizes as very abstract. And it's in the name of all this that thinking's fettered, that any analysis in terms of movements is blocked" (P 166, 122).[2]

At times, Deleuze and Guattari's antirepresentational practice of philosophy leads them to appeal to another kind of adequation between concepts and material states of affairs, in which the open-endedness and mobility of concepts parallel the movement in things themselves. This emerges in remarks such as the suggestion in *A Thousand Plateaus* that the "anexactitude" of mobile concepts is necessary to think a world that is in constant movement:

In order to designate something exactly, anexact expressions are utterly unavoidable. Not at all because these are a necessary step or because one can only advance by approximations: anexactitude is in no way an approximation; on the contrary, it is the precise movement of that which is under way. (MP 31, 20)

Deleuze comments in the same terms in *Dialogues* that inexact words are needed to designate things exactly (D 9, 3). As these remarks imply, his interest in mobile concepts is related to his ontological commitment to a world of events. In *What Is Philosophy?* he insists that philosophical concepts do not represent states of affairs but rather express pure events. Unlike things or states of affairs, events are mobile rather than static phenomena, constantly changing and becoming-other than they were. Deleuze and Guattari understand events in the manner of the Stoics as incorporeal entities that are attributed to things and states of affairs but expressed in propositions or in the infinitive form of the verb: to go, to encounter, to capture, to deterritorialize, and the like. I discuss this concept of pure events further in Chapters 4 and 5. For the moment, however, let us consider further the concept of metaphor.

Deleuze and Derrida on Concept and Metaphor

There is considerable agreement or, as Deleuze and Guattari would say, a "zone of proximity" between Derrida's reasons for relocating the distinction between concept and metaphor within a field of generalized metaphoricity and their own reasons for rejecting the concept of metaphor in favor of a generalized process of concept creation. In the eulogy that he wrote shortly after Deleuze's death, "I'm Going to Have to Wander All Alone," Derrida takes issue with the suggestion that philosophy creates concepts (Derrida 2001d, 193).[3] He does not elaborate on his reasons, but in any case it is not clear that his concerns are justified. If his concern lies with the use of the word *creation* and the implicit suggestion that concepts might be created ex nihilo, then this should be assuaged by Deleuze and Guattari's account of concept creation as comparable to any material process of production.[4] Their characterization of the creator of concepts as a "friend" in the sense that a craftsperson is a friend of his or her chosen material shows that they envisage the creation of concepts as a process of production involving the transformation and combination of certain conceptual or preconceptual raw materials.

Derrida's resistance to the idea that philosophy creates concepts is all the more surprising when we consider that his own deconstructive practice of philosophy involved the creation of a whole series of concepts: writing in general, *différance*, trace, *supplément*, generalized metaphoricity, and so on. He refers to these as "nonconcepts" or "aconceptual concepts" to signal the fact that they are not concepts in the commonly accepted sense of the term but rather successive versions of his attempt to think "beyond the concept" or to think the process of concept formation in terms other than the classical logic of disjunction and inclusion. He accepts the ordinary logic of concept formation, according to which a concept exists only when there is a distinction between what falls under the concept and what does not. However, he notes that, because no two particular objects or occurrences are identical, there is always variation between one instantiation of a given concept and the next. Moreover, because a concept is completely determined only by the potentially infinite series of particular instances to which it applies, it is never fully present on a given occasion. It follows that a more rigorous logic of concept formation would take into account the variation that is involved in the passage from universal to particular, as well as the variation that occurs from one case or one occasion to the next. This variability, along with the nonpresent character of the ideal totality that determines the meaning, implies a necessary openness or indeterminacy in the borders of a given concept at any given moment.

"Iterability" is Derrida's name for the complex relationship that includes both "alterability" of this idealized same in the singularity of an event and recurrence or repeatability of the same from one occasion to the next. Iterability is thus a paradoxical concept that "entails the necessity of thinking *at once* both the rule and the event, concept and singularity" (Derrida 1988, 119; 1990, 216). It is a deconstructive "concept" that points not only to the distinguishing features of all concepts but also to the limits of concept formation understood as the specification of necessary and sufficient conditions for a certain class or kind of thing. Considered as ideal objects defined in terms of the deconstructive logic of iterability, Derrida's philosophical concepts lack the determinacy associated with the traditional concept of concepts.

Deleuze and Guattari invent concepts that exhibit the formal characteristics of Derrida's aconceptual concepts. In *A Thousand Plateaus* they propose a rhizomatic image of thought in which concepts are never stable but in a state of constant flux as they are modified or transformed in the passage from one problem to the next. The concepts put forward are not restricted by the logic of exclusive disjunction that is supposed to govern concept formation in the sciences. Rather, they undergo continuous variation in passing from one plateau to another.[5] *What Is Philosophy?* defines philosophical concepts in a manner that reproduces the formal characteristics of Derrida's aconceptual concepts. Concepts are defined as inherently variable intensional multiplicities, the components of which are further concepts or parts of concepts such as predicates. Within a given concept, these components are arranged in zones of neighborhood or indiscernibility that define the consistency of the concept: "Components remain distinct, but something passes from one to the other, something that is undecidable between them" (QP 25, 19–20). In these terms, we might say that it is precisely such a zone of undecidability between spoken and written signs that defines the deconstructive concept of writing in general. Conversely, we might say that the "zones of undecidability" that render concepts consistent also render them iterable in Derrida's sense of the term. These formal or structural similarities between their respective understanding of philosophical concepts allow Deleuze to count *différance* as a concept and to include it, alongside Bergson's *durée*, Heidegger's *Sein* and Foucault's *énoncé*, among the significant philosophical inventions of the twentieth century: "When Derrida writes 'différance' with an *a*, he is clearly proposing a new concept of difference" (DRF 356, 385).

The parallels between Derrida's aconceptual concepts and Deleuze and Guattari's philosophical concepts point to the underlying affinity between their nonrepresentational views of the nature of language and thought. In "White Mythology," Derrida shows how the concept of metaphor in its canonical Aristotelian sense presupposes a representational view of the primitive relation between words and independently existing things. It is because Aristotle supposes that there is a metaphysically literal language in which the proper concepts or names of things may be formulated that he can define metaphor as the act of calling something by the name of something else. It is because language allows for the imitation of things that both metaphor and literal speech are able to convey truth about what is. However, Derrida argues, because the concept of metaphor relies on the idea of transposing or carrying over the content of a given name onto something else, it is already irreducibly metaphoric. Moreover, to the extent that literal language is understood as a means of conveying that which might be conveyed by other means, this representational conception of meaning involves the very same spatial metaphors of movement and transport. For these reasons, Derrida concludes that Aristotle's conception of language and meaning is thoroughly "implicated in metaphor" and that the quasi-concept of a generalized metaphoricity provides a more appropriate backdrop for the everyday contrast between literal and metaphoric uses of language (Derrida 1972, 287; 1982, 241).

The common ground between Deleuze and Guattari and Derrida emerges when we consider the consequences of abandoning the idea that there is a "proper" relation between particular words and things. This idea is central to Aristotle's version of what Deleuze calls the dogmatic representational image of thought. When it is abandoned, the ground of the distinction between literal and metaphorical uses of words collapses. When a word is transposed from its usual sphere of application and employed in another sphere, there is no more justification for calling this metaphorical than for calling it the creation of a concept. Thus, when Deleuze employs mathematical terms to define his own concept of problematic Ideas in *Difference and Repetition*, he denies that his procedure is metaphorical in any sense other than that which coincides with the creation of new concepts: There is no metaphor here, he writes, "except the metaphor consubstantial with the notion of Ideas, that of the dialectical transport or '*diaphora*'" (DR 235, 181). In the terminology of *A Thousand Plateaus*, there is no metaphor but only the deterritorialization of signs from one location and their reterritorialization in another (see the passage cited above from *Dialogues* 140, 117).

For his part, Derrida adopts the rhetorical term *catachresis*, previously used to describe the "imposition of a sign upon a meaning which did not yet have its own proper sign in language" (Derrida 1972, 304; 1982, 255). In the terms of this definition, taken from Pierre Fontanier, catachresis still relies on the logocentric assumption that meanings exist prior to being named or expressed in language.[6] Derrida therefore uses it "by analogy" to refer to the "discovery" of new objects of thought. He engages in precisely this kind of forced extension of the meaning of words in creating his own series of aconceptual or quasi-concepts. For Deleuze and Guattari, there are no metaphors, only concepts and occasions of their use, which can involve either the unexpected extension, transformation, or variation of an existing concept or, in extreme cases, the coinage of new words to express novel concepts. Where Derrida presents philosophical thought as advancing by catachresis, Deleuze and Guattari present philosophical concepts as inherently subject to variation in the course of being applied to different problems: Concepts developed in relation to one set of problems may be applied in relation to another set of problems, thereby transforming the original concept. However, this propensity for historical movement within and between concepts over time is not the most important sense in which concepts are mobile. Their ambition, as we saw above, is to create concepts that are in themselves mobile. As Deleuze comments in an interview, "It's not enough simply to say that concepts possess movement; you have to also construct intellectually mobile concepts" (P 166,

122). The means by which this task is achieved constitute the philosophical style of a given work because "style in philosophy is the movement of concepts" (P 192, 140). What needs to be explained, however, is just what this style amounts to and what it means to put concepts in motion.

Mobile Concepts 1: The Order-Word

For Deleuze and Guattari, style always involves a procedure of continuous variation, whether in thought, in music, or in the writing of those literary figures who succeed in creating their own minor language within a language. Two things militate against style in philosophy, namely "homogeneous language" and "a heterogeneity so great that it becomes indifferent, gratuitous, and nothing definite passes between its poles" (P 193, 141). *A Thousand Plateaus* embodies a definite philosophical style that seeks to avoid both of these dangers. The book is written in the form of a series of plateaus where *plateau* is not a metaphor but a name for the "zones of continuous variation" in which intellectually mobile concepts are produced (P 194, 142). The heterogeneity of the writing within each plateau produces the openness and instability of the concepts, while the organization of the book into distinct segments of writing allows for movement between the concepts developed in each plateau. In this sense, Deleuze and Guattari write, "we watched lines leave one plateau and proceed to another like columns of tiny ants . . . Each plateau can be read starting anywhere and can be related to any other plateau" (MP 33, 22). The best way to appreciate the practice of creating mobile concepts in this book is to retrace the paths followed in the construction of particular concepts.

Take as an example Plateau 4: "November 20, 1923—Postulates of Linguistics." The mobile concept at the heart of the pragmatic conception of language outlined here is that of the "order-word" (*mot d'ordre*). The plateau is laid out in the form of a series of extended commentaries on postulates shared by a range of approaches within linguistics and the philosophy of language. Four postulates are discussed in detail, but the idea that there could be more is suggested by the manner in which they are discontinuously numbered from I to III and then VI. Those discussed include the postulate that language is informational and communicational; that there is an abstract machine of language that does not appeal to any "extrinsic" factor; that there are constants or universals of language that enable us to define it as a homogeneous system; and, finally, that language can be scientifically studied only under the conditions of a standard or majoritarian language. The rejection of the latter postulate implies abandonment of the view that language may be defined as a system independently of the social and political circumstances of its use. In turn, this implies reversing the traditional relationship between pragmatics and syntacticosemantical theories of language. Deleuze and Guattari appeal to William Labov's sociolinguistic studies of African American English to argue against the idea that the syntactic or semantic structure of language might be defined independently of the pragmatic dimensions of use in particular circumstances. In this manner, through detailed rebuttals of each of these postulates, they develop their own heterogeneous account of the pragmatic conditions and consequences of linguistic utterance. Heterogeneity is ensured by the manner in which they weave together elements of Austin's speech act theory, Stoic logic and its metaphysics of the incorporeal, Hjelmslev's distinction between content and expression, assorted historical and sociolinguistic studies of the politics of language, along with their own theory of assemblages, the abstract machines that govern their operation, and the movements of deterritorialization and reterritorialization to which they are subject. At the same time, the form of commentary on postulates of linguistic theory ensures that the heterogeneity of the text remains within limits.

Austin's speech act theory plays a central role because the aspect of language use that interests them most is the relationship between the acts performed in speaking and the social, institutional, and political conditions of such acts. Deleuze and Guattari's procedure in outlining the concept of the order-word parallels Austin's movement in the course of *How to Do Things with Words* (Austin 1975) from performatives as a class of utterances to illocutionary force as a universal dimension of language use. Initially presented in terms of the function served by explicit or implicit commands, this concept is extended in the course of the plateau so that, by the end, it does not refer to a particular class of utterances but to an entire dimension of language use. In this manner, they pass from explicit commands to a concept of the order-word as "a function co-extensive with language" (MP 97, 76), from there to the acts or incorporeal transformations expressed in utterances, and, finally, to the assemblages of enunciation of which these are the variables. It is from this perspective, they argue, that language must be understood as "the set of all order-words, implicit presuppositions or speech acts current in a language at a given moment" (MP 100, 79).

Deleuze and Guattari further develop the Austinian concept of illocutionary force embedded in their concept of the order-word by recourse to a concept of incorporeal transformation derived from the Stoics. The explicit performatives that Austin used as the basis for his theory of speech acts provide the clearest cases of such transformative events: A judge's sentence transforms an accused person into a convicted felon. What took place before (the murder, the trial) and what takes place after (the punishment) are corporeal changes affecting the passions and interrelations of particular bodies, but

The transformation of the accused into a convict is a pure instantaneous act or incorporeal attribute . . . The order-words or assemblages of enunciation in a given society (in short, the illocutionary) designate this instantaneous relation between statements and the incorporeal transformations or noncorporeal attributes they express. (MP 102–103, 80–81)

All such incorporeal transformations are identifiable by reference to the date and time of utterance; hence the title of this plateau: "November 20, 1923" refers to the day on which, in response to runaway inflation in Germany, it was announced that the existing currency would be replaced by the Reichsmark.[7] History and everyday life are replete with such events. Whether they are world-historical events such as declarations of independence, of war, the assertion of sovereignty over vast areas of land previously unclaimed by European powers, or familiar interpersonal events such as a declaration of love, these incorporeal and "pure" events have lasting consequences for the actions and passions of the material bodies to which they are addressed or attributed.

Two consequences of Deleuze and Guattari's conception of language as the set of order-words current at a given time are significant for their view of the pragmatic character of the relationship between utterances and nonlinguistic components of the world. First, they draw attention to the historical and social character of what is said and suggest that language "always seems to presuppose itself" in the sense that a given utterance always carries the trace of previous utterances of the same form within it. Utterance therefore "does not operate between something seen (or felt) and something said, but always goes from saying to saying" (MP 97, 76). For this reason, they suggest that free indirect discourse rather than declarative judgment is the essential linguistic operation: "Indirect discourse is the presence of a reported statement within the reporting statement, the presence of an order-word within the word. Language in its entirety is indirect discourse" (MP 106, 84).

In other words, it is not the representation of a nonlinguistic reality that is the primary function of language but repetition and therefore transmission of something already said. On this basis, they question the importance that some theorists have attributed to metaphor and metonymy and propose instead that "the translation proper to language is that of indirect discourse" (MP 97, 77). While this remark does not contradict Derrida's appeal to generalized metaphoricity as a means to oppose the representational conception of language, it does highlight the importance of another kind of translative movement that has nothing to do with the structure of metaphor. In this sense, despite the common ground between Derrida's appeal to generalized metaphoricity and their own theory of concept creation, Deleuze and Guattari's pragmatism leads them even further away from the structure of representation that informed both traditional theories of language and the dominant image of thought in philosophy. Commenting in an interview on the fundamental points of his and Guattari's approach to language, Deleuze singles out for mention "the importance of indirect discourse (and the denunciation of metaphor as an unfortunate procedure without real importance)" (P 44, 29).

Second, the manner in which the order-word function of language accounts for the expression of the incorporeal transformations present in a given society at a given time allows Deleuze and Guattari to redescribe the relationship between the world and language use in terms of intervention rather than representation. This is where the everyday sense of *mot d'ordre* as "slogan" is especially significant for this concept. The order-word or slogan-function of language is a matter of effectivity: It refers to the manner in which bodies and states of affairs are transformed by a particular utterance that describes them in a particular way, thereby enabling the participants to perceive things differently and effecting an instantaneous incorporeal transformation. Deleuze and Guattari go on to describe the forms of interaction between language (forms of expression) and the world (forms of content) in terms of the double movement of deterritorialization and reterritorialization, thereby renewing the connection between their pragmatic theory of language and the theory of assemblages developed across the other plateaus that make up this book-rhizome.

To return to the question of the mobility of the order-word concept: The conceptual consistency of the concept can be understood in terms of the complex function that maps linguistic elements such as words and well-formed strings of words onto the circumstances or context of utterance. It is this function, linking language to its outside, that makes the utterance of such linguistic elements a linguistic act or statement. It is in this sense that Deleuze and Guattari suggest that the order-word "effectuates the conditions of possibility of language" (MP 108, 85). At the same time, the heterogeneity of the order-word concept lies in the fact that its meaning cannot be determined apart from its connection to a series of further concepts, such as free indirect discourse, collective assemblages of enunciation, regimes of sign, majority and minority treatments of language, and the concept of events as incorporeal transformations. The inherent mobility of the concept lies in the manner in which it preserves its own unity of composition across the range of differential relations to the other concepts in terms of which it is defined, where the series of these other concepts remains open ended. In this sense, the mobility of the concept is built into its exposition in the text. The series of connections with additional concepts through which it is expounded opens up the order-word concept to a range of potential paths of theorization with regard to the social and political character of language use, the manner in which enunciation or utterance is bound up with discursive as well as nondiscursive conditions of the possibility of saying certain things, and to the manner in which these conditions and therefore the form as well as the content of utterances are subject to constant variation.

Mobile Concepts 2: The War Machine

The concept of the "war machine" outlined in Plateau 12, "1227: Treatise on Nomadology—the War Machine," provides a particularly striking example of a concept in motion. Deleuze and Guattari provide no definitive list of characteristics of the war machine. Instead, they outline a number of defining characteristics by means of a series of axioms and propositions, where there is no reason to suppose that this series is either definitive or closed. They then proceed to demonstrate these axioms using empirical material drawn from the study of mythology, literature, anthropology, historical epistemology, and the history of philosophical images of thought. The first axiom asserts the exteriority of the war machine in relation to the State. By the "exteriority" of the war machine, they mean that it is in all respects "of another species, another nature, another origin" than the State apparatus (MP 436, 352). In other words, these are assemblages of such a completely different kind that no direct comparison between them is possible. Deleuze and Guattari state at the outset the problem that their mode of exposition is designed to address:

The exteriority of the war machine in relation to the State apparatus is everywhere apparent but remains difficult to think. It is not enough to affirm that the war-machine is external to the apparatus. It is necessary to reach the point of thinking the war-machine as itself a pure form of exteriority, whereas the State apparatus constitutes the form of interiority we habitually take as model, or according to which we are in the habit of thinking. (MP 438, 354)

This problem may be stated either from the point of view of the object or from the point of view of the style of thought in which conceptualization is attempted. From the point of view of the object, the State is an apparatus of capture that always involves the constitution of a field of interiority. As such, it is a well-defined entity in the sense that these are the constant features of all forms of State. Despite the differences among ancient empires, early modern monarchies, or contemporary democratic States, they all share a "unity of composition" (MP 532, 427). By contrast, there is no such unity of composition among war machine assemblages. These are the expression of a peculiar kind of abstract machine that "exists only in its own metamorphoses" (MP 446, 360). As such, war machine assemblages are a fundamentally different kind of thing to forms of State. The war machine is less like a well-defined object and more like a function, process, or type of event that recurs differently each time. In other words, it is an entity governed entirely by the logic of iterability that Derrida ascribes to all events. The essentially differential and diverse character of the war machine makes it a paradoxical "object" from the standpoint of the traditional understanding of concepts and concept formation. The war machine is not the kind of thing of which there can be a concept in the traditional sense of a series of features or marks that will determine necessary and sufficient conditions for something to be an assemblage of this kind. It is incapable of being captured in a stable concept, where this implies the specification of necessary and sufficient conditions for something to fall under a given concept. The problem, then, is to arrive at a way of thinking the war machine that is adequate to its nature as a "pure form of exteriority."

From the point of view of the concept, the problem of adequately conceptualizing the war machine is the same as that of arriving at a nonrepresentational style of thought capable of putting concepts in motion. Moreover, this problem arises precisely because the traditional understanding of concepts as the constitution of a form of interiority in thought is modeled on the State form understood as an apparatus of capture. Deleuze and Guattari point to the manner in which the traditional representational image of thought expresses the essence of the State form in general. They apply their concept of the State form as involving two poles or types of capture to the image of thought and point out that "it is not simply a metaphor when we are told of an imperium of truth and a republic of spirits. It is the necessary condition for the constitution of thought as principle, or as a form of interiority, as a stratum" (MP 465, 375). The problem of how to give conceptual expression to a pure form of exteriority therefore calls for another, non-State style of thought that they call "nomad" thought. This would be a mode of thinking that delineates its object not by conceptual capture but by following a variable path of conceptual oppositions. In the case of the war machine concept, Deleuze and Guattari rely on differences such as those between the two poles of sovereignty identified in Dumézil's studies of Indo-European mythology, between the games of chess and Go, and between the different styles of epic drama found in Shakespeare and Kleist. As with the order-word concept discussed above, the war machine concept is defined by retracing a line of continuous conceptual variation through the various kinds of content addressed under the successive axioms and propositions set down in this plateau. In this sense, the mobility of the war machine concept implies an indeterminacy or anexactitude that parallels the differential and dispersed nature of the object.

The Problem of Referentiality

As noted at the outset above, the nonrepresentational character of Deleuze and Guattari's mobile concepts creates a problem for critics. Many tend to assume that they are engaged either in a form of empirical social science or in a form of philosophy that relies on metaphor. Either way, they are supposed to be vulnerable to criticism directed at the empirical basis of their concepts. Kaplan provides an example of the latter reading to the extent that she treats Deleuze and Guattari's nomads as mere metaphors of a deterritorialized mode of existence. To say that the figure of nomadism as it functions in Deleuze and Guattari's text is a metaphor is to imply that it relies on a comparison with real nomadic peoples. Understood in this manner, Deleuze and Guattari's use of the terms *nomad* and *nomadic* in spelling out their concept of the war machine implies a comparison between the characteristics of the war machine and the relations to territory, weapons, and signs found among supposedly nomadic peoples. As a result, their text is open to criticism on the basis of its misrepresentation of one of the parties to this comparison. More generally, it is open to criticism on the basis of its participation in misrepresentations maintained by European colonial discourse. Thus, Kaplan argues that

The nomad as metaphor may be susceptible to intensive theoretical appropriation because of a close fit between the mythologised elements of migration (independence, alternative organization to nation-states, lack of opportunity to accumulate much surplus, etc.) and Euro-American modernist privileging of solitude and the celebration of the specific locations associated with nomads: deserts and open spaces far from industrialization and metropolitan cultural influences. (Kaplan 1996, 90)

The term *mythologised* here makes it clear that, beneath the charge of perpetuating Eurocentric discourse about its colonial others, lies the accusation of misrepresentation of the realities of life among those who came to be called "nomads."

At this point, Kaplan's criticism coincides with Miller's suggestion that the referential authority of Deleuze and Guattari's discourse is threatened by its reliance on colonial anthropological sources (Miller 1998). The question of the referential status of their characterization of nomadism lies at the heart of a recent exchange between Miller (Miller 2003) and Eugene Holland (Holland 2003a, 2003b). In response to Holland's reminder that Deleuze and Guattari's "nomad" is a conceptual persona rather than a social scientific concept, Miller insists that their philosophical concept of nomadism is nevertheless in some sense reliant on anthropological sources and to that extent "derived from" real nomads. To this extent, the "taint of mortal representation remains in *A Thousand Plateaus*" (Miller 2003, 136). He reiterates his earlier criticism that their characterization of nomadism is compromised by the primitivism and colonialism of the anthropological sources on which they rely. Deleuze and Guattari's concept of nomadism is charged with being corrupt because it is epistemologically supported by suspect anthropological material sources. The only alternative to this empirical reading of the concept of nomadism is to treat it as a metaphor. Thus, when he does take into account the concluding remarks of the Nomadology plateau, which deny that nomads "hold the secret" of the war machine, Miller resorts to the metaphorical reading in commenting that "nomads and their war-machine seem to have disappeared into horizonless space, become historical metaphors, inventions serving some other purpose" (Miller 1998, 204). Similarly, in his response to Holland, he accuses Deleuzians of turning real nomads into metaphors in a manner that is "philosophically dubious—producing as it does a 'world without others'—and historically reprehensible—being, as it is, indissociable from colonialism' (Miller 2003, 137).

Miller and Kaplan's criticisms dovetail in supposing either that Deleuze and Guattari present straightforwardly empirical concepts or that they present metaphors. Either way, the argument goes, they are guilty of complicity with colonialism. However, this criticism collapses if we take at face value their claim to produce philosophical concepts rather than metaphors. To persist in treating nomadism, the war machine, the various types of minority-becoming, and so on as metaphors is simply to fail to recognize their nonrepresentational practice of thought. For Deleuze and Guattari, the choice is not between concepts and metaphors understood in terms of the representational image of thought but between this representational image and a new image of thought that allows for the creation of mobile concepts. In these terms, the real issue here is that of the relationship of their concepts to their apparently empirical claims. It is undoubtedly true that they make statements about nomadic peoples and cultural practices in the course of outlining concepts of nomadism, the war machine, and minority-becoming. It may well be true that some of these statements are open to question on empirical grounds. However, the important question is, What is the function of such statements in the text?

The fact that Deleuze and Guattari make it an axiom that the war machine is invented by nomads and their assertion that nomads are defined by the constellation of characteristics that define assemblages of the war machine type suggest that their "nomadism" is only contingently related to the empirical claims made about actual nomadic peoples. They draw on accounts of the life of desert peoples to dramatize the connection between nomadism and smooth space, suggesting that nomadic existence follows paths that distribute individuals and groups across an open and smooth space, unlike the roads and highways that connect the regions of sedentary social space. Sedentary space is striated by enclosures and paths between enclosures, whereas nomadic space is a pure surface for mobile existence, without enclosures or fixed patterns of distribution. However, in the end, these quasi-empirical claims are no more than a means to express the characteristics of smooth space. Ultimately, it is the active relation to smooth space that defines the fundamental nature of the nomad as well as that of the war machine. That is why Deleuze and Guattari can claim that "the nomads make the desert no less than they are made by it. They are vectors of deterritorialization" (MP 473, 382). Their concept of nomadism is not derived from empirical facts about nomads. The statements about nomadic existence in the text serve only to express a concept of nomadism the real sources of which lie in philosophy rather than colonialist social science.

The definition of nomadic existence in terms of its relation to smooth space follows conceptual paths already traced by Deleuze's characterization of a nomadic distribution of being in *Difference and Repetition*, where he refers to a "completely other distribution which must be called nomadic, a nomad *nomos*, without property, enclosure or measure. Here, there is no longer a division of that which is distributed but rather a division among those who distribute *themselves* in an open space—a space which is unlimited, or at least without precise limits" (DR 54, 36). The hostility to figures of unity, totality, and closure expressed in the Deleuzian world of "free differences" is a direct antecedent of the concept of nomadism. This philosophical and moral inspiration, rather than any derivation from anthropological sources, is the real origin of the concept in Deleuze and Guattari's thought. Nomads are not essential to their definition of war machine type assemblages. A political, scientific, or artistic assemblage can be a potential war machine, precisely to the extent that

It draws, in relation to a *phylum*, a plane of consistency, a creative line of flight, a smooth space of displacement. It is not the nomad who defines this constellation of characteristics; it is this constellation that defines the nomad, and at the same time the essence of the war-machine. (MP 527, 422–423).

It follows that their account of the conditions of nomadic existence is really no more than a means to demonstrate key characteristics of assemblages of the war machine kind: the relation to smooth as opposed to striated space, the affinity with lines of flight or deterritorialization, and a capacity for absolute, intensive speed:

The nomad distributes himself in a smooth space; he occupies, inhabits, holds that space; that is his territorial principle. It is therefore false to define the nomad by movement . . . It is thus necessary to make a distinction between *speed* and *movement*: a movement may be very fast but that does not give it speed; a speed may be very slow, or even immobile, yet it is still speed. Movement is extensive, speed is intensive . . . we will say by convention that only nomads have absolute movement, in other words, speed . . . [nomads] are vectors of deterritorialization. (MP 472, 381–382)

In turn, the war machine is really Deleuze and Guattari's term for machines of metamorphosis, outside of and fundamentally opposed to the State-forms that express the forces of unity, totality, and closure in thought or in society (Patton 2000, 109–110). As such, the war machine is an abstract assemblage, an abstract machine of pure exteriority, not to be confused with any concrete social, much less military, apparatus. Its essence is not war but creative displacement, deterritorialization, and the propagation of smooth spaces in which new connections between different forces are possible. The function of this concept is to give expression to the forces and processes of metamorphosis and deterritorialization. Along with the concept of nomadic existence, it is intended to counter-actualize those forces in contemporary society that resist processes of capture. Because the concept of nomadism is definitionally bound to that of the war machine, the characterization of nomadic existence serves to give expression to this paradoxical object. At the same time, however, neither this concept nor its "object" can be considered bound to any given form of expression. Deleuze and Guattari's nomadism is abstract to the same degree that the war machine is an abstract assemblage irreducible to its particular artistic, technological, or political incarnations. The quasi-empirical claims made about nomadic existence serve only to demonstrate these characteristics of this abstract machine.

It follows that the unreliability of these claims is no threat to the task of conceptual specification. Miller may well be correct to suggest that many of the sources for these claims are corrupt. However, the appropriate response to such criticism from the point of view of the task of outlining a nonrepresentational concept of nomadism is to abandon such material and look for other ways to specify the concept. As Miller notes, this amounts to salvaging nomadology from *A Thousand Plateaus* (Miller 2003, 137). However, this response is justified in terms of what I described above as Deleuze and Guattari's pragmatic conception of philosophy. To say that the accounts of nomadism and the war machine serve the philosophical purpose of constructing concepts of a certain kind does not mean that these are good concepts in the sense that they achieve the goal of counter-actualizing certain kinds of transformative agency. The conditions of nomadic social life do not necessarily offer the most effective means to grasp the nature of machines of metamorphosis and deterritorialization in contemporary societies. The strongest reason for rethinking the concept of nomadism comes not from the supposed referential deficiencies of the concept but from the argument, advanced by both Miller and Kaplan, that the choice of nomads to specify the characteristics of war machines and smooth space perpetuates a long tradition of Eurocentric primitivism and a fascination for the Other. To this extent, Kaplan argues, they perpetuate the rhetorical structures of a modernist European imaginary.

As a comment about Deleuze and Guattari's text, there is undoubtedly some truth to this diagnosis, although it engages only with the relatively superficial question of their choice of means of expression. As a comment about their concept of nomadism, these charges are much less compelling because Deleuze and Guattari's association of nomadism with qualitative multiplicity, smooth space, and the conditions of transformation can be seen to controvert the Eurocentric priority attached to sedentary forms of agriculture and social life at the expense of more fluid and mobile relations to the earth. In this sense, their concept of nomadism runs counter to a deep stratum of the modern European social imaginary that we find in Locke's *Second Treatise on Government* as well as in Rousseau's *Essay on the Origins of Inequality*. This Eurocentric prejudice in favor of sedentary forms of life worked its own magic in the justifications it provided for the appropriation of land and the subjugation of so-called primitive peoples (Tully 1994). The absence of sedentary institutions and agricultural practices was considered sufficient reason to relegate indigenous peoples to a condition of primitive savagery and to a cultural time before the advent of "civilization." Deleuze and Guattari's concept of nomadism and its association with processes of deterritorialization and transformation directly challenge this normative structure.

Kaplan further argues that Deleuze and Guattari perpetuate colonial discourse by relying on Eurocentric images of the other rather than allowing the other to speak for itself: "The Third World functions simply as a metaphorical margin for European oppositional strategies, an imaginary space, rather than a location of theoretical production itself" (Kaplan 1996, 88). This argument also assumes that Deleuze and Guattari's oppositional strategies rely on metaphor: Becoming-minor is said to require "emulating the ways and modes of modernity's 'others,'" in much the same way that some feminist critics initially assumed that becoming-woman required men to imitate women.[8] The inappropriateness of the strategy is largely an effect of supposing that it relies on "emulating" the ways of minority groups. If we do not take the concepts of minority or nomadism for metaphors, then no such emulation is implied. In addition, the argument assumes that the authors are responsible for the inappropriate generalization of this oppositional strategy, so that when they recommend minority-becoming for "us all" they speak on behalf not just of Europeans and North Americans but of all peoples everywhere. In this manner, Kaplan argues, a strategy of becoming-minor that only makes sense for those majoritarian figures at the center of power "is presented as an imperative for 'us all'" (Kaplan 1996, 88). However, it is not the authors who are at fault here but rather the reader, who assumes that a book written from within and against one particular cultural tradition can be simply transposed into another context without undergoing significant transformation. Kaplan makes this assumption in claiming that the "utility of their methodology . . . is always generalised," thereby transforming the limitation implicit in Deleuze and Guattari's critical gesture into a defect (Kaplan 1996, 88).

By contrast, if we take their text to be an intervention in a specific cultural context, along the lines suggested by their account of language as the current set of order-words, then it is inappropriate to generalize their critical gesture in this way. As Kaplan herself notes, we need to be aware of the sense in which Deleuze and Guattari's use of the figures of marginality and displacement involves an "attempt to displace the sedimented bulk of European humanist traditions" (Kaplan 1996, 88). There is no guarantee that the means adopted to do so will be effective in all contexts. It is a consequence of the manner of presentation of Deleuze and Guattari's concepts that their critical force remains largely internal to the European cultural imaginary.[9] The interpretation of their practice of philosophy as nonrepresentational and pragmatic, outlined above, teaches us that the effective counter-actualization of processes of metamorphosis, transformation, and deterritorialization requires contextually appropriate means of expression. It shows that the question of metaphor is irrelevant. Finally, it enables us to appreciate the essential mobility of these concepts and to dissociate these from their means of expression. Effective criticism must start from the presumption that "we" do not all have the same relation to such concepts.

2

Deleuze, Derrida, and the Political Function of Philosophy

For Deleuze and Guattari, philosophy is the invention or creation of concepts, the purpose of which is not the accurate representation of how things are but the utopian task of helping to bring about new Earths and new peoples. The creation of concepts "in itself calls for a future form, for a new earth and a people that do not yet exist" (QP 104, 108). In common with Marx, Foucault, and many others, they see the practice of philosophy as serving the larger goal of making the future different from, and in some sense better than, the past. Philosophy serves this goal by virtue of the manner in which the concepts it creates enable us to see things differently. New concepts provide new ways of describing the problems to which philosophical thought is a response, thereby pointing us toward new forms of solution.

The creation of concepts is inseparable from the elaboration of new vocabularies, such as those put forward in *A Thousand Plateaus*. These include the terminology used to describe different kinds of assemblage, where these are defined by their lines of flight or deterritorialization, their particular combinations of content and expression, their forms of stratification, and the abstract machines that they express. They include the battery of terms employed in the characterization of a micropolitics of desire, such as body without organs, intensities, molar and molecular segmentarities. They include the series of terms used to describe various processes of becoming such as becoming woman, becoming animal, and becoming imperceptible. They include the terms used to describe capitalism as a nonterritorially based axiomatic, in contrast to territorial systems that overcode flows of consumption and production. They include the terms used to describe states as apparatuses of capture in contrast to the abstract machines of metamorphosis (nomadic war machines) that are the agents of social and political transformation. As we saw in Chapter 1, these are philosophical rather than social scientific vocabularies, pragmatic rather than truth oriented. They enable a form of description that is intended to be immediately practical. Even though the aim is change rather than truth, they provide new ways of describing everyday events and processes and therefore new ways of understanding and acting on the world. For example, it makes a difference whether we are dealing with the effective deterritorialization of a given apparatus of capture or simply a modification of its mechanism. The characterization of the different kinds of line that define individual or collective bodies enables questions such as: "What are your lines? What map are you in the process of making or rearranging? What abstract line will you draw, and at what price, for yourself and for others? What is your line of flight?" (MP 249, 203).

For Derrida too, the aim of philosophy is practical: It does not seek truth but rather the deconstruction of established institutions and practices. In "Force of Law" he proposes a formula that parallels Deleuze and Guattari's utopian conception of the function of philosophy when he affirms that deconstruction seeks to intervene to *change* things, not "in the rather naïve sense of a calculated, deliberate and strategically controlled intervention, but in the sense of maximum intensification of a transformation in progress" (Derrida 1992a, 8–9; 1994a, 24). Even though he does not claim that deconstruction serves that aim by inventing concepts, he does say that deconstruction aspires to be inventive. In "Psyche: Invention of the Other," he addresses the widespread negative perception of his earlier work by asking in what sense can the movement of deconstruction "far from being limited to the negative or destructuring forms that are often naively attributed to it, be inventive in itself, or at least be the signal of an inventiveness at work in a sociohistorical field?" His unequivocal reply is that deconstruction "is inventive or it is nothing at all" (Derrida 1987, 35; 2007a, 23). Deconstructive inventiveness involves the opening, uncloseting, or destabilization of "foreclusionary structures" so as to allow both for the movement toward the other and for the coming of the other (Derrida 1987, 60; 2007a, 45).

Contrary to the suggestion that he is an anti-Enlightenment thinker, Derrida affirms his belief in perfectibility and progress, insisting that nothing seems to him "less outdated than the classical emancipatory ideal" (Derrida 1992a, 28; 1994a, 62). Similarly, in response to questions about the possibility of improving existing law in relation to hospitality put to him by Penelope Deutscher in Sydney in 1999, he declared: "I am for the Enlightenment, I'm for progress, I'm a progressist. I think the law is perfectible and we can improve the law" (Derrida 2001c, 100). Just as Deleuze and Guattari remain silent about the character of the new Earths and peoples that philosophy helps to bring into being, so Derrida says almost nothing about the direction of progress. We could understand *progress* here to be defined negatively and say that deconstruction is progressive in the same nonteleological sense that Foucault ascribes to the ethos of enlightenment when he defines this as a commitment to freedom from past constraints or to the possibility of passing beyond "the contemporary limits of the necessary" (Foucault 1997, 313). In these terms, the sense or direction of progress can be retrospectively understood only as the achievement of freedom from prior constraints that impose conscious or unconscious limits to available ways of thinking or acting. However, like Deleuze and Guattari, Derrida endorses an even more radically antiteleological conception of the future as open. For example, in *Specters of Marx* he endorses a form of Marxism that is heir to the spirit of the Enlightenment and that in turn justifies a "radical and interminable" critique of the present. This critique, he continues, "belongs to the movement of an experience open to the absolute future of what is coming" (Derrida 1993, 148; 1994b, 90). I will comment further on this idea of the absolute future in the final section of this chapter.

In the eulogy that he wrote after Deleuze's death, Derrida acknowledges their "affinity" with regard to certain "theses" about difference and the simulacrum, even as he "grumbles" about others such as the idea that philosophy consists in creating concepts (Derrida 2001d, 193).[1] I argued in Chapter 1 that it is not clear that he is entitled to grumble about this issue given the number of "aconceptual" or nonconcepts proposed in his early works (see above, p. 24). Nevertheless, it will be objected that deconstruction does not invent new concepts, much less provide new means of description. On the contrary, and above all in its affirmative phase, deconstructive analysis is applied exclusively to already existing concepts such as invention, justice, democracy, friendship, the gift, hospitality, and forgiveness. Surely this indicates a fundamental difference between deconstruction and Deleuze and Guattari's constructivism? Without wishing to deny the real differences of style and method that remain between them, I argue that Deleuze and Derrida share an ethicopolitical conception of philosophy as oriented toward change in the sense of working on the limits of the present.

There are at least two respects in which their respective approaches to the political function of philosophy converge in the kind of proximity (*voisinage*) that Deleuze and Guattari ascribe to the components of philosophical concepts when they suggest that these remain distinct but that something undecidable passes between them (QP 25, 19–20). First, for both approaches philosophy is a political activity oriented toward the future, where the future is understood as open rather than determined by the past or, as Foucault suggests, defined by its potential difference from the present. Second, both rely on a certain usage of the absolute or the unconditioned to maintain the critical function of political philosophical concepts. In this manner, over and above the differences between their respective philosophical vocabularies, we can perceive a zone of convergence or undecidability with respect to their concepts or "theses" relating to the political function of philosophy.

Deconstructive Analysis of Ethical
and Political Concepts

The practice of "affirmative" deconstruction relies on at least two distinct strategies with regard to the analysis of concepts. The first of these involves a genealogical study of the history and interpretations of a given concept, along with the interconnections it has to other concepts or philosophemes. Thus, the analysis of the concept of invention in "Psyche: Invention of the Other" includes a discussion of history of the concept and the different ways in which invention has been recognized in legal, literary, intellectual, and technological domains (Derrida 1987, 35–49; 2007a, 23–36). Similarly, the examination of law and justice in "Force of Law" alludes to the need to recall "the history, the origin and subsequent direction" of the different concepts of law, right, and justice inherited within the European tradition. Derrida argues that deconstruction implies the need for "a historical and interpretative memory" that would undertake a genealogy of these concepts, the norms and values associated with them, and the wider network of concepts to which they are connected: responsibility, property, intentionality, will, freedom, conscience, consciousness, and so on (Derrida 1992a, 19–20; 1994a, 44–45). More generally, whenever he sets out the research program that would be required for a deconstructive practice of philosophy, political philosophy, or the humanities in general, this always includes the study of the history of the concepts that have defined their object: the concept of man as opposed to animal or to woman; concepts of sovereignty and democracy; and so on (Derrida 2002b, 230–231). In this regard, *Politics of Friendship* undertakes a detailed study of this kind in relation to the concept of friendship and the network of concepts surrounding its relation to the political and to democracy: concepts of kin and family, masculinity, love, and enemy. *Rogues* also makes a number of suggestions with regard to the connections between democracy and sovereignty.

A second form of deconstructive analysis, on which I propose to focus here, offers a redescription of existing concepts that reproduces versions of a distinction between a contingent or conditioned form of the concept and an absolute or unconditioned form. In each case the absolute or unconditioned form of the concept is paradoxical or impossible. In this manner the aporetic analysis of invention in "Psyche: Invention of the Other" leads to a distinction between two kinds of invention, namely ordinary invention, which is always the invention of the possible, and an extraordinary or pure invention, which would involve the appearance of something truly or radically other. This other is literally impossible, in the sense that it implies the appearance of something beyond or outside the order of the possible. In this form of deconstructive analysis, everything is organized around the invention of the other, which John Caputo takes to mean the "in-coming of the other, the promise of an event to come, the event of the promise of something coming" (Caputo 1997, 42). In other writings, Derrida offers parallel analyses of the gift, justice, responsible decision, democracy, hospitality, and a number of other such phenomena. In each case, affirmative deconstruction invents or reinvents a distinction between two poles of the concept in question to argue two things: first, that the difference between these two poles is irreducible; and, second, that the ever-present possibility of invention, reconfiguration, or transformation in our existing, historically conditioned, and contingent ways of understanding the phenomenon in question is guaranteed by the existence of the absolute or unconditioned form of the concept.

In each case, too, this aporetic analysis also leads to a phenomenology of the "experience" of this impossible act. For example, in "Psyche: Invention of the Other," Derrida writes that "the interest of deconstruction . . . is a certain experience of the impossible" (Derrida 1987, 27; 2007a, 15). If experience is understood as a passage toward a given destination, then because an aporia is a nonroad, a blocked passage, it is by definition not something of which we can have experience. Caputo points out that this experience of the impossible is not experience in the "traditional, dusty phenomenological sense" where this means to perceive what appears or presents itself but rather experience in a deconstructive sense, in which it means running up against the limits of the unpresentable and unrepresentable (Caputo 1997, 33). For example, in "Force of Law" the difference between a conditioned and an unconditioned form of the concept appears in the form of the distinction between law and justice. The law, which is subject to historical conditions and is therefore open to modification or change, is contrasted with justice, which is that in the name of which the law is modified and which therefore remains essentially undeconstructible. Justice is manifest both in particular applications of the law and in particular improvements or modifications of the law, but neither of these implies an experience of justice as such. Justice as such, supposing there is such a thing, is an impossible object of experience if only because of the contradictory injunctions implicit in the idea of doing justice to a particular individual or to a particular case. In so far as deconstruction is concerned with justice, it is concerned with the experience of that which we are not able to experience or the experience of the impossible (Derrida 1992a, 16; 1994a, 38). This experience of the impossible should not be understood simply in a negative sense as a barrier or limit but also in a positive sense as an ordeal or test through which we have to pass to realize some new iteration of the concept in question. For Derrida, the experience of the impossible "is not simply the experience of something which is not given in actuality, not accessible, but something through which a possibility is given'" (Derrida 2001c, 64). In effect, any decision involves an experience of this kind. On the one hand, if it is to be properly a decision and not simply a mechanical procedure, it must involve more than simply acting in accordance with a given rule. On the other hand, a decision must have some relation to a rule and not be simply capricious or unmotivated. In these terms, we might say that this form of aporetic analysis provides new means of describing the decision that is always implicit in occasions or situations of this kind.

To give a more concrete ethical and political sense to this form of analysis, consider Derrida's discussion of the concept and the politics of forgiveness. "On Forgiveness" takes its point of departure from the proliferation of "scenes of repentance, confession, forgiveness or apology" entered into by governments, heads of state, churches, and other corporate bodies in the closing years of the twentieth century.[2] Examples of such "geopolitical" scenes in which the concept of forgiveness played a central role include the South African Truth and Reconciliation Commission (1995–1998) and the Australian reconciliation process (1991–2000). Derrida argues, in accordance with Deleuze and Guattari's account of the nature of concepts and his own logic of iterability, that forgiveness is a complex and open-ended concept. It is uncertain whether it applies in the first instance to acts or to persons. It is unclear whether is it only the wronged party who can offer forgiveness or whether it can or must involve some third party who intervenes between victim and perpetrator. On the one hand, there is reason to accept that forgiveness "in the strict sense" must be a direct and unmediated matter between the parties involved. On the other hand, there is reason to say that forgiveness can be realized only by virtue of the mediation of some universalizing instance such as the state, the law, or language. After all, there can be no scene of forgiveness without a common language in which to understand the nature of the wrong or the identity of the parties involved: "When the victim and the guilty share no language, when nothing common and universal permits them to understand one another, forgiveness seems deprived of meaning" (Derrida 2001a, 122; 2001b, 48).

The second form of deconstructive analysis reappears when Derrida argues that the Christian or Abrahamic tradition, from which our uses of the term *forgiveness* are derived, is fundamentally divided between a concept of unconditional, infinite forgiveness and a forgiveness that is possible only on certain conditions, such as the repentance of the perpetrator. Under this condition, the guilty party recognizes the crime and in so doing becomes transformed, so that it is no longer the guilty as such who seeks forgiveness. At the same time, he argues, it is only the limit case that gives force, or meaning, to the idea of forgiveness. This includes both the idea of the truly unforgivable act and the idea of forgiveness without conditions: "Must one not maintain that an act of forgiveness worthy of its name, if ever there is such a thing, must forgive the unforgivable and without condition?" (Derrida 2001a, 114; 2001b, 39). The reason is that if one forgave only that which is forgivable, the concept of forgiveness would lose its force, just as it would if one forgave only subject to certain conditions. In the same way, the concept of a gift would lose its force if one gave only that which one was able to give without cost or if one gave only in the expectation of a return. Similarly, the concept of justice would lose its force if it were reduced to the idea of procedural justice in accordance with law, just as the concept of hospitality would lose its force if it did not imply a relation to an unconditional hospitality.

It follows from this analysis that true forgiveness, forgiveness properly so-called, is strictly speaking impossible and therefore paradoxical: How can one forgive the unforgivable? For Derrida, however, to say that the logic of forgiveness relies on this paradox is not to disqualify it. On the contrary, it is to draw a line between the logic of forgiveness as such and all forms of conditional forgiveness. In *Of Hospitality*, he identifies a parallel antinomic structure within the law or the concept of hospitality. On the one hand, hospitality as it is practiced in particular contexts is always conditional. It is always offered to certain determinate others, endowed with a particular social status, and subject to certain reciprocal duties in relation to the rights of the host. On the other hand, the conditional practice of hospitality derives its force and its meaning from a concept of absolute or unconditional hospitality that would welcome the other in the absence of any conditions such as knowledge of name, status, or provenance, and without any restrictions with regard to their movements or behavior while in the domain of the host:

> Absolute hospitality requires that I open up my home and that I give not only to the foreigner (provided with a family name, with the social status of being a foreigner, etc.), but to the absolute, unknown, anonymous other, and that I *give place* to them, that I let them come, that I let them arrive, and take place in the place I offer them, without asking of them either reciprocity (entering into a pact) or even their names. The law of absolute hospitality commands a break with the hospitality of right, with law or justice as right. (Derrida 1997b, 29; 2000, 25).

Derrida draws several consequences from this analysis of the relationship between the conditional and unconditional poles within such ethicopolitical concepts. The first is that there is always an irreducible gap between the conditional and unconditional. Forgiveness proper remains heterogeneous to the order of political or juridical thought, just as absolute hospitality remains irreducible to ordinary, conditional hospitality: "as strangely heterogeneous to it as justice is heterogeneous to the law to which it is yet so close, from which in truth it is indissociable" (Derrida 1997b, 29; 2000, 27). On the one hand, he acknowledges that we could never "in the ordinary sense of the words" found a politics or law on forgiveness in this unconditional sense (Derrida 2001a, 114; 2001b, 39). On the other hand he argues that, in all the geopolitical scenes of forgiveness or reconciliation referred to earlier, there is an implicit appeal to "a certain idea of pure and unconditional forgiveness, without which this discourse would not have the least meaning" (Derrida 2001a, 119; 2001b, 45). In practice, it is never a question of pure forgiveness because there is always some kind of "transaction" or exchange involved. In the case of the Australian reconciliation process, for example, the exchange might be described as involving the legitimacy of a nation-state that aspires to be postcolonial in return for some special rights on the part of the indigenous inhabitants. "It is always the same concern: to see to it that the nation survives its discords, that the traumatisms give way to the work of mourning, and that the nation-State not be overcome by paralysis" (Derrida 2001a, 116; 2001b, 41).

The second consequence Derrida draws from this analysis is that the indissociable bond between these two heterogeneous poles of the concept in question serves to keep open the possibility of change. In this manner, the intimate relationship between law and justice guarantees that existing laws can always be criticized as unjust, just as the implicit relation to unconditional forgiveness ensures that the conditions under which forgiveness can occur remains open. With regard to the law, he argues that the deconstruction of existing law "takes place in the interval that separates the undeconstructibility of justice from the deconstructibility of *droit* (authority, legitimacy and so on)" (Derrida 1992a, 15; 1994a, 35). By the same token, while absolute or unconditional forgiveness is irreducible to the order of conditions, it is manifest only insofar as it engages with the conditions that obtain in particular historical scenes of forgiveness. The resolution or nonresolution of particular processes of reconciliation or forgiveness necessarily takes place in the interval between these two poles. In effect, the indissociability of these two poles amounts to a call for the invention of new protocols of forgiveness capable of meeting the demands of a particular situation: "It is between these two poles, *irreconcilable but indissociable*, that decisions and responsibilities are to be taken" (Derrida 2001a, 119; 2001b, 45). Far from paralyzing the desire for resolution or improvement in a given situation, Derrida suggests that this distinction requires us to invent new intermediate schemas in the Kantian sense of protocols that serve to actualize concepts in the field of the sensible (Derrida 1997b, 131; 2000, 147). In the specific case of the law of hospitality,

It is a question of knowing how to transform and improve the law, and of knowing if this improvement is possible within an historical space which takes place *between The* Law of an unconditional hospitality, offered *a priori* to every other, to all newcomers, *whoever they may be*, and *the* conditional laws of a right to hospitality, without which *The* Law of unconditional hospitality would be in danger of remaining a pious and irresponsible desire, without form and without potency, and even of being perverted at any moment. (Derrida 1997a, 57: 2001b, 22–23)

Finally, the third consequence that Derrida draws is that the unconditioned is necessary to inflect politics or to bring about change. Just as it is it is by appealing to justice or to "a certain beyond of the law" that the law can be modified or improved, so it is by reference to the paradoxical idea of the unforgivable that we can "orient" an evolution of the law or inspire new forms of responsibility. Thus, for example, when in 1964 the French Government decided that there should be no statute of limitations for crimes against humanity, they did so on the basis of an appeal to a certain idea of the unforgivable and an implicit reference to the transcendent order of the unconditional (Derrida 2001a, 127; 2001b, 53). The case for the establishment of an international criminal court might also be supposed to involve an appeal to the idea of unforgivable crimes that justify a recourse to law over and above that of sovereign states.

In all cases, the distinction between these two indissociable but heterogeneous orders is a reason to think that we are not "defined" by the statutory forms of our belonging to a nation-state, by citizenship, or by the existing practices that determine our political being: "Must we not accept that, in heart or in reason, above all when it is a question of forgiveness, something arrives which exceeds all institution, all power, all juridico-political authority?" (Derrida 2001a, 128; 2001b, 54). This "beyond" is what interests Derrida throughout his analyses of ethicopolitical concepts. It appears under a variety of names: the Other, justice, unconditional or absolute hospitality, and so on. Another way to describe the achievement of this form of conceptual analysis would be to say that it invents, in a variety of specific vocabularies tailored to fit the needs of a particular occasion, a series of descriptions of this "beyond." In all cases, it provides the aporetic assurance of an open future: at once both the condition of possibility and the condition of impossibility of change.

The characterization of the absolute form of the concept as an unconditioned suggests a possible correspondence with Kant's transcendental Ideas that Derrida often takes pains to disavow. He argues that justice in itself or democracy-to-come both have the structure of a promise rather than that of a regulative Idea, especially where the latter is understood in a sense that is not strictly Kantian to imply a determinate and in principle realizable form. For Derrida, the unconditioned in all its manifestations must be understood to be impossible in the sense that all aporetic experience involves an experience of the impossible. It is not an ideal form against which particular acts may be measured or toward which our present social arrangements might be said to progress. For this reason, he argues, the deconstructive concept of justice "has no horizon of expectation (regulative or messianic). But for this very reason it *may* have a future (*avenir*), a 'to-come' (*à-venir*) which I rigorously distinguish from the future that can always reproduce the present" (Derrida 1992a, 27; 1994a, 60). The phrase *to-come* here functions as a name for the future understood in such a way that it is not to be identified with any future present but rather with a structural future that will never be actualized in any present, even though it remains capable of acting in or on the present. It is precisely because justice remains to come that justice is not only a juridical or political concept but a philosophical concept that opens up the possibility of transforming, recasting, or refounding law and politics. In other words, the *to-come* stands for a perpetually open, yet to be determined future, understood as "the space opened in order for there to be an event, the to-come, so that the coming be that of the other" (Derrida 2002a, 180). It is this constant orientation toward the other or toward the open future that is named by the phrase *to-come* and that underwrites the political function of this form of deconstructive analysis.

Derrida's concept of the unconditional bears a certain resemblance to Richard Rorty's concept of the cautionary use of the word *true*. Rorty defines this cautionary sense of *true* as "the use we make of the word when we contrast justification with truth and say that a belief may be justified but not true" (Rorty 2000, 4).[3] Because he accepts the historical character of justification and rejects any transcendent concept of truth, he takes this cautionary use of *true* to serve only to mark the ever-present possibility that what we now consider justified may not be so before different audiences in the future. It is a gesture toward "an unpredictable future" that serves to remind us of the gap between what we now consider to be justified and "truth" in any strong metalinguistic or metaphysical sense. Similarly for Derrida, the irreducible gap between the conditional and unconditional forms of the concept, combined with the inevitable reference to the unconditional, remind us of both the possibility and the importance of departing from existing forms of thought or practice. Whenever the question of the purpose or the politics of deconstruction is raised, he points to the undesirability of having a "good conscience" about established ways of acting and thinking. In other words, he points to the desirability of being willing to question and challenge what is currently accepted as self-evident in our ways of thinking and acting. In this sense, he shares with both Deleuze and Guattari and Foucault a commitment to what the latter referred to as the "undefined work of freedom" (Foucault 1997, 316). In other ways, too, despite their quite different philosophical vocabularies, the critical impulse at the heart of deconstruction may be compared with Deleuze and Guattari's pragmatic constructivism. As I will show in what follows, both rely on a concept of the unconditional, and both draw attention to the normative ambivalence implicit in their understanding of the future and the condition of possibility for change.

Absolute and Relative Deterritorialization

Deleuze and Guattari's version of the distinction between conditioned and unconditioned poles of the concept emerges in their definition of the concept of deterritorialization. This concept lies at the heart of the metaphysical normativity elaborated in their collaborative work. In the concluding statement of rules governing certain key concepts in *A Thousand Plateaus*, deterritorialization is defined as the complex movement or process by which something escapes or departs from a given territory (MP 634, 508), where a territory can be a system of any kind, conceptual, linguistic, social, or affective. On their account, such systems are always inhabited by "vectors of deterritorialization," and deterritorialization is always "inseparable from correlative reterritorializations" (MP 635, 509). Reterritorialization does not mean returning to the original territory but rather refers to the ways in which deterritorialized elements recombine and enter into new relations in the constitution of a new assemblage or the modification of the old. Absolute and relative deterritorialization are distinguished on the basis that relative deterritorialization concerns only movements within the actual—as opposed to the virtual—order of things. By contrast, absolute deterritorialization takes place in the virtual—as opposed to the actual—order of things. In itself, absolute deterritorialization remains an unrealizable or impossible movement, manifest only in and through relative deterritorialization. Conversely, relative deterritorialization occurs only because there is "a perpetual immanence of absolute deterritorialization within relative deterritorialization" (MP 74, 56). In this sense, absolute deterritorialization is the underlying condition of all forms of actual or relative deterritorialization. At one point, they describe it as "the deeper movement . . . identical to the earth itself" (MP 178, 143). The relationship between these two heterogenous but indissociable movements of deterritorialization parallels the relationship that Derrida discerns between the conditioned and unconditioned poles of the various ethicopolitical concepts he discusses.

Another version of the distinction between the conditional and unconditional emerges in Deleuze and Guattari's concept of becoming, which involves a distinction between a conditioned or sensible form of becoming and an absolute or conceptual form. In *What Is Philosophy?* they define sensible becoming as "the action by which something or someone continues to become other (while continuing to be what it is)" (QP 168, 177). In effect, this amounts to a process very similar to what Derrida calls "iteration." By contrast, conceptual becoming is "the action by which the common event itself eludes what is. Whereas conceptual becoming is heterogeneity grasped in an absolute form, sensible becoming is otherness (*alterité*) engaged in an expressive material" (QP 168, 177). In *A Thousand Plateaus*, they describe a whole series of sensible becomings: becoming-animal, becoming-child, becoming-woman, and so on. These are specific and conditioned processes by which something or someone becomes other in relation to the real or imagined capacities of something else. These different becomings may be ordered in various ways. For example, in relation to the masculine standard of European cultural and political normality, they argue that "all becomings begin with and pass through becoming-woman" (MP 340, 277). Along another axis, however, these forms of sensible becoming may be contrasted with the unconditioned form or "immanent end" of all becomings, which they call "becoming-imperceptible" or "becoming-world." This is the form of becoming in which an individual is reduced to an abstract line that can connect or conjugate with other lines thereby making "a world that can overlay the first one, like a transparency" (MP 343, 280). It is a paradoxical becoming in which the individual is divorced from everything that constitutes its worldly identity, albeit in its own way. The individual is no longer considered from the point of view of movement, which refers only to relative deterritorialization, but from the point of view of the intensive process of absolute deterritorialization (MP 345, 282).

Deleuze and Guattari do not dwell on the aporetic character of the extreme or unconditioned form of the concepts outlined in *A Thousand Plateaus*. However, it is not difficult to find the elements of paradox in each case. For example, consider the ambiguous status of relative deterritorialization that can be either positive or negative. It is negative when the deterritorialized element is immediately subjected to forms of reterritorialization that enclose or obstruct its line of flight. It is positive when the line of flight prevails over secondary reterritorializations, even though it may still fail to connect with other deterritorialized elements or enter into a new assemblage. Relative deterritorialization therefore can lead either to effective change or transformation within a given territory or system or to defeat and immediate reterritorialization. Because absolute deterritorialization is the underlying condition of relative deterritorialization in all its forms, it follows that it may be described in terms of the Derridean formula as at once both the condition of possibility of change and the condition of its impossibility (see Chapter 7, p. 148).

To take another example, consider the ambiguous status of the lines of flight along which individual or collective assemblages break down or become transformed. At one point, they refer to the "paradox" of fascism, understood in terms of the ambiguity of the line of flight (MP 281, 230). Lines of flight or deterritorialization are at once both the source of the highest creativity and the affect associated with this state, namely joy, and the source of "a strange despair, like an odour of death and immo-lation, a state of war from which one returns broken" (MP 280, 229). The molecular as opposed to the molar line already constitutes a mortal threat to the integrity of a subject with a given set of desires, aspirations, or notions of the good. It is along this line that the subject undergoes "molecular changes, redistributions of desire such that when something occurs, the self that awaited it is already dead, or the one that would await it has not yet arrived" (MP 243, 199). The freedom expressed in this kind of becoming other is incompatible with the continued existence of the stable subject of liberal political philosophy. In *Deleuze and the Political*, I called this "critical freedom," following James Tully's use of this term, to distinguish this capacity for metamorphosis from the standard liberal concepts of positive and negative freedom (Patton 2000, 83–87). The free-dom expressed in Deleuze and Guattari's third line, the line of flight or absolute deterritorialization, is monstrous in the way that Derrida once argued that the future "can only be anticipated in the form of an absolute danger. It is that which breaks absolutely with constituted normality and can only be proclaimed, *presented*, as a sort of monstrosity" (Derrida 1967, 14; 1974, 5).[4] The freedom expressed in Deleuze and Guattari's becoming-imperceptible is just such a form of "absolute danger." Once embarked on this line, "One has become imperceptible and clandestine in motionless voyage. Nothing can happen, or can have happened, any longer . . . Now one is no more than an abstract line, like an arrow crossing the void. Absolute deterritorialization" (MP 244, 199–200).

Pure Events and the Event to Come

In *What Is Philosophy?* Deleuze and Guattari provide another vocabulary in which to express the distinction between conditioned and unconditioned forms of a given concept when they define the objects of philosophical concepts as pure events. Philosophical concepts, they say, express pure events. While pure events are expressed or incarnated in bodies and states of affairs in the course of everyday or historical events, the pure event in itself exists independently of these impure incarnations: "The event in its becoming, in its specific consistency, in its self-positing concept, escapes History" (QP 106, 110). So, for example, the political philosophical concept of a social contract might be supposed to express the pure event of incorporation of a political and legal system with certain features—guaranteed personal freedoms, rights to property, equal treatment before the law, and so on. This pure event is expressed in different concepts of the nature of the social contract and more or less imperfectly actualized in societies founded on a rule of law, but it remains irreducible to this series of expressions and actualizations. Understood in this manner, the concepts set out in *A Thousand Plateaus* are, in the first instance, the expression of pure events: deterritorialization, becoming, incorporeal transformation, capture, metamorphosis, and the like. In themselves, and in accordance with the paradoxical character of the unconditioned described above, such pure events are unrealizable or "unlivable" forms (QP 148, 156). They are actualized only secondarily, through their incarnation in particular historical phenomena as contingent and conditioned versions of such events: *this* form of capture, *this* process of deterritorialization, becoming-animal as opposed to becoming-child or becoming-non-European, and so on.

In his earlier work, Deleuze pointed to the paradoxical character of the objects of specifically philosophical thought. For example, in *Difference and Repetition*, he drew on Kant's suggestion that the transcendental Ideas that are the objects of reason are like problems that have no solution, in order to describe the objects of philosophical thought as transcendental Ideas or problems. Just as pure events are supposed to be independent of their actualizations, so transcendental problems were considered to be irreducible to the particular solutions in which they are incarnated. The clearest cases of irresolvable problems are of course paradoxes; and, at one point, Deleuze refers to the transcendental object of the faculty of sociability, revolution, as "the paradox of society" (DR 269, 208).

In *The Logic of Sense*, he introduced the concept of pure events via a discussion of the Stoics and the paradoxes that they identified in relation to the temporal identity of events. Thus, in his discussion of Lewis Carroll in the opening paragraph, Deleuze points to the paradoxical nature of events from the perspective of ordinary time. When we say that Alice grew (she became taller), this implies that she became taller than she was before. By the same token, however, she also became shorter than she is now (assuming that she continued to grow). The realm of becoming thus admits contradictory predicates (becoming taller, becoming shorter) in a manner inconceivable within linear time. Although she is not taller and shorter at the same time, she becomes taller and shorter at the same time: "This is the simultaneity of a becoming whose characteristic is to elude the present" (LS 9, 1). Pure events are coextensive with such becomings.

The concept of the pure event does not feature prominently in Derrida's work, although in *Signature, Event, Context* he does explain the "enigmatic originality" of every signature by reference to "the pure reproducibility of a pure event" (Derrida 1972, 391; 1988, 20). In effect, all of his deconstructive aconceptual concepts might be supposed to refer to pure events or to variations on the one pure event of sense or meaning as given by the structure of iteration: writing, the trace, *différance*, dissemination, metaphoricity, and so on. In *Spectres of Marx*, he speaks of the concept of democracy in terms that resemble Deleuze and Guattari's talk of pure events, namely as the concept of a promise that can never be fully realized in any actual society, however democratic (Derrida 1993, 110–111; 1994b, 64–65). Just as Deleuze and Guattari distinguish the idea of revolution from the bloody historical events associated with this concept (QP 96–97, 100–101), so Derrida distinguishes the idea of democracy from its more or less inadequate historical determinations (Derrida 2002a, 179). Deleuze and Guattari do not refer to the pure event of democracy, but they do make reference to a "becoming-democratic" that is irreducible to an existing form of constitutional state (QP 108, 113). In his later work, Derrida prefers to speak of a perpetually inaccessible "democracy to come," where what is important is not so much the "democracy" as the "to come" (Derrida 2002a, 182). In the same way that justice is not a determinate ideal, "democracy to come" is not the name of any future democracy but the paradoxical combination of a promise, which implies deferred presence, and the effectivity of the event of that promise in the singular now that is irreducible to any present (Derrida 2002a, 180). This is a concept of democracy understood in terms of the logic of *différance* or iterability that, according to Derrida, characterizes any event. It stands to the pure event of democracy as Deleuze and Guattari's sensible becoming stands to pure or conceptual becoming.

I suggested above that what motivates deconstruction in its aporetic analysis of concepts is the relation that emerges in each case to something beyond. This beyond is invariably associated with an experience of the impossible in the sense that an invention properly so called would involve the coming about of something that does not belong to the existing order of possibilities. The beyond is an impossible object of experience to the same degree and in the same sense that the truly other or the pure event are impossible. Derrida argues that events only happen "under the aegis of the impossible. When an event, efficiency, or anything is deemed possible, it means that we have already mastered, anticipated, pre-understood and reduced the eventhood of the event" (Derrida 2002a, 194). In this sense, the event is not something that comes from the future present but from an absolute future that is necessarily monstrous: "A future that would not be monstrous would not be a future" (Derrida 1992b, 400; 1995, 387).

At this point, the common political orientation that informs both Derrida's and Deleuze and Guattari's practice of philosophy manifests itself in a partial convergence of their respective vocabularies with regard to the future and the pure event. As we saw above, there is an internal connection between Deleuze and Guattari's ethic of deterritorialization and the orientation toward a perpetually open future or "to-come." This is apparent in the role played by the concept of absolute deterritorialization in the ontology of assemblages outlined in *A Thousand Plateaus*: Even though in itself it is an impossible or "unliveable" state, absolute deterritorialization is like a reserve of freedom or movement in reality that is activated whenever relative deterritorialization takes place. Absolute deterritorialization is the underlying principle that ensures that the future will be different from the past or that the future must be understood as inhabited by the permanent possibility of otherness or monstrosity. In political terms, absolute deterritorialization is manifest as revolution or the minor forms of becoming-revolutionary, which are not to be confused with the past, present, or future of actual revolutions but which nonetheless call for new Earths and new peoples (QP 97, 101).[5]

In *What Is Philosophy?* this orientation toward an open future is transposed onto philosophy itself. Deleuze and Guattari call the process of inventing concepts that extract events from existing states of affairs the "counter-effectuation" of those events: "The event is actualized or effectuated whenever it is inserted, willy-nilly, into a state of affairs; but it is *counter-effectuated* whenever it is abstracted from states of affairs so as to isolate its concept" (QP 150, 159). In counter-effectuating events, we attain and express the sense of what is happening around us. To think philosophically about the present is therefore to counter-effectuate the pure events that animate everyday events and processes. Conversely, to describe current events in terms of such philosophical concepts is to relate them back to the pure events of which they appear only as one particular determination, thereby dissociating the pure event from the particular form in which it has been actualized and pointing to the possibility of other determinate actualizations. But philosophy as the creation of untimely concepts does not extract just any event from things but "new" events, meaning events that are forever new, like justice, unconditional forgiveness, absolute hospitality, or democracy to come.[6] Herein lies the utopian vocation of philosophy, which Deleuze and Guattari redefine as the manner in which philosophy engages with the present. Even as they admit that perhaps *utopia* is not the best word for what they mean, they assert its etymological connection with the now-here, the singular moment at which absolute deterritorialization meets the present relative milieu of bodies and states of affairs (QP 96, 100). This is the same singular and paradoxical moment at which, for Derrida, the event of the promise implied in the "to-come" takes place in the present (Derrida 2002a, 180).[7] It therefore comes as no surprise that Deleuze and Guattari should describe the object of philosophical creation, the concept, as "the contour, the configuration, the constellation of an event to come" (QP 36, 32–33).

Philosophy, they argue, is a vector of deterritorialization to the extent that it creates concepts that break with established or self-evident forms of understanding and description. For Derrida, too, the irreducible gap between the conditioned and unconditioned forms of the concept, combined with the inevitable reference to the unconditioned, serves to remind us of both the possibility and the importance of departing from existing forms of thought or practice. Whereas his deconstructive analysis seeks to identify conditional and unconditional poles within existing ethicopolitical concepts, Deleuze and Guattari's philosophical constructivism seeks to create untimely concepts that serve the overriding aim of opening up the possibility of transforming existing forms of thought and practice. The concepts that they invent, such as becoming, capture, lines of flight, and deterrritorialization, are not meant as substitutes for existing concepts of justice, rights, democracy, or freedom. Nevertheless, they serve the political task of philosophy only to the extent that they assist in bringing about another justice, new rights, or novel forms of democracy and freedom.

3 ▚▚▚▚▚

Redescriptive Philosophy:
Deleuze and Rorty

In one of his last essays on Derrida, Richard Rorty called for a "syncretic, ecumenical perspective" that would minimise differences between his own pragmatism and the "postmodernism" of French philosophers such as Foucault and Derrida (Rorty 1998b, 338). Any serious pursuit of this program would have to include Deleuze and Guattari at the head of the list of those French philosophers who have much in common with Rorty's pragmatism. Because Rorty wrote very little on either Deleuze or Guattari, and almost nothing that is favorable, this might seem an implausible extension of his ecumenical perspective. At an early stage in his engagement with French "postmodern" philosophers he wrote a brief review of Deleuze's *Nietzsche and Philosophy* together with Richard Schacht's *Nietzsche,* in which he painted a rather unflattering picture of a Parisian silliness that was supposed to have cultivated and imitated "the more fatuous side of Nietzsche" (Rorty 1983, 620). Deleuze's crime was to have taken seriously Nietzsche's metaphysical system-building tendency and to have elaborated the theory of will to power in a manner that ultimately "dissolves everything into a mush of reactive forces in order to bring out their underlying nastiness" (Rorty 1983, 619). Thereafter, references to Deleuze in Rorty's work are scarce and mostly consist of adding his name to lists of French "postmodernist" philosophers alongside Foucault, Lyotard, and Derrida.[1]

Rorty's ignorance of Deleuze was matched by the latter's cursory attention to his work as expressed in occasional ironic comments about "the Western democratic popular conception of philosophy." The introduction to *What Is Philosophy?* abruptly asserts that the idea of philosophy as a "Western democratic conversation between friends has never produced the slightest concept" (QP 12, 6).[2] Deleuze later identifies the leading proponent of this conception of philosophy in suggesting that it provides no more than the occasion for "pleasant or aggressive dinner conversations at Mr Rorty's" (QP 138, 144). Disagreement over the nature of concepts and their role in philosophy provides one of the striking points of difference between them. Deleuze's insistence that philosophy creates concepts appears to be directly contradicted by Rorty's insistence that there are no such things as concepts, only the more or less systematic uses made by people of particular words. Because for Deleuze the invention of concepts is inseparable from the deployment of new vocabularies and new uses of words, it is not clear how far this is a serious difference between them. In any case, there are more than enough far-reaching similarities between their approaches to philosophy to make the lack of any sustained engagement between them regrettable. Their mutual misrecognition amounted to an unfortunate *rendez-vous manqué* in contemporary social and political philosophy.

My aim in this chapter is to offer some reasons for thinking that, of all the French "postmodernists," Deleuze is the one who comes closest to many of Rorty's views. I begin by suggesting that, appearances to the contrary, Deleuze is a pragmatic and ironist rather than metaphysical thinker in Rorty's sense of these terms. I then discuss their shared opposition to representational approaches to thought and language and the parallels between Deleuze and Guattari's constructivism and Rorty's descriptivism. In the third section, I argue that Deleuze's apparently metaphysical conception of meaning and pure events implies an intimate connection between everyday events and their descriptions. The final section discusses the "politics of redescription" implied by Deleuze and Guattari's pragmatism along with some significant differences between their approach to politics and Rorty's liberal ironism.[3]

Postmetaphysical Ironism

Exposing the common ground between Rorty and Deleuze requires an effort of translation between different philosophical idioms of the kind Rorty imagines when he calls for a book about Derrida that would meet analytic philosophers halfway and not treat concepts as quasi-persons (Rorty 1998b, 329–330). Reconciling idioms in this manner, he suggests, would contribute to breaking down barriers to international communication that are the result of nothing more than "the very different courses

of reading that different countries demand of their philosophy students"
(Rorty 1998b, 329). To take one example of their parallel trajectories
within very different philosophical vocabularies, Deleuze and Rorty both
develop powerful critiques of the representationalism that has dominated
the philosophical tradition. However, whereas in *Philosophy and the Mirror of Nature* Rorty follows the later Wittgenstein, Sellars, and Quine in
completely abandoning transcendentalism in its Kantian form, Deleuze
repeatedly argues in transcendentalist terms against the representational
image that has dominated philosophy from Plato onward. In *Difference
and Repetition*, he proposes an alternative account of the transcendental
conditions of thought, following the post-Kantian path opened up by
Salomon Maïmon that transforms these from conditions of possibility to
conditions of actuality.

Does this reliance on the language of transcendental philosophy
mean that Deleuze is a metaphysician in Rorty's sense of the term? Not at
all. While he continues to make use of metaphysical distinctions such as
that between a virtual and an actual realm of existence, or metaphysical
concepts such as the idea of a pure event, he does so in a manner that is
entirely consistent with the antimetaphysical ironism that Rorty outlines
in *Contingency, Irony, Solidarity.* His solo writings display a highly developed and self-conscious ability to move from one philosophical vocabulary to another. From one book to the next, he changes his use of particular terms in accordance with the requirements of the problem or problems
to be addressed. It is in this sense that he suggests that philosophy should
be conceived as part detective novel part science fiction (DR 3, xx). Giving
up on the idea of accurately representing the world leaves us with the task
of replacing the forms of description practised by our predecessors with
new vocabularies or replacing old descriptions with new ones that enable
us to cope better with the world.

Unlike metaphysicians, who believe that there are real essences and
an intrinsic nature of things that it is the task of philosophy to discover,
Rorty's ironists are nominalists who believe that nothing has an intrinsic
nature or real essence. They are also historicists who believe that all our
descriptions of events and states of affairs are couched in the terms of particular vocabularies that are subject to change: "Ironists agree with Davidson about our inability to step outside our language in order to compare
it with something else, and with Heidegger about the contingency and
historicity of that language" (Rorty 1989, 75). As such, an ironist is aware
of the contingency of his or her own "final vocabulary" and also aware

that such vocabularies can be neither justified nor refuted by argument but only replaced by other vocabularies. Rorty's ironist pragmatism abandons any orientation toward a true theory of how things are in favor of the creation of new vocabularies that enable more useful descriptions of the world. He recommends that we give up talk of truth and falsity in philosophy and instead talk about the degree to which a new vocabulary is interesting, where "interesting" philosophy is usually "a contest between an entrenched vocabulary which has become a nuisance and a half-formed new vocabulary which vaguely promises great things" (Rorty 1989, 9). Redescription rather than argument is the only appropriate method of criticism of an existing vocabulary, and as a result ironists are those who "specialise in redescribing ranges of objects or events in partially neologistic jargon, in the hope of inciting people to adopt and extend that jargon" (Rorty 1989, 78).

For Deleuze too, the practice of philosophy is inseparable from the elaboration of new vocabularies. He makes this point in his commentaries on Foucault, for example, in showing how his concept of the "diagram" of disciplinary power concept is inseparable from the vocabulary of power, forces, and bodies developed in *Discipline and Punish* and related texts, as well as from the vocabulary developed to describe discursive formations in *The Archaeology of Knowledge* (DRF 235, 256). He often singles out Foucault's concept of "utterance" (*énoncé*) as one of his most important conceptual inventions (DRF 356, 385). In his own case, as we noted in Chapter 2 (pp. 41–42), the prodigious exercise of concept creation undertaken with Guattari in *A Thousand Plateaus* provided a whole series of vocabularies in terms of which we can describe significant features of the natural and social world. These include the terminology used to describe different kinds of assemblages, the terms employed in the elaboration of a micropolitics of desire, and a typology of different processes of becoming. They also include the terms used to describe capitalism as an axiomatic of flows and those employed in the description of apparatuses of capture and metamorphosis machines. The philosophical method followed throughout this collaborative work is one that eschews argument in favor of the deployment of new vocabularies that enable new forms of description. *What Is Philosophy?* makes it clear that Deleuze shared Rorty's pragmatic conception of the aim of philosophy as providing intellectual tools for particular human ends rather than for the pursuit of truth. In *Difference and Repetition*, he had already described the act of thought as a dice-throw, by which he meant that thinking is a form of experimentation, the success or failure of which lies outside the control of the thinker. In *What Is Philosophy?* he and Guattari suggest that philosophy is a form of experimentation that proceeds via the creation of new concepts. The usefulness of philosophical concepts can be measured by the ways in which they help to change what can be said or written about a given issue and by the degree to which elements of their related vocabularies are taken up in the social sciences and in different varieties of practical reason. For Deleuze no less than for Rorty, philosophy contributes to making the future different from the past by affording new forms of description and therefore new possibilities for thought and action. As a result, the adequacy or inadequacy with which philosophy fulfills its vocation is assessed not in terms of truth and falsity but in terms of categories such as interesting or important (QP 80, 82). Philosophy can offer guidelines for well-formed as opposed to flimsy concepts, but it cannot offer criteria for judging the value of concepts or the importance of the events they express. Philosophy as the invention of concepts is a form of experimentation with regard to what is underway: "To think is to experiment, but experimentation is always [concerned with] that which is in the process of coming about—the new, remarkable and interesting—which replace the appearance of truth and which are more demanding" (QP 106, 111).

Rorty appears to acknowledge the convergence between his work and that of Deleuze in one tantalizingly brief but positive remark in which he suggests that "James and Dewey were not only waiting at the end of the dialectical road which analytic philosophy travelled, but are waiting at the end of the road which, for example, Foucault and Deleuze are currently travelling" (Rorty 1982, vxiii). Once we acknowledge the family resemblance in their approaches to philosophy, additional points of convergence soon emerge. For example, the introduction to *A Thousand Plateaus* shows that they held similar conceptions of text and interpretation. Deleuze and Guattari's claim that there is no philosophically significant difference between what a text is made of and what it talks about parallels Rorty's rejection of the distinction between using and interpreting texts or, more generally, the distinction between signifying bits of the world such as signs and texts and other objects such as trees and quarks. Rorty claims that reading texts is a matter of placing them in relation with "other texts, people, obsessions, bits of information or what have you" (Eco 1992, 105). In remarkably similar terms, Deleuze and Guattari defend the idea of a book that should be regarded as an assemblage with the world rather than an image or representation of it: "We will never ask what a book means, as signified or signifier, we will not look for anything to understand in it. We will ask what it functions with, in connection with what other things it does or does not transmit intensities . . . A book itself is a little machine" (MP 10, 4). The pragmatism of their conception of philosophy is especially evident in the earlier version of this introduction, published separately as *Rhizome*, where they invoke Foucault's conception of a book as a toolbox and Proust's conception of a book as a pair of spectacles in support of their stated aim of producing "a functional, pragmatic book" (R, 72, 67).[4]

Antirepresentationalism

Criticism of the idea that knowledge should be understood as "an assemblage of representations" was a constant theme in Rorty's work from *Philosophy and the Mirror of Nature* onward (Rorty 1979, 136). Deleuze too had long been a critic of the idea that thought should be understood in terms of the representation of an external reality. *Difference and Repetition* criticizes the representational image of thought that dominates the tradition from Plato to Kant and outlines an alternative nonrepresentational conception of thought. At one point he suggests that philosophy understood as the theory of thought remains in the position that modernist painting found itself half a century earlier: "It needs a revolution like the one that took art from representation to abstraction" (DR 354, 276). Deleuze argued in this book, as he had already done in *Nietzsche and Philosophy*, that philosophical reflection on the nature of thought had long been dominated by a single "dogmatic" image that identified thinking with knowing and supposed that knowledge was ultimately a form of recognition. One of the central presuppositions of the dogmatic image is the idea that "thought is the natural exercise of a faculty . . . that there is a natural capacity for thought endowed with a talent for the truth or an affinity with the true" (DR 171, 131).[5] Like Rorty, he follows Heidegger in tracing the origins of this conception to particular metaphors used by Plato in describing knowledge, in particular the analogy between knowledge and perception (Rorty 1979, 158–159).

Deleuze objects that this dogmatic image is a timid and conformist conception of thought, based on the most banal acts of everyday thinking and bound up with the recognition of existing epistemic, moral, and political values. He does not deny that recognition occurs but seeks to retain the name of thinking for the different activity that takes place when the mind is provoked by an encounter with the unknown or the unfamiliar. He points to a passage in *The Republic* in which Plato draws attention to phenomena that force us to think, thereby raising the question whether it is not precisely when we are unable to recognize that we truly think (DR 181, 138). He takes his own preferred model of thought from the situation of the apprentice struggling to come to terms with unfamiliar materials and techniques. He changes the terms of the enquiry to address the real conditions that give rise to thought rather than its conditions of possibility.

In *Nietzsche and Philosophy* he took the will to power as the basis for a genealogical analysis of thought, with the result that thought would no longer be assessed in terms of truth and falsity but in terms of "the noble and the base, the high and the low, depending on the nature of the forces that take hold of thought itself" (NP 118, 104). Nietzsche's approach breaks the connection between thought and truth assumed by the dogmatic image. In so far as it is concerned with the forces that determine thought to take a particular form and to pursue particular objects, it points to the possibility of a genetic and differential analysis of the real conditions that give rise to thought. Having argued that, for Nietzsche, the sense and value of all things is determined by the qualities of the will to power expressed within them, Deleuze concluded that truth is a human construct and that we "always have the truths we deserve as a function of the sense of what we conceive, of the value of what we believe" (NP 119, 104). His point was not to deny the possibility of true statements about the world within a given system of sense and value but rather to suggest that truth is no more than an "abstract universal," the precise content of which remains undetermined (NP 118, 103).

In *Difference and Repetition* he outlined a theory of "transcendental" problems as the ground of thinking and the source of all truths, suggesting that "problems are the differential elements in thought, the genetic elements in the true" (DR 210, 162). Problems here are understood in a sense close to that in which Kant referred to Transcendental Ideas as the problematic horizons of speculative thinking. In these terms, the task of philosophy is to specify the elements and structure of the Ideas or Problems that govern thought in a particular field. Deleuze's conception of transcendental problems as the genetic elements of thought implies a twofold genesis: a logical genesis of truths in the form of solutions to particular problems and a transcendental genesis of the act of thinking in the discovery or constitution of Ideas or Problems. Both geneses are implicated in the activity of apprenticeship that Deleuze takes as his model for thought: "The exploration of Ideas and the elevation of each faculty to its transcendent exercise amounts to the same thing. These are two aspects of an essential apprenticeship or process of learning" (DR 213, 164).

In the terms of the differential and genetic conception of thought that Deleuze outlines in *Difference and Repetition*, there is no reason to believe that the transcendental problems that find expression and determination in the concepts and vocabularies of philosophers exist out there in the world independently of those forms of expression. Nor is there any reason to believe that philosophy, which identifies and describes such Ideas or problems, is moving toward a final vocabulary in terms of which we will be able to represent the world as it really is. Deleuze never embraced the idea that philosophical descriptions of the world can or should converge on a unique true theory. On the contrary, he defended the idea of a transcendental *empiricism* according to which what problems there are is an open question to be answered by the exploration of the field of thought in a given society at a given time. Just as there are Ideas or Problems that correspond to the physical and biological realities studied by natural science, so there are Ideas of psychic structures, languages, and societies that are the objects of social sciences. For Deleuze, the limits of thought are set neither by the ahistorical nature of human reason nor by the nature of reality as such but by the set of problems thrown up by history, by social life, or by the development of particular sciences. In this sense, we can accept that even the vocabulary of the transcendental empiricism outlined in *Difference and Repetition* is entirely consistent with Rorty's historicism.

Philosophical Constructivism

Rorty suggests that, because ironists do not believe in the existence of a final vocabulary that philosophy aims to discover, their self-descriptions will be "dominated by metaphors of making rather than finding, of diversification and novelty rather than convergence to the antecedently present" (Rorty 1989, 77). Deleuze's later work is even more overtly ironist in Rorty's sense of the term than the early work discussed above. *What Is Philosophy?* proposes a definition of philosophy as "the art of forming, inventing or fabricating concepts" (QP 8, 2). The authors explicitly endorse

Nietzsche's characterization of concepts as things that philosophers must not accept as gifts, nor merely purify and polish, but first "*make* and *create*" (QP 11, 5). Their elaboration of this concept of philosophy focuses on a "horizontal" account of the nature of concepts and the process by which they are made rather than a vertical account of the relation of such concepts to the world. In any concept, they suggest, "there are usually bits or components that come from other concepts, which correspond to other problems and presuppose other planes" (QP 23, 18). They argue that concepts are always related to other concepts and to the problems to which they constitute a response: "A concept lacks meaning to the extent that it is not connected to other concepts and is not linked to a problem that it resolves or helps to resolve" (QP 76, 79). Concepts therefore possess a history, which includes the variations they undergo in their migration from one problem to another. Thus, for example, throughout the tradition of contractarian approaches to political philosophy, the concept of the social contract is transformed as a result of being rethought in relation to new problems, while retaining elements of its former incarnations. This concept is transformed by virtue of the differences between Hobbes's and Locke's accounts of the constitution and legitimation of coercive political authority. It is transformed again in Rousseau, Kant, and Rawls.

Deleuze and Guattari's definition of philosophy is stipulative insofar as the creation of concepts serves to distinguish philosophy from other forms of intellectual activity such as science and art: "The concept belongs to philosophy and only to philosophy" (QP 37, 34). Echoes of Kant's distinctions between thought (Ideas) knowledge (concepts), and sensation (intuitions) may be heard in the differences that are spelled out in *What Is Philosophy?* among philosophical concepts, scientific functions, and artistic "blocks of sensation" on the one hand and their respective objects on the other. Science aims at the representation of states of affairs by means of mathematical or propositional functions, while art does not aim at representation but at the capture and expression, in a given medium, of the objective content of particular feelings and sensations. Philosophy falls somewhere in between. It is like science in that it fulfils a cognitive rather than an affective function. At the same time, it is like art, especially modern art, in that it does not seek to refer or to represent independently existing objects or states of affairs. The "decisive" definition of philosophy, they suggest, is that it is the form of thought that produces "knowledge through pure concepts" (QP 12, 7).

The kind of knowledge that philosophy produces is pragmatic rather than metaphysical in Rorty's sense of the latter term. It is not knowledge of the way the world is independently of human concerns and human resources. For Deleuze and Guattari, scientific functions are referential in the limited sense that they refer to bodies or states of affairs that are supposed to exist independently of the function concerned, although not independently of the plane of reference that provides the axes along which functions are defined. The history of science provides a succession of such planes. The independence of the variables on a given scientific plane of reference establishes an external relation between a function and its object, such as a particle with a given position, energy, mass, and spin. This referential relation is rendered explicit in the propositional functions and sentences of formal languages where there is a corresponding domain of interpretation in which the objects that constitute the extension of a given concept are also the referents of singular terms.

By contrast, the objects of philosophical concepts are pure events, and the relation of such concepts to events is not referential but expressive. Concepts express events in the sense that Descartes' *cogito* expresses the event of thought or Hobbes's social contract expresses the event of the establishment of civil society. It is this feature of the relation between concepts and their objects that Deleuze and Guattari have in mind when they claim that the concept is "real without being actual, ideal without being abstract. The concept . . . has no *reference*: it is self-referential; [*in the sense that*] it posits itself and its object at the same time as it is created" (QP 27, 22). In other words, there is no vertical relation between philosophical concepts and the world, only the horizontal relation between concepts and particular characterizations of states of affairs. Philosophical concepts are formulated on the basis of historically variable "planes of immanence," which involve high-level presuppositions about what the world is like, of the kind that Deleuze earlier pointed to in suggesting that philosophy since Plato has largely taken place under the influence of a particular image of thought: "In the end, does not every great philosophy lay out a new plane of immanence, introduce a new substance of being and draw up a new image of thought . . . " (QP 52, 51). Such planes of immanence on which philosophical concepts are constructed are like nets or sieves that filter the chaos that lies on the other side of thought. Deleuze and Guattari suggest that philosophy, science, and art each in their own way cast nets or planes over chaos, thereby aligning themselves with Rorty's historicist and nominalist philosophers who see themselves as providing descriptions for human purposes rather than representing "the way that the world is in itself" (Rorty 1989, 4).

Even though it is presented in a quite different vocabulary, the conception of philosophy outlined in *What Is Philosophy?* in many respects resembles Deleuze's earlier transcendental empiricism. The cognitive function of philosophy as Deleuze and Guattari define it is bound up with their concept of the pure events that philosophical concepts are supposed to express. The vocabulary of this book does not relate the creation of concepts to transcendental Ideas or problems in the manner that Deleuze did in *Difference and Repetition*. Nevertheless, we can still perceive the connections between the different philosophical vocabularies that make this a successor to his earlier account. In *Difference and Repetition* he remarks at one point that "problems are of the order of events" (DR 244, 188). The equivalence of transcendental problems and pure events is reaffirmed in *The Logic of Sense*, where both of these are further identified with sense or the "what is expressed" in propositions (LS 148, 123). Following the Stoics, Deleuze took the "sayable" or sense that is expressed in a proposition and attributed to bodies and states of affairs to be an incorporeal entity that subsists independently of its linguistic expression. In this manner, he outlined a concept of sense as "an incorporeal, complex and irreducible entity, at the surface of things, a pure event which inheres or subsists in the proposition" (LS 30, 19).

The concept of pure events that Deleuze and Guattari put forward in *What Is Philosophy?* also relies on this Stoic distinction between corporeal states of affairs and incorporeal events that "rise like a vapour from the states of affairs themselves" (QP 120, 127). This way of thinking about events is the basis for the distinction between history and becoming throughout Deleuze's work with Guattari (see Chapters 4 and 5). In these terms, pure events are incorporeal entities that subsist over and above the particular forms in which they are expressed in statements and actualized in bodies and states of affairs. An example that Deleuze frequently uses to illustrate this difference is Blanchot's distinction between death as a realizable event toward which "I" may have a personal relation and death as impersonal and inaccessible event towards which "I" can have no relation (LS 178, 151–152; DR 148, 112). Political philosophy provides a fertile field for further examples of such pure events: Insofar as the concept of the social contract may be considered to express the pure event of incorporation of a legal and political system, this contract is irreducible to its incarnation in particular forms of political or civil society. Kant draws a contrast of this kind in *The Contest of the Faculties* when he distinguishes between the concept of a revolution in favor of universal rights of humankind and the manner in which that concept was actualized in the bloody events of 1789. In Deleuze's terms, he showed that "the concept of revolution exists not in the way which revolution is undertaken in a necessarily relative social field but in the 'enthusiasm' with which it is thought on an absolute plane of immanence" (QP 96, 100). In this sense, pure events, whether they apply to individuals (marriage, illness, or death), or to societies (the social contract, colonization, war, or revolution) are incorporeal abstractions that may be actualized in different places at different times but that are not exhausted by such particular determinations. It is as though actual historical events were doubled by a series of ideal or virtual events from which they draw the resources for endless modification. It is for this reason that they can describe the philosophical concepts that express such pure events in terms that recall Derrida's concept of the unconditional, suggesting that the concept is "the contour, the configuration or constellation of an event to come" (QP 36, 32–33).

Deleuze and Guattari contrast the effectuation of a given pure event in particular circumstances with the "counter-effectuation" that occurs when a new concept is extracted from things. They acknowledge that material events are indistinguishable from the bodies and states of affairs in which they are actualized. However, the events that are expressed in philosophical concepts are not material but pure events that exceed their actualization in particular material processes and states of affairs. To counter-effectuate everyday events is therefore to consider them as processes the outcome of which is not yet determined. It is to relate them back to the pure event of which they appear only as one determination or specification or to consider them in the light of the transcendental problem to which they constitute only one particular solution. Because of this, Deleuze and Guattari can suggest that pure events represent a "reserve" of being and the guarantee of an open future (QP 148, 156).

Events and Language

It follows from the account of incorporeals as the "expressed" of statements that the individuation of events as events of a particular kind is dependent on language. There is a parallel here with Elizabeth Anscombe's view that intentional actions are always actions under a description. Anscombe argues that because actions involve intentions; and, because having an intention presupposes some description of what it is one intends to do, it follows that the same spatiotemporal occurrence may correspond to a series of actions: One and the same series of arm movements can correspond to the actions of moving a lever up and down, pumping water, poisoning a well, and so on (Anscombe 1959). Human actions can be identified as actions of a particular kind only by taking descriptions into account. This thesis about the dependence of actions on descriptions implies that the nature of actions is not exhausted by any particular description or set of descriptions. More generally, it implies that the same spatiotemporal occurrence or series of states of affairs may incarnate an open-ended series of actions. Ian Hacking explores some surprising consequences of this thesis. One is the phenomenon to which Nietzsche and Foucault drew attention, namely that new forms of description of human behavior make possible new kinds of action. Only after the discursive characterization of behavior in terms of juvenile delinquency or multiple personality was established did it become possible for individuals to conceive of themselves and therefore to act as delinquents or to switch personalities: "Inventing or molding a new kind, a new classification, of people or of behavior may create new ways to be a person, new choices to make, for good or evil. There are new descriptions, hence new actions under a description" (Hacking 1995, 239). A further surprising conclusion that Hacking draws from this account of the identity of actions is that there is no simple fact of the matter that enables us to say whether a given redescription of a past action is correct or incorrect: "If a description did not exist, or was not available, at an earlier time, then at that time one could not act intentionally under that description" (Hacking 1995, 243).

Deleuze's Stoic conception of pure events involves no reference to intentions; however, it does imply that the specification of everyday events as events of a certain kind is a function of the manner in which they are described. As a result, generalizing Anscombe's thesis about the relation between actions and descriptions points in the same direction as Deleuze's Stoic thesis about the relationship between pure events and the forms of their linguistic expression. On Anscombe's view, because the same spatiotemporal occurrence may constitute more than one action and therefore be described in a variety of ways, it follows that the nature of spatiotemporal events considered as actions is essentially indeterminate. For Deleuze, there is a similar indeterminacy associated with the event proper or pure event because this is not reducible to the manner in which it is incarnated in particular states of affairs. Conversely, there is no limit to the variety of events that may be incarnated in a given spatiotemporal occurrence or series of states of affairs. In other words, whether we consider everyday incarnate or impure events as spatiotemporal occurrences under a description or as the actualization in bodies and states of affairs of a given pure event, their character as events of a particular kind will be determined by the way in which they are described.[6]

The Politics of Redescription

Because the manner in which a given occurrence is described or "represented" within a given social context determines it as a particular kind of event, there is good reason for political actors to contest accepted descriptions. In their discussion of language use in *A Thousand Plateaus*, Deleuze and Guattari describe the changes in the status of a body or in its relations to other bodies that occur when it is subject to a new description as moments of "incorporeal transformation." The explicit performative statements that provided Austin with the point of departure for his theory of speech acts are the clearest cases of such events. A judge's sentence transforms an accused person into a convicted felon. What took place before (the murder, the trial) and what takes place after (the punishment) are corporeal events. These involve changes of state that affect bodies, their passions, and their interrelations, but "the transformation of the accused into a convict is a pure instantaneous act or incorporeal attribute" (MP 102, 81). Deleuze and Guattari argue that the pragmatic function of language consists in the attribution or effectuation of the incorporeal transformations current in a society at any given time: reaching adulthood, becoming unemployed, improving efficiency, restoring accountability, and so on. Understood in these terms, language use is not primarily the communication of information but a matter of acting in or on the world. Event attributions do not simply describe or report preexisting events; they help to actualize particular events in the social field. That is why politics frequently takes the form of struggle over the appropriate description of events: Was that a terrorist act or an act of war? Is this a legitimate defence of national interest or an illegitimate act of aggression?

Deleuze's Stoic conception of events not only points to the role of language and other forms of representation such as electronic media in the actualization of everyday events; it also points to a critical role for philosophy in relation to the commonsense understanding of events. The conception of philosophy outlined in *What Is Philosophy?* implies a constructivist and critical engagement with what Rorty calls the final vocabularies that characterize a particular society at a particular time. For Rorty, irony is opposed to common sense, where the latter is understood as the attitude of those who take for granted "the final vocabulary to which they and those around them are habituated" (Rorty 1989, 74). Similarly, for Deleuze and Guattari the attitude of common sense is the very antithesis of philosophy as they understand it. Common sense is the domain of opinions, where these are by definition wedded to the final vocabulary of a given milieu. On their account, philosophy is untimely and "worthy of the event" when it does not simply respond to events in the terms of common sense but rather creates *new* concepts that enable us to counter-actualize present events and historical processes and to propose new descriptions of events and situations.

Critical engagement with current self-evidence regarding the nature of events may take a variety of forms. Baudrillard's ironic theory-fiction exemplifies a purely negative manner of problematizing the commonsense representation of historical events. In his essay on the first Gulf War, he argued that what took place was not a war because the military operations undertaken on either side demonstrated such enormous disparities in technology and strategy that direct encounters between opposing forces rarely took place. The overall effect was more in the nature of a police operation than a war (Baudrillard 1995). He was not simply making a rhetorical point that relied on an essentialist concept of war. Rather, he pointed to the fundamental indeterminacy in the pure event of armed conflict. New forms of military technology have made possible a type of engagement at a distance that no longer fits existing descriptions of war. In this sense, Baudrillard enabled us to say that the real is in advance of its representations. From Deleuze and Guattari's point of view, we might say that a new concept is required to give expression to the new type of event that took place in the Gulf.

Foucault provides another example of a philosopher who consciously seeks to break with common sense. In "Polemics, Politics and Problematizations: An Interview," he described his work as attempting to "problematize" aspects of present social reality without attempting to spell out an alternative politics that might contain "the just and definitive solution" (Foucault 1984, 384). By "problematize," he meant proposing new concepts and new descriptions of social phenomena, such as criminal punishment or sexuality, to disturb habitual ways of thinking and talking. In an earlier interview dealing with the method of his historical philosophy, he used the term *eventalisation* to describe this procedure. Foremost among the several meanings he attached to this term was the "breach of self-evidence" that occurs when what was taken to be part of a continuous unbroken history turns out to be singular and contingent (Foucault 2000, 226).

Deleuze and Guattari's conception of philosophy as the invention of concepts amounts to a further means of breaking with self-evidence. Like Rorty, they see philosophy as providing new vocabularies and new means of description. However, their conception of philosophical concepts as means of expression of pure events, that is to say of events that are always yet "to come," implies a more radical break with existing vocabularies. Their agreement with regard to the pragmatic function of philosophy and the politics of redescription this implies only highlights the differences between their respective approaches to politics and the political role of philosophy. Even here, the differences between Rorty's relatively complacent and Deleuze and Guattari's critical pragmatism come into relief against a common background. They share a commitment to broadly "liberal" or progressive politics. They agree with Marx that the job of philosophers is "to help make the future different from the past" (Rorty 1995, 198). Deleuze and Guattari's persistent support for Marx's critique of the inequalities generated by capitalism is matched by Rorty's concern with issues of material social justice.

Beyond this broad agreement, however, they have different views of the manner in which redescriptive philosophy can play a political role. Rorty sees the kind of redescription made possible by the work of philosophers such as Foucault, Deleuze, or Derrida as essentially a private affair. He thinks that there is a tension between the kind of philosophical commitment to the cause of freedom embodied in their work and the commitment to not inflicting pain on others that is part of a liberal public political culture. Because redescription can humiliate and cause pain in others, a liberal public political culture should not impose such redescriptions on others. Rather, it should allow people to be taken on their own terms (Rorty 1989, 88–91). However, the fact that redescription may humiliate and cause pain in others is not sufficient to show that redescriptive philosophy should be regarded as private. The exercise of standard liberal freedoms such as freedom of speech can have the same effects, as a number of recent controversies over offences to religious sensibilities have shown. This does not imply that these are private affairs: On the contrary, it is a reason why the forms of exercise of such freedoms should be subject to public control.

Rorty also thinks that redescriptive philosophy can have no bearing on the political culture of liberal democracies because this is a pragmatic culture concerned principally with issues of public policy, issues on which this kind of philosophy has little to say. Hence the view expressed in *Achieving Our Country* that "the Left should put a moratorium on theory. It should try to kick its philosophy habit" (Rorty 1998a, 91). But many of Rorty's own examples of the kinds of progress achieved by what he calls the cultural left might be taken as evidence for precisely the opposite view. The kinds of conceptual, historical, and social analysis that made it possible to write about the oppression of women, blacks, and gays were not carried out independently of new uses of existing words and the subsequent transformation of philosophical concepts such as exploitation, discrimination, and liberation. This kind of intellectual activity made it possible to invent new forms of description that have contributed to changes in public attitudes and, as a result, eventually to changes in the law and public institutions. Even though he shares the view that the ultimate goal of philosophy is freedom rather than truth, Rorty believes that, at least insofar as social philosophy is concerned, this goal has been reached with the conceptual framework of liberal democratic society. At one point, he suggests that "Western social and political thought may have had the last *conceptual* revolution it needs" (Rorty 1989, 63, emphasis added).

Deleuze and Guattari hold the opposite view: The explicitly political vocation of philosophy lies in its contribution to permanent conceptual revolution. Philosophy's task is the creation of "untimely" concepts in Nietzsche's sense of this term: "acting counter to [our] time, and therefore acting on our time and let us hope, for the benefit of a time to come" (QP 107, 112; see Nietzsche 1983, 60). From *Nietzsche and Philosophy* onward, Deleuze always aligned his conception of philosophy with that of Nietzsche on two points: opposition to those whose ultimate aim is the recognition of what exists and preference for an untimely thought that seeks to invent new possibilities for life. The definition of philosophy put forward in *What Is Philosophy?* is utopian in the strong sense that it is supposed to contribute to the emergence of new forms of individual and collective identity or to summon forth "a new earth and a people that does not yet exist" (QP 104, 108). Rorty suggests that this kind of utopian politics has been the rule rather than the exception among intellectuals ever since the French Revolution fired their romantic imagination and led them to set aside questions about the will of God or the nature of man in favor of the dream "of creating a hitherto unknown form of society" (Rorty 1989, 3). This only partially correct diagnosis allows him to align Foucault and other poststructuralist thinkers with a failed revolutionary utopianism. He then draws a line between his own liberal politics and the utopianism of those who yearn for a kind of autonomy that could never be embodied in social institutions (Rorty 1989, 65).

However, Rorty's diagnosis misrepresents Foucault in attributing to him "the conviction that we are too far gone for reform to work—that a convulsion is needed" (Rorty 1989, 64–65). It ignores the development in Deleuze's political thinking that led him to abandon the Marxist concept of revolution in favor of a "becoming-revolutionary" that is a permanent possibility open to all. Like Foucault, he views this kind of individual and collective self-transformation as our only way of "responding to what is intolerable," where the limits of what is intolerable are themselves historically determined and subject to change (P 231, 171). In this sense, Deleuze and Guattari agree with Foucault that the pursuit of freedom implies a constant effort to detach ourselves from past ways of thinking and acting. On their view, social and political change is played out in the indirect interaction that takes place between forms of becoming minoritarian, in which individuals and groups differentiate themselves from majoritarian political culture, and the norms of that majoritarian culture (see Chapter 8).[7] Rorty's diagnosis relies on a misleading contrast between those who remain in the grip of a Kantian conception of freedom as an inner realm exempt from natural necessity and those who view freedom only as the recognition of contingency (Rorty 1998a, 326). In fact, Foucault, Deleuze, and Guattari share his conception of freedom as the recognition of contingency, along with a commitment to the ever-present possibility of agency within relations of power. This implies the permanent possibility of resistance to forms of domination and exclusion, which they argue is partially realized in the ongoing process of pushing back the limits of what it is possible to do or to be but never finally or entirely achieved. In this manner, change is often brought about by particular reforms, and the redescription made possible by the invention of new concepts contributes to local and specific ways in which the future will be unlike the past.

PART II   COLONIZATION AND DECOLONIZATION
IN HISTORY AND LITERATURE

4

History, Becoming, and Events

Deleuze and Guattari appear ambivalent toward history and historians. *Anti-Oedipus* advocates a universal history that would retrospectively understand all human societies in the light of capitalism (AO 163–164, 153–154). *A Thousand Plateaus* draws extensively on the work of historians of Europe and Asia as well as specialized works of economic and military history and histories of science, mathematics, technology, music, art, and philosophy. At the same time, this book asserts the need for a nomadology that would be "the opposite of a history" (MP 34, 23). Like so many of the other disciplines proposed in *A Thousand Plateaus* (rhizomatics, pragmatics, schizoanalysis, and so on), nomadology is essentially the study of certain kinds of assemblages, in this case states and war machines, as well as the relations between them. What is the relationship between these assemblages and historical processes? What is the function of so much historical material in works of philosophy devoted to the description of abstract machines or assemblages?

In his 1990 interview with Antonio Negri, Deleuze comments that he had become "more and more aware of the possibility of distinguishing between becoming and history" (P 230, 170). In *What Is Philosophy?* this distinction took the form of a contrast between a historical realm in which events are actualized in bodies and states of affairs and an ahistorical realm of pure events, where these are the "shadowy and secret part [of an event] that is continually subtracted from or added to its actualization" (QP 147, 156). Deleuze and Guattari's final collaborative work draws a parallel distinction between Philosophy and History, where the former is understood as the practice of thought that produces concepts that express these pure events, while "what History grasps of the event is its effectuation in states of affairs or in lived experience . . . the event in its becoming, in its specific consistency, in its self-positing concept, escapes History" (QP 106, 110). The pure event is never a determinate kind of event but rather becoming itself, or the process by which something comes about. As such, it is the condition of all change. That is why Deleuze and Guattari suggest that to think by means of concepts is to experiment, where experimentation always involves that which is coming about. By contrast, history (*L'histoire*) is not experimentation but only "the set of almost negative conditions that make possible the experimentation of something that escapes history" (QP 106, 111).[1]

For Deleuze and Guattari, Philosophy is not representational and not directed at discovering ahistorical truths. Rather, it is a kind of practical reason undertaken in pursuit of new Earths and peoples that do not yet exist. Philosophy fulfills its critical function when it creates concepts that give expression to the evental realm of becoming. It achieves its utopian aim when the absolute deterritorialization expressed in its concepts connects with one or other form of relative deterritorialization present in the historical milieu. Philosophy's privileged relation to the pure event and becoming implies that it takes precedence over History, at least in relation to this utopian goal. At the same time, this apparent devaluation of History is tempered by Deleuze and Guattari's account of the manner in which Philosophy fulfils its critical function. They draw on historical knowledge about the circumstances under which Philosophy emerged as a specific form of thought in ancient Greece, about the evolution of capitalism and its relationship to states, and about the kinds of relative deterritorialization present in modern societies.

However, questions remain about the distinction between becoming and history. How does it relate to other distinctions that Deleuze draws between becoming and the corporeal realm of bodies and states of affairs? How does it relate to the differences set out in *Difference and Repetition* and *The Logic of Sense* between the virtual and the actual, between problems and solutions, between effects and causes, between the sense or meaning of propositions and the actualities they describe? How does it relate to the distinction drawn in *A Thousand Plateaus* between the plane of organization and the plane of consistency on which there are no longer species or kinds of body but only body-events or haecceities, or to other distinctions of this kind developed in the course of this book? Here we encounter the difficult problem of how to read Deleuze's texts in relation to one another and in relation to the problems and concepts they appear to share. My approach does not take his successive books to be expressions of a single, uniform philosophy in which there is no change from one project to the next but rather a succession of experiments in which the same issues and concepts are taken up and reworked from a different angle. This is particularly evident in relation to his successive discussions of pure events, their relation to transcendental problems and to becoming. There are many indications that we should proceed with caution, taking into account the different problems from one book to the next as well as the relative constancy of some of the resources and resultant formulations.

Structure, Genesis, and Sense:
The Metaphysics of Pure Events

History is not a primary concern in *Difference and Repetition*, where Deleuze is more concerned with the traditional image of thought in Philosophy and its treatment of sameness and difference, recurrence and repetition. Nonetheless, an early version of the distinction between the realm of becoming and history is implicit in his discussion of the ideational synthesis of difference in Chapter 4. Following Kant, he identifies the Ideas that are the ultimate objects of thought with quasi-transcendent problems that orient human thinking. His transcendental empiricism allows him to go beyond Kant and propose an open-ended list of Ideas that includes the ultimate objects of physical, biological, social, linguistic, and other domains of thought. He defines these problematic Ideas as differential multiplicities or structures and suggests that they are "of the order of events" (DR 244, 188). He also proposes that the relationship between the determinants of a problem and its solutions be understood as a relation between two series of events that develop on parallel planes, echoing without resembling one another: "real events on the level of the engendered solutions and ideal events embedded in the conditions of the problem" (DR 244, 189). In this manner, following Geoffroy Saint-Hilaire, real organisms might be said to actualize the "differential relations between pure anatomical elements" that make up the Idea of the organism as such. Or, following Marx, the real social relations of a given society might be said to actualize the differential relations of production that make up the social Idea (DR 239–241, 184–186).

Insofar as Deleuze provides here the barest outlines of a conception of history, he follows the contours of the structuralist conception proposed by Althusser and his collaborators. They were, he suggests, "profoundly correct in showing the presence of a genuine structure in *Capital* and in rejecting historicist interpretations of Marxism" (DR 241, 186). He takes the capitalist mode of production to be a differential multiplicity or structure whose virtual, internal movements determine the real events that succeed one another in historical time. For this reason, he denies that there is any difficulty in reconciling structure and genesis so long as we understand that genesis does not take place between actual things but "between the virtual and its actualisation." In other words, the genesis of actual states of affairs takes place in a "suprahistorical" time that goes from the differential elements of an ideational structure to real things and the "diverse real relationships that constitute at each moment the actuality of time" (DR 238, 183).[2]

Deleuze's conception of history at this point follows Althusser's suggestion that there would be different kinds of historicity corresponding to particular modes of production: a temporality of the feudal mode, a temporality of the capitalist mode of production, and so on.[3] However, because capitalism is only one solution to the problem or pure event of society as such, this structural-Marxist conception of history was also obliged to account for the transition from one social structure to another. It implied a distinction between those events that express the unfolding in history of a given mode of production and those that express the transition from one mode of production to another. In a phrase that recalls the Althusserian concept of "overdetermination," Deleuze suggests that the historical transition from one solution to another occurs by way of the "condensation" of the singular points of a given structure into a "sublime occasion, *Kairos*, which makes the [new] solution explode like something abrupt, brutal and revolutionary" (DR 246, 190).[4] He equates these revolutionary moments at which the pure event of society breaks through into history with the manifestation of a freedom, "which is always hidden among the remains of the old order and the first fruits of a new" (DR 250, 193).

In *The Logic of Sense* we find the same identification of pure events with problems, and the spatiotemporal actualization of those events with solutions, as in *Difference and Repetition*. However, the concepts do not appear in the same configuration, and they are not mobilized in response to the same problems.[5] Deleuze was more concerned here with the nature of sense or meaning, understood as the depthless surface between words and things. He was concerned with the relation of sense to the structures of signification in which it is produced, to non-sense, and to the impersonal transcendental field on which he locates the corporeal as well as the incorporeal intensities that provide the raw material and subject matter of psychoanalysis. Although history is not a primary concern in *The Logic of Sense* any more than it was in *Difference and Repetition*, the reference to Novalis's distinction between ideal Protestantism and real Lutheranism does give a historical illustration of the distinction between pure events and their actualization in a given context (LS 68, 53).

Bearing in mind the overriding concern with language and the problematics of surface, *The Logic of Sense* still provides one of the most detailed accounts of the incorporeal realm of becoming and the pure event to be found anywhere in Deleuze. The equivalence between sense and pure (ideal) events or becomings is established at the outset, where it is also allied with a particular relation to time. Lewis Carroll's example of Alice's growing—in which her becoming taller is coextensive with her becoming shorter, depending on the temporal direction in which we view this event—is taken to show "the simultaneity of a becoming whose characteristic is to elude the present" (LS 9, 1). This paradoxical simultaneity of contradictory processes provides a reason for distinguishing a historical time within which events occur (*Chronos*) from a time of the event (*Aion*) that remains irreducible to the former (LS 14, 5; 77, 61).

This conception of events and their relationship to time owes much to the Stoics, for whom events were considered to be incorporeal effects of bodily causes. It implies that a pure event such as the event of battle is something over and above the movements of soldiers, horses, and equipment on a given occasion. The pure event is expressed in these particular elements while nevertheless remaining irreducible to them. As Deleuze explains in his comments on Stoicism in *Dialogues*:

The event is always produced by bodies which collide, lacerate each other or interpenetrate, the flesh and the sword. But this effect itself is not of the order of bodies, an impassive, incorporeal, impenetrable battle, which towers over its own accomplishment and dominates its effectuation (D 79, 64).

The Logic of Sense offers reasons why battle functions as an exemplary event in so much of modern literature: because it can be actualized in different ways on different occasions and because, on any given occasion, different participants will grasp different levels of its actualization. As a consequence, in any flesh and blood battle, "the event hovers over its own field, being neutral in relation to all of its temporal actualizations, neutral and impassive in relation to the victor and the vanquished, the coward and the

brave" (LS 122, 100). This conception of pure events as real but nonac-
tual entities, expressed in the successive configurations of material bodies
but irreducible to any particular set of such configurations, continues to
inform the distinction between becoming and history up until Deleuze's
final work. However, its precise meaning is not self-evident.

Some of the formulations employed in these early texts suggest a
substantive distinction between two distinct realms of being. On this
reading, pure events might be understood on the model of Platonic forms
that can be only imitated but never fully realized in any actual thing,
event, or state of affairs. A literal reading of the event of battle hovering
over its particular incarnations and participants might suggest this way of
understanding the extracorporeal realm of pure events, as might Deleuze's
examples of pure events of society, atomism, organism, psychic structure,
language, and so on in *Difference and Repetition*. The same is true of Joë
Bousquet's remark that his wound "existed before him" and Deleuze's suggestion that events of this kind that determine the fate of an individual life
must be understood as "not what occurs (an accident)" but rather as "inside what occurs, the purely expressed. It signals and awaits us" (LS 175,
149).[6] In these terms, pure events would be real and apparently transcendent objects only partially expressed in their spatiotemporal incarnations.
At best, actual historical events would approximate the pure event without
ever incarnating it completely.

Of course, Deleuze's overturning of Platonism and his identification
of pure events with transcendental problems would imply a number of
modifications to this model. Pure events are modelled on certain kinds
of mathematical problem rather than, as with Plato, the pure form or
idea of a given quality: the Just as that which is only just, and so on. It
follows that pure events require specification in ways that already determine the kinds of solution available. However, if we follow this line of
thought through *The Logic of Sense* and its Stoic metaphysics, we encounter a whole universe of banal everyday events such as being-cut-with-a-
knife, the becoming-green of trees, walking, sinning, being-eaten, and so
on. This way of understanding the realm of pure events seems to lead to a
Meinongian universe of intensional objects in which neither their identity
conditions nor their number is well defined. We might wonder how the
event of being cut is related to my accident with the razor this morning
or whether there is a pure event of walking down the stairs to my apartment as well as a pure event of walking. Sometimes Deleuze's overturned
Platonic world of simulacra does appear to evoke this kind of ontological

madness. But is this the best way to understand the distinction between becoming and history?

There are several reasons to be wary of this quasi-Platonic model of the extrahistorical realm of becoming. One has to do with the essential connection that Deleuze asserts between events and language (see Chapter 1, pp. 71–72). *The Logic of Sense* identifies the pure event with the sense or the "expressed" in what is said and argues that it is in the very nature of events to be "expressed or expressible" in propositions. Because what is expressed in a proposition is its sense, it follows that sense and event are two sides of the same incorporeal surface: Sense is the event, "*on the condition that the event is not confused with its spatio-temporal realization in a state of affairs*" (LS 34, 22). Deleuze does not draw a distinction between two sorts of events but rather between events or the sense of what happens and the material unfolding or actualization of events or, as he says: "the event, which is ideal by nature, and its spatio-temporal realization in a state of affairs" (LS 68, 53). In the same way, he insists that the difference between historical time and event time is not an ontological distinction between two temporal orders but a distinction between two "readings" of time (LS 77, 61).

A further reason to question the Platonizing interpretation of pure events is Deleuze's increasingly resolute hostility to transcendence in all its manifestations. This is one of the significant changes that takes place in his thinking alongside his growing commitment to the distinction between becoming and history. In *Difference and Repetition* he was happy to treat Ideas or problems as both immanent and transcendent and to attribute to the ideal series of events "the double property of transcendence and immanence in relation to the real" (DR 219, 169; 244, 189). By contrast, in *What Is Philosophy?*, transcendence is described as a constant temptation, one of the forms of which is "the illusion of the eternal when it is forgotten that concepts must be created" (QP 51, 49–50). The metaphysical reading of pure events above succumbs to precisely this temptation. That is no doubt why he is careful to specify that although the pure event might seem to be transcendent, it is "pure immanence of what is not actualized or of what remains indifferent to actualization, since its reality does not depend upon it. The event is immaterial, incorporeal, unlivable: pure *reserve*" (QP 148, 156).

A final reason to be wary of the substantive understanding of the realm of pure events relates to the task of Philosophy as this is outlined in *What Is Philosophy?* The purpose of creating concepts is to give linguistic expression to the pure event expressed in actual events. However, we encounter difficulties if we try to understand this process in terms of the Platonic model. For this implies that pure events must be discovered in the states of affairs that express them. Yet there appears to be a radical indeterminacy of the event in relation to the historical occurrence or, to put it another way, the state of affairs appears to underdetermine the event or events expressed in it. Controversies in history and political science are made of this. Consider the event of colonization in a particular country: Did this amount to invasion or peaceful occupation? In its purest form, is this a problem of capture of territory, peoples, and resources by a technologically superior power, or is it a problem of encounter between different peoples that might have taken very different forms to those that it took historically? (See Chapter 5, pp. 116–117.) The question becomes even more complex when we take into account the utopian aspiration of Philosophy as Deleuze understands it: The goal is not just the creation of concepts but the creation of concepts that call for new Earths and new peoples. What determines which concepts will serve this purpose? As we saw above, for Deleuze successful philosophical concepts are those that give expression to what is happening now, to the new, remarkable and interesting (QP 106, 111). But how do we determine what is in the process of coming about? In practice, what is the task of Philosophy as opposed to History, and how does this relate to becoming?

Events Untimely and Sublime

One way to approach these questions is suggested by Deleuze's recurrent comparisons between Nietzsche's *untimely* and his own conception of philosophical thought as experimentation. In a 1967 interview, "Nietzsche's Burst of Laughter," he argued that Nietzsche located all his work in a dimension that was neither that of history, even dialectically understood, nor that of the eternal, but the *untimely*, "which operates both in time and against time" (ID 180, 129). He went on to suggest that perhaps a reason for the "return to Nietzsche" in France around this time was the rediscovery of his concept of the untimely dimension. This was certainly true of Deleuze's own philosophy. His 1968 preface to *Difference and Repetition* described the task of modern Philosophy as that of overcoming "the alternatives temporal/non-temporal, historical/eternal and particular/ universal" by following Nietzsche's discovery of the untimely: not to be a philosophy *of* the untimely but to be itself untimely, that is, to act on the present but against it, "let us hope, for the benefit of a time to come" (DR 3; xxi).[7] As we saw above, *What Is Philosophy?* aligns Philosophy with the experimental function of thought, apparently at the expense of History in so far as this is concerned only with the "almost negative conditions" that make it possible to create something new. Deleuze repeats the same lines from Nietzsche's *Untimely Meditation* in describing the "unhistorical vapour that has nothing to do with the eternal" but that is rather "the becoming without which nothing would come about in history but that does not merge with history" (QP 107, 112). What does this identification of becoming with the untimely tell us about Philosophy and its relationship to becoming and history but also its differences from History?

One response is suggested by Deleuze's remarks in "Nietzsche's Burst of Laughter" about those moments at which the untimely and the historical coincide. He gives examples from the successful struggles for the liberation of colonized peoples carried out in Egypt and Cuba in the 1950s and Vietnam in the 1960s (ID 180–181, 130). The parallels between these events and the moments of transition from one historical structure to another referred to in *Difference and Repetition* are evident. They are all turning points in history, after which some things will never be the same as before. Toward the end of this interview, which took place in Paris in April 1967, he laments the absence of such Earth-shattering events in France. After the May uprising less than a year later, he often referred to this event in terms that suggest it was another of those moments at which the untimely and the historical coincide. For example, he described May 1968 as "of the order of a pure event" (DRF 215, 233); as "a becoming breaking through into history" (P 209, 153); and as "a demonstration, an irruption, of a becoming in its pure state" (P 231, 171).[8] Events of this kind express the creative power of becoming or the untimely to transform or reinterpret historical reality. For Nietzsche, Deleuze points out, things are already interpretations, so to reinterpret is to change things: "Politics, too, is in the business of interpretation" (ID 180, 130). It follows that in those moments where becoming breaks though into history that "there is always a coincidence of poetic acts and historical events or political actions, the glorious incarnation of something *sublime* or *untimely*" (ID 180, 130; emphasis added).

Deleuze's characterization of these untimely events as sublime relies on the necessary relationship between events and interpretation. It also points to a new kind of sublimity that it is helpful to explain by means of a comparison with some of Derrida's remarks on the event. In *The Critique of the Power of Judgment* Kant distinguished two kinds of sublime. The "mathematical sublime" is the feeling aroused in us by those sensory experiences of phenomena in which nature conveys "the idea of its infinity" (Kant 2000, 138). By contrast, the dynamical sublime is produced in us by those appearances of nature's might and power that are so overwhelming that the prospect of human resistance to them is inconceivable (Kant 2000, 143–148). To these two kinds of experience of the sublime we can add a third, not discussed by Kant but consistent with his overall conception of the mental faculties, namely the hermeneutical sublime. This is the experience produced by those phenomena that threaten to overwhelm not just our powers of imagination or the capacity of the human will to resist even the threat of annihilation but also our capacity to understand or identify the phenomena in question. Several commentators suggested that the terrorist attacks of September 11, 2001, were sublime events because of the magnitude of the forces that brought about the collapse of the towers, the suffering inflicted on so many people, and the fear and terror that all this inspired (Battersby 2003; Derrida 2003; Kearney 2003). However, Derrida was the only one to point to the hermeneutic dimension, suggesting that part of what made this such an extraordinary and sublime event was the damage wrought on "the conceptual, semantic, and one could even say hermeneutic apparatus that might have allowed one to see coming, to comprehend, interpret, describe, speak of, and name 'September 11'" (Derrida 2003, 93).

Derrida went on to generalize this hermeneutically sublime dimension of September 11 by arguing that every event implies the possibility of resistance to our existing means of representation. In other words, for there to be an event, we must be able to recognize, identify, interpret, or describe a given occurrence as a certain kind of event. At the same time, however, to the extent that an event is a new occurrence at a given moment in time, it must also be endowed with the potential to resist this kind of incorporation within our existing systems of recognition, interpretation, and description. In this sense, he argues, every event, in so far as it is an event, carries the potential to break with the past and to inaugurate a new kind of event:

The event is what comes and, in coming, comes to surprise me, to surprise and to suspend comprehension: the event is first of all *that which* I do not first of all comprehend. Better, the event is first of all *that* I do not comprehend. (Derrida 2003, 90)

For Derrida, this indeterminate and paradoxical future—the "to come" that is the condition of there being events at all—ensures that there is an element of the hermeneutical sublime, a degree of hermeneutical sublimity, in every event. He understands the "to come" as a structural future, presupposed by but irreducible to any actual future present. What Derrida refers to as the "to come," Deleuze calls "becoming" or "absolute deterritorialization." He aligns this with Nietzsche's "untimely" and Foucault's "actual." In each case, it is a question of the pure "event-ness" that is expressed in every event and that is, for that reason, immanent in history. It follows that every event raises with greater or lesser urgency the hermeneutic question "what happened?" In this sense, as Deleuze pointed out in *The Logic of Sense*, all events are signs requiring interpretation. This enigmatic character of events might also be derived from the ambiguous relationship they have to time. On the one hand, they occur at a more or less precise moment in historical time (*Chronos*). On the other hand, it is difficult to pinpoint a precise moment at which a given event takes place. This is because the unactualized part, the pure event-ness of the event, belongs to a different order of time (*Aion*), in which it

> retreats and advances in two directions at once, being the perpetual object of a double question: What is going to happen? What has just happened? The agonizing aspect of the pure event is that it is always and at the same time something which has just happened and something about to happen; never something which is happening. The *x*, with respect to which one feels that *it* just happened, is the object of the "novella"; and the x which is always about to happen, is the object of the "tale." The pure event is both tale and novella, never an actuality. It is in this sense that events are *signs*. (LS 77, 63)

All events are signs in the sense that they provoke the questions that History and historians have sought to answer: What has happened? What is going to happen? Explanations can be given of particular events at different levels: macropolitical, micropolitical, long *durée*, short term, and so on. But these are never conclusive, if only because they work within a given hermeneutical framework. Most historical events are readily assimilable within such frameworks, but every now and then something happens that we cannot assimilate or understand. The events that Deleuze calls instances of "becoming breaking through into history" are instances of this kind. They exhibit the hermeneutical sublime in the highest degree insofar as they realize the potential to break with existing frameworks of understanding. Far from being the actualizations of a particular preexisting event, they are eruptions of "eventality," pure eventness, becoming, or absolute deterritorialization. On other occasions, however, we pass over such thresholds of sense almost without being aware that we have done so. For example, in societies established by colonization, such as Australia, a succession of subtle changes to the political imaginary renders problematic the character of this foundational event. The removal of overt discrimination and the inclusion of the aboriginal inhabitants as full members of the political community mean that "we" now have to understand what happened from the point of view of the colonized as well as the colonizers. Colonization was also invasion. It is no longer evident that there is a coherent, single answer to the question, "What happened?"

It is in relation to these almost imperceptible events that genealogical explanation can be most useful. Consider Nietzsche's response to the epochal event of which he was convinced that few in Europe in the late nineteenth century were even conscious, let alone aware of what it meant: the death of God.[9] This event raises the historical question par excellence—*What has happened?*—but also the prospective, diagnostic question: *What is going to happen?* In effect, the death of God is something that has already happened but also something that is yet to come. *The Genealogy of Morals* sketches an answer to these questions by answering the prior question posed by the demise of European Christianity, namely, What was the meaning of belief in God? Nietzsche points to the peculiar opposition between good and evil and the "inversion of the value-positing eye" that is bound up with this "slave revolt" in morality; to the origins of bad conscience and to the manner in which this was used by various priesthoods in their efforts to contain the worst effects of human *ressentiment*; and finally, to the character of the ascetic ideal, by which he means the belief in a world behind the actual world that allows for a variety of forms of imaginary expression on the part of a human will to power that prefers to will nothingness than not will (Nietzsche 1994, 28). His response is an effort to comprehend both the nature and magnitude but also the meaning of this cataclysmic event. In other words, the genealogical response to historical events that we find in Nietzsche is an interpretative exercise.

Much of Foucault's work takes a similar form. He reinterprets past practices, institutions, and forms of knowledge, but always from the perspective of a hitherto unnoticed distance. His genealogies describe the discursive and nondiscursive formations (*dispositifs*) from which we are separated by hitherto imperceptible fractures in the hermeneutical frameworks within which we live and experience the historical present. In this manner, he shows up the madness of incarcerating the insane, the arbitrariness and injustice of imprisoning convicts, the irrationality of making our identity as subjects depend on our sexual behavior. These are all examples of practices that were previously considered unproblematic or unavoidable but that we can now perceive as contingent and open to change (Foucault 1997, 315). Deleuze argues that, whereas he identifies becoming and Nietzsche identifies the untimely as the source of change, Foucault writes from the perspective of the actual (*actuel*). He does not mean *actuel* in the ordinary French sense of this word, which refers to that which is current or present. He points to a passage in *The Archaeology of Knowledge* in which Foucault draws a distinction between the present (*notre actualité*) and "the border of time that surrounds our present, overhangs it and indicates it in its otherness" and suggests that Foucault writes from this border between present and future (Foucault 1969, 172; 1972, 130). Even though Foucault's text does not describe it in this way, this border region is what Deleuze means by the *actuel*.[10] *What Is Philosophy?* spells out the proximity of Deleuze's "becoming," Nietzsche's untimely (*l'inactuel* or *l'intempestif*), and Foucault's supposed *actuel* in suggesting that all three terms refer to "that which is in the process of coming about": not what we presently are or recently were but rather to "what we are in the process of becoming—that is to say, the Other, our becoming-other" (QP 107, 112). However, while Deleuze regularly compares Nietzsche's untimely and Foucault's *actuel* with the realm of becoming and pure eventness that is the object of his own philosophy, he nowhere undertakes the same kind of genealogical interpretation of events. His comments on a text by Charles Péguy suggest that there is an important difference between the historical responses to the question "What happened?" undertaken by Nietzsche and Foucault and his own philosophical response.

The Internal Dynamics of Events

In *Difference and Repetition*, *The Logic of Sense*, and *What Is Philosophy?* Deleuze cites the same passage from Péguy's *Clio*, an essay in the form of a dialogue between History and a pagan soul, written between 1909 and 1912 but not published until 1932. Péguy refers explicitly to Bergson in presenting History as proceeding on two levels: that of a public, worldly time in which different peoples and distinct periods acquire their character, and that of a *durée* that has its own rhythm, its own periods of contraction and relaxation, its own points of crisis, of suspension and of relief (Péguy 2002, 265). Péguy's muse, History, admits to the existence of moments in public life as in personal memory when all of a sudden a problem that had long proved intractable disappears, and it is as if we became a different person or entered into a different world. The former person or the old world suddenly becomes foreign to us. And yet, in terms of the wordly time of historical events, nothing has happened:

Suddenly, we felt that we were no longer the same convicts. Nothing had happened. Yet a problem in which a whole world collided, a problem without issue, in which no end could be seen, suddenly ceased to exist and we asked ourselves what we had been talking about. Instead of an ordinary solution, a found solution, this problem, this difficulty, this impossibility had just passed what seemed like a physical point of resolution. A crisis point. At the same time, the whole world had passed what seemed like a physical crisis point. There are critical points of the event just as there are critical points of temperature: points of fusion, freezing and boiling points, points of coagulation and crystallisation. There are even in the case of events states of superfusion which are precipitated, crystallised or determined only by the introduction of a fragment of some future event. (Péguy 2002, 269)[11]

In *Difference and Repetition*, Deleuze cites this passage immediately after the assimilation of structures-problems with events and the distinction referred to above between two series of events, one real and one ideal, where the ideal series is described as both transcendent and immanent in relation to the real. He presents Péguy's description of the event as illustrating these two series by deploying "two lines, one horizontal and another vertical, which repeated in depth the distinctive points corresponding to the first, and even anticipated and eternally engendered these distinctive points and their incarnation in the first" (DR 244, 189). *The Logic of Sense* recounts broadly the same concept of structures as determined by the communication or resonance of two series, where a series is a set of singular points or singularities. Within any such structure, the redistribution, displacement, and transformation of these singular points will determine a particular form of historicity. Deleuze here cites the same passage in support of his claim that Péguy "clearly saw that history and events were inseparable from those singular points" (LS 68, 53). In both texts, this passage is used to support the idea that there are two levels or dimensions of time. The surrounding comments focus on the idea that historical events are the expression of singularities that are located in a virtual structure, one that lies outside the order of worldly time.

What Is Philosophy? refers to the same passage in support of a different thesis. Much of the passage cited in *Difference and Repetition* is deleted, and another line from further down Péguy's page is added: "Nothing happened and we are in a new people, in a new world, in a new humanity" (Péguy 2002, 269; QP 107, 111). Here, the emphasis is not so much on the conditions that render possible such experiences but on the experience itself and the question: How should Philosophy respond to such events? Péguy is said to have explained that there are two ways of considering an event. One is the way of the historian that consists in "going over the course of the event, in recording its effectuation in history, its conditioning and deterioriation in history." The other is the way of the philosopher. *Clio* is described as "a great work of philosophy," and the passage is cited to illustrate a way of considering an event that consists in "reassembling the event, installing oneself in it as in a becoming, becoming young again and aging in it, both at the same time, going through all its components or singularities" (QP 106–107, 111).[12] The focus of Deleuze and Guattari's comments on this passage in *What Is Philosophy?* is not so much the distinction between virtual and actual, becoming and history, but the philosophical response to the complexity that we find in all events. Péguy presents us with one of those occasions when, although on the historical surface nothing has happened, there has nonetheless been a sudden and unanticipated break with the past. Something happened on another level such that we find ourselves in a new world with new problems. The hermeneutical challenge is to "make sense" of the event, to answer the question: What happened?

On Deleuze's account here, it is clear that History and Philosophy respond to this question in different ways. History makes sense of the event by characterizing it and providing an explanation. It tells us how the event came about, at some level of generality or duration, what prepared the way for it and made it possible, how it unfolded and eventually dissipated over time. In these terms, genealogy is still a form of historical explanation. Even with all due acknowledgment of the contingency and discontinuity it admits into history, and taking into account the structural rather than the linear causal character of genealogical explanations of an event, it remains close to what Deleuze describes in the passages cited above as an historical approach.[13] While History tells us what actually happens and why, the task of Philosophy is to give expression to the pure event in what happens. As we noted above, Deleuze defines the pure event as that part of every event that escapes its own actualization. Pure eventness in this sense is the highest object of historical thought. It is what must be thought from a historical point of view but at the same time that which can never, or never exhaustively, be thought because it is given to us only through what actually happens. A different approach is needed, one that creates concepts that take us inside the event, one that allows us to "install" ourselves in the event as in a becoming.

This is the approach to the nature of events followed by Deleuze and Guattari. One of the clearest examples is provided by their analysis of the different kinds of line of which individuals and groups are composed.[14] *A Thousand Plateaus* takes up Deleuze's argument in *The Logic of Sense* that the novella is a literary genre devoted to the "What happened?" question that is posed by every event. As a result, the novella stands in a special relationship to the realm of pure eventness or becoming:

> It evolves in the element of "what happened" because it places us in a relation with an unknowable or an imperceptible (and not the other way around: it is not because it speaks of a past about which it can no longer provide us knowledge). (MP 237, 193)

The novella brings us into a relation to becoming by virtue of its treatment of the three kinds of line of which individuals and groups are composed. First, there is a molar or rigid line of segmentarity that corresponds to the social and institutional identities within which our public, private, and professional lives are lived: family, school, work, and so on. It is on this line that are defined the significant events that make up the biography of a given person or the history of a particular country. Second, there is a line of molecular or supple segmentation that is not divided into distinct segments but into quanta of deterritorialization. On this line, Deleuze and Parnet suggest, we encounter a different kind of event: "becomings, micro-becomings, which don't even have the same rhythm as our 'history' . . . another politics, another time, another individuation" (D 151–152, 124). This line involves a conception of time closer to the *Aion* that Deleuze earlier defined as the time of the event. It involves a present "whose very form is the form of something that has already happened, however close you might be to it, since the ungraspable matter of that something is entirely molecularized" (MP 240, 196). In F. Scott

Fitzgerald's *The Crack-Up*, Deleuze's favored example of the novella genre, these events are the imperceptible cracks in a person's makeup that occur independently of the signifying breaks that otherwise define the progress of a life. They are changes in the molecular structure of a personality or "redistributions of desire such that when something occurs, the self that awaited it is already dead, or the one that would await it has not yet arrived" (MP 243, 198–199). The "something" that is referred to here can only be a "historical" event of the kind that takes place on the first kind of line.[15]

Even so, the different kind of event that takes place on this second line still only amounts to a relative deterritorialization of the segmentarity found on the first line. Deleuze and Guattari point to the existence of a third line that represents an even greater distance from the historical entities and identities of the first line, namely the line of flight or absolute deterritorialization. This is a purely abstract line on which

not only has the matter of the past volatilized but the form of what happened, of an imperceptible something that happened in a volatile matter, no longer even exists. One has become imperceptible . . . (MP 244, 199)

If the very form of the historical question has been lost, then it is on this line that individuals or groups escape history and enter into the element of becoming or pure eventness. They become imperceptible in the sense that they are identifiable only as haecceities or pure events, indistinguishable from one other but each in its own way.[16] They are reduced to an abstract line capable of actualization in a multiplicity of traits. In this sense, as Deleuze and Guattari clarify later in *A Thousand Plateaus*, the imperceptibility of the line of flight or becoming is a way "to enter the haecceity and impersonality of the creator" (MP 343, 280).

Describing these lines as involving different kinds of event is only a first approximation. They might just as readily be described as referring to three levels within any event. Deleuze and Guattari indicate the intended scope of this analysis of the internal structure of events when they propose that the three kinds of line "could equally be the lines of a life, a work of literature or art, or a society, depending on which system of coordinates is chosen" (MP 249, 203–204). Lines of flight are primary in relation to the other two kinds but, as Deleuze and Parnet point out, this primacy is neither chronological nor eternal: It is rather "the fact and right of the untimely" (D 164, 136). In *A Thousand Plateaus* Deleuze and Guattari assert that there is no act of creation that is not trans-, sub- or superhistorical, with reference to Nietzsche's "unhistorical atmosphere" without which creative acts would not be possible (MP 363, 296). The prefix is less important than the fact that this *Untimely* is aligned with the eventlike forms of individuation (*haecceity*), time (*Aion*), and change (absolute deterritorialization) that are associated with the mobile transformative dimension of every assemblage. It is another name for "the innocence of becoming (in other words, forgetting as opposed to memory, geography as opposed to history, the map as opposed to the tracing, the rhizome as opposed to arborescence)" (MP 363, 296). Even history is said to advance by way of the actualization of absolute deterritorialization in a given society at a given time: It follows lines of flight rather than "signifying breaks" (MP 250, 204).

We can now see more clearly the purposes served by the historical material in *A Thousand Plateaus*. On occasions, Deleuze and Guattari describe complex historical phenomena such as Nazism, the Crusades, or the decline of the Roman Empire in terms of their explication of the inner structure of events. In this manner, for example, a passage from Henri Pirenne's *Mohammed and Charlemagne* is used to illustrate the relationship between the rigidly segmented lines of the Roman Empire, the fluid lines of flight or deterritorialization of "the nomads who come in off the steppes," and the supple but ambivalent segmentarity of the migrant barbarians who oscillate between these two poles, sometimes becoming settled, occupying land and being incorporated into the Empire; sometimes allying themselves with the deterritorializing nomads and embarking on a line of conquest and pillage (MP 271–271, 222). Similarly, the work of Mikhail Griaznov is used to show that their concept of nomadism does not refer to an anthropological or sociological kind of peoples but to "a movement, a becoming that affects sedentaries, just as sedentarization is a stoppage that settles nomads" (MP 536, 430).

The continuity with Deleuze's earlier embrace of a structuralist conception of history is apparent in the remark that nomadism is a becoming and that all history does "is to translate a co-existence of becomings into a succession" (MP 537, 430). In *A Thousand Plateaus*, Deleuze and Guattari say that lines of flight express different states of the abstract machines that define particular assemblages rather than the displacements and redistributions of singular points in ideal structures. Nevertheless, their conception of history still relies on the schema according to which virtual movements find expression in actual historical processes. Their overall concern is not to provide historical explanations, genealogical or otherwise, or even to characterize particular historical events but rather to delineate the internal dynamisms of events and the manner in which these unfold in reality. History provides them with one series of examples, alongside others, of surface phenomena where these are produced by the interaction of inner, virtual events or processes. Musical, psychological, anthropological, and other phenomena also provide examples of different kinds of relationship between virtual and actual events and processes, for example when they draw upon Pierre Clastres' description of the mechanisms found in nonstate societies that both anticipate and ward off the emergence of state power (MP 537, 431).

Deleuze and Guattari sometimes rely on a narrow sense of the term *history* that restricts it to molar and majoritarian identities and the processes that unfold in linear time. While history understood in this manner may be a surface phenomenon, the events that unfold in history cannot be dissociated from the "unhistorical atmosphere" that surrounds them. The aim of philosophy as Deleuze defines it is to create concepts that express the virtual dynamics of historical and other kinds of event. However, the point is not to oppose history and becoming but to distinguish between them and to show that there are "all kinds of correlations and movements back and forth between them" (DRF 353, 381).[17] Even though Philosophy is experimental thought and experimentation is not historical, "without history experimentation would remain indeterminate, lacking any initial conditions" (P 231, 170). The line of flight or absolute deterritorialization is the primary object of their analysis of the virtual dynamics of assemblages—whether as nomadology, schizoanalysis, pragmatics, micropolitics, or noology—precisely because it is the source or condition of the emergence of the new. The exploration and elaboration of the realm of pure eventness or becoming is important because this dimension is immanent to the social field, its history, and its public forms of individuation. Far from being opposed to history, or a matter of flight from the world, becoming, eventness, and lines of flight are the condition of movement or change within the world.

The Event of Colonization

Colonization was not a topic that figured largely in Deleuze's published work, which does not mean that he was uninterested or uninformed about the issue.[1] He made occasional passing remarks about the process of colonization, such as those in a 1982 interview with Elias Sanbar. In discussing an analogy drawn between the Palestinians and Native Americans, he contrasts the situation of colonized peoples who are retained on their territory to be exploited with the situation of those who are driven out of their territory altogether. He suggests that the Palestinian people are like the indigenous inhabitants of North America in that they are a people driven out from their territory (DRF 180–181, 195–196).[2] This analogy is limited in a number of respects. First, as Deleuze himself notes, the Palestinians, unlike the Native Americans, do have an Arab world outside of Israel from which they can draw support. Second, like indigenous peoples in many parts of the world, neither the Native Americans nor the Palestinians are completely in the situation of refugees. Rather, they are peoples who are often displaced from their traditional homelands but who, whether displaced or not, remain captives of the colonial state established on their territories. In this sense, they are subject to "internal" colonization of the kind practiced in North and South America, Australia, and parts of Africa rather than the "external" colonization practiced by European powers in other parts of Africa, Asia, and the South Pacific.

Despite this relative lack of concern with colonial issues, Deleuze and Guattari do provide conceptual resources for thinking about the problems of internal colonization and decolonization.[3] I argued in *Deleuze and the Political* that the theory of the state as apparatus of capture is especially helpful in understanding the mechanisms by which new territories and peoples are subsumed under the sovereignty of existing states (Patton 2000, 120–131). Their concepts of deterritorialization and the resultant metamorphosis of assemblages are suggestive in relation to the challenges to existing forms of capture of land and resources, such as those posed by legal means on the basis of the doctrine of Aboriginal or native title. As with any such process of deterritorialization, the outcome will depend on the kinds of deterritorialization and reterritorialization in play within a given context.

In this chapter I pursue further the question of the usefulness of Deleuze and Guattari's philosophy in relation to postcolonial issues, with particular regard to Deleuze's way of thinking about events. I outline some of the principal recurrent theses about the nature of events put forward from *The Logic of Sense* onward and then apply these to the historical event of colonization. As in my earlier discussion, a focus will be the legal dimensions of colonization as it occurs in common-law countries such as Australia. My interest in bringing the jurisprudence of colonization together with Deleuzian theses about the nature of events is twofold: first, to ask whether, and if so in what ways, these theses can help us to understand the historical phenomena associated with such large-scale historical events; second, in keeping with the methodological counsel Deleuze offers to Jean-Clet Martin, to ask whether the colonial example helps us to understand some of the more puzzling aspects of Deleuze's thinking about events.[4] After setting out the key elements of Deleuze's concept of events, I will ask how, in Deleuzian terms, we should understand the event of colonization.

Stoicism and Events

Deleuze's thinking about the nature of events has always relied heavily on the Stoics who, he suggests, were the first to create a philosophical concept of the event (LP 71, 53). They drew a fundamental distinction between a material or physical realm of bodies and states of affairs and a nonphysical realm of incorporeal entities that included time, place, and the sense, or the "what is expressed" (*Lekta*), in statements. They took the sense of a statement to be identical with the event expressed in it: "Sense, *the expressed of the proposition*, is an incorporeal, complex and irreducible entity, at the surface of things, a pure event which inheres or subsists in the proposition" (LS 30, 19). This Stoic metaphysics implies that events stand in an essential relationship both to bodies and states of affairs, on the one hand, and to language, on the other: "The event subsists in language, but it happens to things" (LS 37, 24). As a result, it implies a number of further theses about the relationship between incorporeal events and physical configurations of bodies, about the relationship between events and time, and about the relationship between incorporeal events and language. I begin with the relationship between events and bodies.

The Stoic conception of events implies a distinction between pure events and their actualization or, as Deleuze and Guattari later say, their "incarnation" in particular bodies and states of affairs. Deleuze insists on the irreducibility of events to bodies and states of affairs, just as he does on the irreducibility of sense to the proposition in which it is expressed: Sense is only identical to the event *"on the condition that the event is not confused with its spatio-temporal realization in a state of affairs"* (LS 34, 22). As I argued in Chapter 4, this is not a distinction between two kinds of events but a distinction between events proper and their spatiotemporal realization in states of affairs. Events are not ideal forms or universals abstracted from the specific features of any one occasion. Rather, they are singular but incorporeal entities, different in kind from physical bodies but capable of being expressed in particular configurations and movements of bodies. In this way, for example, an actual battle is made up of the movements of certain bodies and pieces of equipment at a particular place and a particular time, but the event of battle is not confined to these elements because it can recur on other occasions when it would be expressed in entirely different elements.

This distinction raises further questions about the nature of pure events and the nature of their relationship to particular occurrences or instantiations of those events. As both singular and recurrent entities, events must be supposed to be identifiable as the same event even as they vary from one occasion to the next. In this sense, they are open-ended and indeterminate idealities, characterized by their "iterability" in Derrida's sense of the term. In this manner, for example, in "Signature Event Context" he speaks of the "pure event" of a signature, reproducible and recognizable on different occasions but at the same time irreducible to any determinate number of such occasions (Derrida 1972, 391; 1988, 20). Derrida's distinction between particular occurrences and the "pure reproducibility of a pure event" mirrors Deleuze and Guattari's distinction between historical events as these are incarnated in bodies and states of affairs and the pure events that are only imperfectly actualized in the linear time of history: "What History grasps of the event is its effectuation in states of affairs or in lived experience, but the event in its becoming, in its specific consistency, in its self-positing concept, escapes History" (QP 106, 110).

Colonization is clearly a pure event in these terms. Successive iterations of the concept reveal important differences between the object, methods, rationalizations, and aims of colonization in different parts of the world. As a preliminary characterization, let us say that it is a recurrent, asymmetrical encounter between Aboriginal societies and more powerful peoples organized into forms of sovereign state. This already distinguishes colonization from incursions, raids, and other forms of attack by nomadic or other peoples not organized as territorial states. Historically, colonization has tended to involve the incorporation or at least the subordination of a territory along with its peoples and resources by the colonizing state. European nations colonized much of the Americas, Africa, and parts of South-East Asia between the sixteenth and nineteenth centuries. Incorporation and subordination are forms of capture, which is the pure event in terms of which Deleuze and Guattari define sovereign statehood: "The State is sovereignty. But sovereignty only reigns over what it is capable of internalizing, of appropriating locally" (MP 445, 360). Nation-states were formed in Europe by the capture of local territories and the transformation of these into more or less uniform lands and peoples. The essential elements of capture as they define it are the constitution of a general space of comparison and the establishment of a center of appropriation. The uniformities of land, labor, and people are essential conditions for the extraction of rent, profit, and taxes that provided the financial basis for the development of modern nation-states. Like those at home, newly colonized territories outside of Europe were usually encumbered by indigenous populations with their own distinctive social organization and relations to Earth and its products. These typically involved particular varieties of what Deleuze and Guattari called "territorial" social machines, in contrast to the despotic and axiomatic machines that gave rise to European capitalism (AO 163–227, 153–210). As such, they needed to be "deterritorialized" before they could be reterritorialized as dependent colonies of the relevant European state. The simultaneous deterritorialization and reterritorialization of newly "discovered" territories took a variety of forms: economic, technological, affective, and pathogenic as well as political transformations followed one upon the other in the early stages of contact.

Events and Time

Deleuze's distinction between the pure event and its actualization in particular circumstances is further reinforced by the distinction drawn in *The Logic of Sense* between a historical time within which events occur (*Chronos*) and a "time of the event" (*Aion*) that cannot be reduced to the former time. This distinction provides further support for the view that events proper in some sense "escape History." However, this remains one of the most puzzling aspects of this concept of the event. Why draw this distinction in the first place and, having done so, how does the resultant untimely or "aternal" concept of the event shed light on the historical events that determine our present and future possibilities?[5] To see how the event of colonization helps to illuminate Deleuze's concept of the untimely or "aternal" character of events, let us consider his reasons for distinguishing historical time and event time.

A first reason advanced in the opening paragraph of *The Logic of Sense* has to do with the paradoxical character, from the perspective of ordinary time, of pure events. Deleuze takes an example from Lewis Carroll to show that events imply contradictory properties of a thing in a manner inconceivable within linear time. When we say that Alice grew (she became taller), this implies that she became taller than she was before. By the same token, however, she also became shorter than she is now (assuming that she continued to grow). Although it makes no sense to say that she is taller and shorter at the same time, we can say that she *becomes* taller and shorter at the same time, thereby exhibiting "the simultaneity of a becoming whose characteristic is to elude the present" (LS 9, 1). It follows that, for Deleuze, events are coextensive with becomings and that becomings exhibit contradictory properties in the absence of further specification of the temporal perspective from which we examine them. Considered from the point of view of her smaller self engaged in growing, Alice becomes larger. Considered from the point of view of her larger self, Alice continues to become smaller than she is, although progressively less so. To take another example, consider what happens to H_2O at zero degrees Celsius: water becomes ice, or ice becomes water, depending on whether temperature is increasing or decreasing. In other words, whether we witness the freezing of water or the melting of ice depends on the temporal direction from which we view the becoming.[6]

The paradoxical nature of pure events such as justice, hospitality, forgiveness, or democracy-to-come is a prominent theme in Derrida's later work (see Chapter 2, p. 46). He characterizes each of these events in their "unconditional" form as impossible experiences. Deleuze's understanding of events, becomings, and problems also draws attention to the paradoxes associated with their pure form. For example, in *Difference and Repetition* he describes the pure event of society as a paradoxical event that cannot be lived within actual societies but "must be and can only be lived in the element of social upheaval (in other words, freedom, which is always hidden among the remains of the old order and the first fruits of a new)" (DR 250, 193). The paradoxical character of the freedom expressed in such moments of revolutionary social upheaval emerges when we consider how it may be described from the point of view of the old order as the descent into chaos or from the point of view of the new as the necessary chaos from which new forms of order may emerge.

The situation of indigenous peoples who become colonized provides many examples of such contradictory properties. For example, with regard to their status as people subject to a rule of law, they pass from a law-governed state to one of complete lawlessness and at the same time from a state of complete lawlessness to a law-governed state, depending on whether we view the event from the point of view of indigenous law and custom or from that of the law of the colonizer. With regard to Canada, John Borrows points out that from the point of view of Aboriginal peoples the Crown's assertion of sovereignty is an exercise of arbitrary power. It was carried out without consultation or consent. In consequence, taking seriously the principle that the rule of law stands as a bulwark against arbitrariness and oppression would invalidate the Crown's claims to sovereignty and support the continued sovereignty of the Aboriginal peoples: "Canada's laws should be declared invalid, though enforceable, by the application of the rule of law until the parties resolve this situation through negotiation" (Borrows 2001, 54).

In the Australian colonies in the early nineteenth century, it was widely believed that colonization had been effected merely by the settlement of European peoples. Under the eighteenth and nineteenth doctrine of "extended *terra nullius*," it was possible for European powers to acquire sovereignty over territories that were inhabited by "primitive" peoples living in accordance with customs that could not properly be considered laws. As a consequence, there was considerable scope for ambivalence with regard to the legal status of the indigenous people within the newly founded colony. The colonists could not help but observe that Aboriginal people lived according to their own customs, but they could deny these customs the status of law and consider them "only such as are consistent with a state of greatest darkness and irrational superstition."[7] On the one hand, under the British law imposed in the colonies, the natives were regarded as subjects of the Crown and thus protected in the sense that crimes against them were not supposed to go unpunished. On the other hand, because they were considered to be savages incapable of swearing oaths, courts were not bound to take into account evidence they might have offered. This anomalous status was eventually resolved by the implementation of statutory regimes for the "protection" of Aboriginal peoples that assigned them to a special legal status and deprived them of almost all the ordinary rights and duties of subjects (Chesterman and Galligan 1997, 11–57).

Similar kinds of paradoxical transformation occurred with regard to the property rights of the indigenous inhabitants. Consider the consequences of colonization as these are now defined in terms of the doctrine of Aboriginal or native title under Canadian or Australian law. Subjection to the British Crown involved at once both the loss of entitlements as they existed under indigenous law and the acquisition of entitlements under common law. The paradox inherent in becoming dispossessed while simultaneously becoming bearers of common-law native title is reflected in some of the legal formulations offered by colonial courts. For example, in the *Mabo* case that belatedly introduced the concept of native title into Australian law, one of the judges described native title as a concept that straddles indigenous and common law.[8] As such, it is a concept that expresses the paradoxical logic of Derrida's "nonconcepts" that are at once both the same and different (*différance*), present and absent (*trace*), or poison and remedy (*pharmakon*). Justice Brennan expressed the peculiar nature of this concept at the frontier between common law and indigenous legal orders in suggesting that "Native title, though recognised by the common law, is not an institution of the common law" (Bartlett 1993, 42). Similarly, in the 1997 *Delgamuukw* case, in which the Canadian Supreme Court finally settled some of the questions relating to the nature and limits of Aboriginal title, the court took the view that Aboriginal title was sui generis and arose from the relationship between common law and preexisting systems of Aboriginal law.[9] They sought to resolve the paradox of simultaneously becoming dispossessed while becoming possessed by suggesting that Aboriginal title "crystallized" at the time sovereignty was asserted (Persky 1998, 101). These strange formulae produced in the course of efforts to make sense of the legal event of colonization may be taken as signs of the fact that, wherever it occurred, this was one of those moments at which, in Deleuze's phrase, "becoming breaks through into history."

A second reason for drawing a distinction between "event time" and "linear time" emerges when we consider the paradoxes involved in identifying, in historical time, the precise moment at which events occur. Suppose we take a time before the event and a time after: The infinite divisibility of the series of moments implies that there are two converging series on either side of the event but no point at which these series meet. Thus, from the perspective of historical time, there is no present moment at which the event takes place. As Deleuze expresses this point in *The Logic of Sense*: "The agonizing aspect of the pure event is that it is always and at the same time something which has just happened and something about to happen; never something which is happening" (LS 79, 63).

Colonial acquisition of new territory is elusive in precisely this manner. When did the British colonization of Australia occur? Was it during the exploratory voyage of Captain Cook, specifically the moment in 1770 when he raised the British flag on a tiny island off the northern tip of Cape York and claimed sovereignty over half the continent in the name of King George III? Afterward, as if to reinforce the claim, he named this rocky outcrop "Possession Island" (Day 1996, 27). If we accept that Cook's flag raising and naming ceremony effectively imposed British sovereignty, why then did Governor Phillip repeat the ceremony after the arrival of the first fleet of convicts, not once but twice, on the shores of Sydney Cove on January 26, 1788? (Day 1996, 38). The reality is that such singular events, taken in isolation, are insufficient to effect even the legal event of colonization. Like declarations of war or independence, these events make sense only in anticipation of the process and the institution that follows. This brings us back to the elusive character of the precise moment at which the event occurs. At the moment of Cook's or even Phillip's flag ceremonies, it is too soon to say that colonization has taken place. At any moment thereafter it can be said that colonization has already taken place.

The elusive temporality of the event of colonization also points to its complexity. This is an event that exhibits the kind of differential contamination between acts of institution and acts of preservation described by Derrida in "Force of Law" (Derrida 1992a, 38–44; 1994a, 93–105). The initial acts of proclamation and arrival anticipate the subsequent acts of invasion, dispossession, and settlement, while, at the same time, the subsequent policies and actions of colonial governors, magistrates, police, and the settlers under their protection reproduce and reinforce the initial act of foundation. The imposition of a new law, new culture, and new forms of government on the territory and its indigenous inhabitants continues the work of colonization that was only nominally carried out by the initial assertion of sovereignty. The colonial example thus illustrates the inner complexity of events that is often imperceptible from the point of view of ordinary historical time. By the same token, this example points toward a third reason for regarding event time as another kind of time or another dimension within time, namely that this enables us to make sense of the internal structure and complexity of events. Their relations to other events structure them externally while, as Deleuze often comments, events can involve long periods when it appears that nothing is happening, then suddenly everything changes and nothing is the same as before.

The passage from Péguy's *Clio* that is cited in *Difference and Repetition*, *The Logic of Sense*, and *What Is Philosophy?* puts forward another version of the idea that events are always structured by their own internal singularities (see Chapter 4, pp. 93–96). It is because events possess their own internal structure and logic independently of their actualization in historical processes that critical moments in a long-term process of transformation are sometimes precipitated by the introduction of some fragment of a future event. The transformation of Nietzsche's Zarathustra proceeds in this manner by a series of partial ruptures. These occur at those moments in the narrative when Zarathustra is exposed to some fragment of the future event that is his overcoming. This event, which never arrives, would involve his becoming free from the bonds of resentment and reconciled to human finitude.

The elusive temporality and inner complexity of events has a further consequence, namely the variability of the relations between the pure event and its historical manifestations. A variety of relations are possible between the virtual and the actual course of events: Pure events might be effective in history either from the direction of the past or from that of the future, and in each case either as poles of attraction or repulsion. Deleuze and Guattari provide examples of different kinds of interaction between historical events and pure events or between the realms of history and becoming. For example, the pure event as attractor is manifest in the sense in which the universalization of capitalist production, the real subsumption of labor to capital and the generalized decoding of social processes stands as the tendential outcome of all of the subsidiary forms of capital that emerged beforehand. Deleuze and Guattari describe capitalism as the only form of society that operates by means of a generalized decoding of flows. As a result, the forms of decodification made possible by earlier systems of codification appear in retrospect to lead inevitably to this point. In this sense, they follow Marx in suggesting that "capitalism has haunted all forms of society" (AO 164, 154).

A relation to a future event as limit or threshold is evident in the manner in which the complete deterritorialization of social life appears at once as the inevitable yet unattainable limit of capitalism. Capitalist societies simultaneously deterritorialize forms of social life and reterritorialize by resuscitating or reinventing fragments of earlier social codes. In some primitive nonstate societies, Deleuze and Guattari suggest that we find equally complex relations toward the future event of capture. These are societies in which there are mechanisms that both anticipate and ward off the historical emergence of some form of state: "These societies simultaneously have vectors moving in the direction of the State, mechanisms warding it off, and a point of convergence that is repelled or set outside as fast as it is approached" (MP 537, 431).

Deleuze often draws a distinction between two kinds of occurrence that he characterizes in terms of the mathematical distinction between ordinary and singular or remarkable points on a line. In historical terms, this corresponds to the difference between "normal" events, as defined within an established frame of reference and a set of rules, and "extraordinary" events that involve shifting from one frame to another or replacing one set of rules by another. Variants of this kind of distinction may be found, for example, in Thomas Kuhn's contrast between normal and revolutionary science or in Walter Benjamin's contrast between violence of foundation and violence of conservation. It is a matter of perspective as to whether we describe this as a distinction between two kinds of event or as a distinction internal to a given pure event. From the perspective of the realm of becoming in which events unfold their inner complexity, this distinction is not so much between conservation and creation as between two kinds of relative deterritorialization or transformation of an existing assemblage.

On the one hand, there are sudden transitions to a different structural frame and, with this, the possibility of actualizing a new kind of event. On these occasions, fundamental social change occurs through the sudden eruption of events that mark a turning point in history and inaugurate new fields of social, political, or legal possibilities. Deleuze points to such poetic or sublime moments at which the historical and the untimely coincide in his 1967 interview, "Nietzsche's Burst of Laughter." All of his examples come from successful anticolonial struggles: Egypt's nationalization of the Suez Canal in 1956, the Cuban revolution in 1959, and the Vietnamese war of independence in the 1960s (ID 180–181, 130). After May 1968, he often suggested that this was also a moment of "becoming breaking through into history" (P 209, 153). In this case, what occurred was a momentary expression of pure eventness that French society proved unable to assimilate. The people showed themselves to be incapable of undertaking the collective self-transformation required to give historical reality to the new possibilities for life glimpsed in the events that unfolded (DRF 215–217, 233–236). Despite the historical failure, the potential for radically different forms of social relation remains. Such poetic or sublime moments, when becoming breaks through into history, testify to the manner in which pure eventness or becoming persists alongside the historical sequence of states of affairs.

On the other hand, fundamental social change sometimes happens by degrees, as with the steady erosion of myths and prejudices about sexual difference and its implications for social and political institutions under the impact of feminism throughout the twentieth century. Change of this kind may come about through processes of "continual variation" or deterritorialization in which novelty emerges in the course of the repetition of established acts and kinds of event under different circumstances or in different contexts. This is what enables institutions such as the law to be transformed even as they are maintained and reproduced. It follows that not all world-changing events are violent or bloody. Following Nietzsche's Zarathustra, who points out that the greatest events are not always the noisiest but sometimes the most quiet moments, Deleuze also draws attention to the "tiny silent events" that testify to the poetic or creative underneath the historical and that bring about the formation of new worlds (ID 181, 130).[10]

The pure event of colonization can take either of these forms. While it is often an event of the noisy, Earth-shattering kind, this does not exclude the possibility that it is also an ongoing, silent event. Even once it has been achieved, it continues to operate inaudibly, often in ways that pass unnoticed to those not directly affected. It is an event that haunts the societies established on the territory of Aboriginal peoples, who remain caught in a form of internal exile. The event of colonization may reemerge into history in unexpected ways, for example in efforts to renegotiate through legal and political means the terms of the original solution to the jurisprudential problem. This is what occurred in Australia with the 1992 *Mabo* decision and the sudden introduction of native title jurisprudence into Australian law. A decision by the High Court reactivated an event that had never entirely passed away but continued to hover over the history of relations between indigenous and nonindigenous Australians "like mist over breaking waves."[11] The historical moment in which this decision took place involved a return to earlier events of colonization, collapsing elements of the colonial past into the present and making these parts of the ongoing elaboration of the future. At such moments, we glimpse the possibility of an altogether different relationship between indigenous and settler communities, premised on mutual recognition and equality rather than incorporation and subordination. In Deleuzian terms, the philosophical challenge is to extract a new concept from the colonial encounter and its aftermath, to counter-actualize this event in a manner that might open up the possibility of a genuinely postcolonial society.

Events, Language, and Concepts

As we saw in Chapter 3, Deleuze's Stoic conception of the relation between events and language has implications for our understanding of the pragmatic and political function of language. The intimate relationship between events and the forms of their linguistic expression forms the basis for his argument that language use contributes to the effectuation of the "incorporeal transformations" current in a given society at a given time (MP 95–139, 75–110). Incorporeal transformations are events. They typically involve changes in the properties of the body concerned, such as changes of status or changes in relations to other bodies. The transformation of the accused into a convict at the conclusion of a criminal trial is an incorporeal transformation, as is the transformation of a vast area of land into the sovereign territory of a given European power.

Like many world historical events, colonization is a complex process involving different kinds of incorporeal transformation, such as the naming of prominent geographical features along a newly discovered coast or flag-raising ceremonies accompanied by proclamations of possession in the name of the colonial sovereign. The latter appear to be modern equivalents of the "magical capture" that Dumézil describes as one of the two poles of sovereignty in Indo-European mythology (MP 434–435,

424–425). Stating, claiming, or naming something is never sufficient to actualize a particular event, but these purely linguistic acts of declaration or attribution are often important and sometimes necessary conditions of actualization. The pragmatic dimension of language outlined by Deleuze and Guattari explains why politics frequently takes the form of struggle over appropriate terminology with which to describe events. Disagreements over what happened often take the form of disputes over the appropriate event attribution. Was the colony "settled" by brave pioneers or was it "invaded" without regard for the lives or property of the indigenous inhabitants? Did the ensuing destruction of peoples and cultures amount to "genocide," or were they simply "swept away by the tide of history"?

I argued in Chapter 4 that Deleuze's concept of pure eventness or becoming forms the basis for his conception of philosophy. The usefulness of Deleuzian theses about events is intimately bound up with this highly political conception of the purpose and function of philosophy. Philosophy creates concepts on a plane of immanence, where these concepts express pure events: "The concept is obviously knowledge—but knowledge of itself, and what it knows is the pure event, which must not be confused with the state of affairs in which it is embodied. The task of philosophy when it creates concepts, entities, is always to extract an event from things and beings" (QP 36, 33). Events are actualized in states of affairs, bodies, and the lived experience of people, but as philosophers we "counter-effectuate" events when we step back from states of affairs, bodies, and experiences to isolate or extract a concept. It follows that philosophy creates many of the events in terms of which we understand and react to the processes and states of affairs that condition our lives: concepts of fairness, equality, and justice; concepts of social contract, revolution, democracy to come: or, to take an example from Rawls, the concept of a well-ordered society governed in accordance with principles of justice. The counter-effectuation of historical events expresses the sense of what is happening by extracting a pure event. This is what happens, for example, when a philosopher tells us that we live in a time of enlightenment, of revolution, of reconciliation, of globalization or empire, and so on. But the creation of concepts does more than this. By separating out the pure event from the determinate form in which it has been actualized, it allows us to perceive actual historical events as particular determinations or effectuations of a given pure event and, by implication, the possibility of other determinations of the same event. Philosophy is "utopian" because it creates concepts that give expression to this incorporeal reserve that is the condition of all change. Already, in *The Logic of Sense*, Deleuze characterized the doubling of the actualized event that is achieved by means of its philosophical counter-effectuation with reference to Nietzsche's untimely: "To the extent that the pure event is each time imprisoned forever in its actualization, counter-actualisation liberates it, always for other times" (LS 188, 161).[12]

Deleuze understands the one–many relation between such pure events and their actualizations along the lines of the relation between a problem and its solutions. In *Difference and Repetition* he writes that "problems are of the order of events" (DR 244, 188). In *The Logic of Sense*, he describes events as "problematic and problematizing" (LP 69, 54). By "problem" here he means a virtual structure the nature of which is never entirely captured in any given specification or determination of its conditions. In this sense, he aligns the distinction between an ideal event and its spatiotemporal realization, with the distinction between a problem as such and its determination in a manner that permits a solution. In these terms, he can speak of the problematic Idea of society prior to any determinate set of relations of production and exchange or the problematic Idea of language as such, prior to any determinate language (DR 240–241, 186; 262–265, 203–206). In the same vein, we might add, one could speak of the problematic Idea of political community prior any determinate form of political organization. Specification is necessary for the production of particular solutions, but the pure problem-event is not thereby dissolved or exhausted because there always remains the possibility of other specifications and other solutions. This is a reason to insist on the distinction between the empirical event, which is a particular determination of the problem, and the problem-event that, in its pure form, remains "immaterial, incorporeal, unlivable: pure reserve" (QP 148, 156).

The concepts that philosophy creates are not assessed for their truth or falsity but for the degree to which they are "Interesting, Remarkable, or Important" (QP 80, 82). Concepts are interesting, remarkable, or important when they give expression to new problems or perhaps to new solutions to problems that have already been posed. However, the conditions of the problems addressed by philosophy are not found in the empirical reality of things, as they are for the sciences, but in the "intensional conditions of consistency" of the concepts themselves. In these terms, Deleuze suggests that if the concept is a solution, "the conditions of the philosophical problem are found on the plane of immanence pre-supposed by the concept" (QP 78, 80–81). On this basis, we can ask, "What is the problem to which the concept of colonization offers a solution? What are the conditions of this problem and how might a better understanding of those conditions help us to reformulate existing concepts of colonization?"

The Problem of Colonization

In the case of European colonization by states that saw themselves as subject to an impersonal rule of law, one of the most important elements of the problem of colonization was juridical. Colonization was presumed to be legitimate in so far as the sovereign asserted a justifiable legal claim to the territory in question. This in turn implied an incorporeal transformation of the territory, transforming it into a uniformly appropriable and exploitable resource over which the new sovereign reserved its right to allocate property in land. It follows that a fundamental problem of colonization is that of the jurisprudential means by which the imperial sovereign imposed control over foreign territories and indigenous peoples.

Different solutions to this problem have been adopted in different parts of the world. These amount to different legal mechanisms for transferring sovereignty from the indigenous inhabitants to the colonial sovereign. They include treaties and purchase of tracts of land, along with simple appropriation of the land in those cases where it was considered empty of inhabitants with any legitimate claim (*terra nullius*). A common feature of all such instruments was the "right of preemption" that reserved the right to acquire land from the natives for the sovereign. Along with the power of the sovereign to allocate titles to land, this ensured the constitution of a uniform smooth space of potential real property where before there had been only foreign territories and foreign peoples with their own customs and laws. The sale of land often provided a means to finance the establishment of colonial governments and the settlement that followed.[13]

None of this precludes the possibility of resistance to such regimes of colonial capture. On the contrary, the fact that the violence of colonization is institutionalized in the form of law means that the colonial institutions themselves are open to reinvestment by other forces. Which of the various solutions to the jurisprudential problem was adopted determines the basis of the colonial sovereignty, the legal form of the settlements with indigenous peoples that follow, and the possibilities for reinterpretation of these legal settlements to accommodate greater freedom for the colonized. In these terms, contemporary efforts to undo the legal and political institutions of internal colonization in countries with captive indigenous populations may be understood as attempts to return to the original conditions of the problem. They seek to "problematize" existing solutions to the problem of colonial society to arrive at new ones.

Consider the jurisprudential transformations that have occurred with regard to the legal recognition of Aboriginal entitlements to land in Australia and Canada in recent years. In those territories acquired under the "extended" version of the *terra nullius* principle in international law, which allowed territory to be considered empty for legal purposes even when it was inhabited, it had long been assumed that indigenous peoples never had any rights to the land because on colonization it became the property of the British Crown. Part of the justification for this view was the so-called barbarian hypothesis, according to which at the time of colonization there were no recognizable legal owners of the land because the indigenous occupants were considered too low in the scale of civilization to be considered as having any legal rights. Canadian courts had begun to dismantle this particular form of legal capture with the *Calder* case in 1973.[14] In Australia, it was not until the *Mabo* case in 1992 that the High Court decided that this was mistaken in law as well as in fact and that the indigenous inhabitants of the continent had retained some entitlements to land in accordance with their traditional laws and customs. Australian law henceforth recognized a form of Aboriginal or native title to land, although this remained a lesser form of entitlement than property ownership under the common law. The possibility of claiming native title was subject to a range of further restrictive conditions, including the existence of an ongoing connection with the land on the part of the claimants and the absence of any acts by the Crown that might have extinguished native title over the land in question. Despite these limitations, this landmark decision represented a break with nineteenth-century assumptions about the nature of Aboriginal societies and with the longstanding nonrecognition of indigenous law and custom.

For reasons internal to the relationship between sovereign power and domestic courts, the *Mabo* decision did nothing to undermine the legal basis of the initial claim to sovereignty.[15] However, in terms of the broader historicopolitical event of colonization, it was widely regarded as having discredited the principle of *terra nullius* that had underpinned the imposition of British sovereignty. This principle was now considered to be the product of particular racist assumptions embedded in earlier decisions from colonial courts all the way up to the Privy Council. The historicopolitical significance of the *Mabo* case was greatly enhanced by the fact that it was decided in the context of an existing national debate over reconciliation between indigenous and nonindigenous peoples. The decision had the effect of broadening the public debate beyond questions of property and land to include fundamental questions about the rule of law and the requirements of justice in the aftermath of extensive historical injustice. It unleashed a judicial and legislative process that effectively rewrote the legal terms on which colonization had taken place in Australia. Subsequent cases involved the revisiting of the terms of nineteenth-century pastoral leases and a reconsideration of the ongoing relationship that many Aboriginal peoples had maintained with their traditional lands.[16] While the outcome of these cases was not always favorable to the indigenous claimants involved, they nevertheless amounted to a renegotiation of the terms in which the jurisprudential problem of colonization was originally solved.

Following Deleuze's conception of the pure event in its distinction from actual historical processes, we might conceive of the politicolegal event surrounding *Mabo* as a process of transition from one determination of colonial society to another. As such, it is a process in which we glimpse the possibility of an altogether different relationship between indigenous and settler communities, premised on mutual recognition and equality rather than incorporation and subordination. This process is unevenly advanced by small leaps and bounds, where these are also occasioned by our exposure to fragments of some future event, namely a just reconciliation between colonizers and colonized. This points to the possibility that the pure event of which the actual forms of colonization represent particular determinations is not an event of incorporation but one of encounter between peoples and cultures largely unknown to one another. The unexpected legal event that was the *Mabo* decision might be said to have returned the nation to the problem of colonization from which it emerged, not only to renegotiate the terms under which Aboriginal lands and Aboriginal people were subordinated to the authority of the British Crown but eventually to question whether the colonial encounter need to have taken the form of the imposition of sovereignty at all. This is the import of the widespread demands in Australia for a treaty or some other document of reconciliation that would recognize the right of Aboriginal peoples to self-determination and self-government.

This is also the import of the argument of Canadian political theorist James Tully that history provides us with other principles in terms of which the encounter between European nation-states and indigenous peoples might have taken place. These include the principles of recognition, consent, and continuity that had long formed the basis of European as well as Native American interstate or international relations (Tully 1994, 169–180; 1995, 116–139; 1998). Tully's principles of a fair and just constitutional association and the demand of indigenous peoples for a treaty relationship provide reason to suppose that the problem to which colonization provided a solution is not in its purest form a problem of capture but one of encounter. For European colonists throughout the modern period, the problem was posed on the basis of the belief that non-European peoples ranked lower on the scale of civilization. The obligation to improve the condition of those lower on the scale went hand in glove with the right to annex their territory. However, if this belief is abandoned, the problem appears in its pure state as that of the conditions of coexistence of different peoples. There are many inequalities on both sides of the divide between state-governed European societies and territorially governed indigenous societies, but the encounter between them need not have taken the forms of legal incorporation that it so often did. The event of colonization might have unfolded on the basis of mutual respect and cooperation between equals. It might have been an encounter that was also an event of reconciliation between peoples and cultures largely unknown to one another. To reconceptualize the event in this manner is to counter-effectuate the historical process of colonization in a manner that calls for new peoples and new relations between them on the land they share.

Becoming–Animal and Pure Life
in Coetzee's *Disgrace*

Although he does not propose any systematic philosophy of literature, Deleuze engages with literary works throughout his career from *Proust and Signs* to *Essays Critical and Clinical*. As Ronald Bogue suggests, much of his writing is "a thinking alongside literary works, an engagement of philosophical issues generated from and developed through encounters with literary texts" (Bogue 2003, 2). *What Is Philosophy?* treats literature as a form of thinking no less valuable than philosophy for the manner in which it pursues the political vocation of resistance to the present, everyday servitude, the intolerable, and the shameful. Philosophy and literature serve this vocation in different but parallel fashion, by virtue of their particular methods of calling for new Earths and peoples to come (QP 104, 108). Whereas philosophy breaks with everyday opinions through the invention of concepts, literature breaks with everyday perceptions and affections by capturing hitherto unrecognized percepts and affects. In this sense, the novelist is a "seer" who experiences new kinds of "becoming" (*un voyant, un devenant*) (QP 161, 171). In "Literature and Life," Deleuze suggests that good literature is always a kind of world-historical delirium, the collective expression of people caught up in a perpetual becoming-revolutionary. The "ultimate aim" of such literature is to "set free, in the delirium, this creation of a health or this invention of a people, that is, a possibility of life" (CC xx, 4).

It is because of the importance of this concept of impersonal life to his philosophy that Deleuze is rightly regarded as a vitalist thinker. In a chapter of *Dialogues*, he justifies his preference for the English and American literature of Thomas Hardy, D. H. Lawrence, Herman Melville, F. Scott Fitzgerald, Virginia Woolf, Henry Miller, and others by reference to the manner in which it invents new possibilities for life. His favored writers are those who portray life as a process of self-transformation or escape from established identities in favor of flight toward another world. For these authors, writing is a matter of tracing lines of flight or processes of becoming that have the potential to lead to the creation of new forms of life. Individuals realize this potential when they manage to break out of existing forms of life and gain access to the primary and transformative power of pure, impersonal life. It is because his preferred literature retraces these becomings that Deleuze can say that *"writing does not have its end in itself precisely because life is not something personal. Or rather, the aim of writing is to carry life to the state of a non-personal power"* (D 61, 50). It is in the spirit of this conception of literature and Deleuze's own encounters with literary works that I propose to read J. M. Coetzee's 1999 Booker Prize–winning novel *Disgrace*. I argue that *Disgrace* deserves to be added to the Deleuzian literary canon for the way in which the central protagonist embarks on a line of flight or deterritorialization that promises to transform his sense of who he is. In the case of this character and his daughter, personal transformation takes place by means of a becoming-animal. My aim is not only to outline a Deleuzian reading of *Disgrace* but also to use the novel to explore the personal and political dimensions of key concepts such as becoming-animal, becoming-minor, and the concept of a pure life that is immanent in the everyday existence of humans and animals alike.[1]

South Africa, Becoming-Animal, and the People to Come

Disgrace is set in postapartheid South Africa where the lives of the central characters are conditioned by the historical divide between colonizing and colonized peoples. The painful transition to a new South Africa is directly implicated in many of the events that befall these characters, even if their concerns and those of the novel are not confined to the difficult process of dismantling the former colonial regime.[2] The central character, David Lurie, is an aging male professor of English literature who is as out of touch with himself as he is with the requirements of life in the new vocational and professional university. He is increasingly out of touch with the new social relations emerging between men and women, European and other Africans. While he is conscious of his age, his life is also a self-centred denial of his mortality and his dependence on others.

Lurie remains an unredeemed and in many ways unredeemable character. Nevertheless, in the course of the novel he enters into a becoming-animal, which opens up the possibility of transformation in his relation to himself, to other people and to animals. These intimations of change suggest that, in addition to its concern with the ongoing effects of colonization, *Disgrace* is also a novel about relations between the sexes, human finitude, and the natural life we share with animals.

The novel opens with an account of his weekly assignation with a prostitute, which he likes to believe is more than an exchange of sexual favors for money. The arrangement ends after they accidentally meet in a public place: The look in her eyes is enough to shatter his self-serving illusions about the nature of their relationship. His efforts to maintain a Romantic idea of his virile self lead him into a predatory sexual relationship with a colored female student, Melanie Isaacs, for which he is subsequently charged and found guilty of sexual harassment. This sets him on a line of flight that eventually leads to the deterritorialization of his personal, social, professional, and intellectual world. He refuses any form of contrition or apology and is eventually forced to resign from his position at the university. He goes to visit his daughter, Lucy, who lives on a small farm in the country where she makes a modest living growing produce and flowers and operating a boarding kennel for dogs. While at his daughter's farm, Lurie helps out with the kennel and begins to care for the Dobermanns, German shepherds, ridgebacks, bull terriers, and Rottweilers that Lucy describes at one point as "Watchdogs, all of them" (Coetzee 1999, 61). His sympathy for these abandoned former guard dogs is nourished by the sentiment that they, like him, are part of the debris of history: animals out of place in the new South Africa.

The presence of these dogs does not prevent an attack on the farm by a gang of young African men in which Lucy is subjected to a brutal sexual assault and Lurie is beaten and set alight with methylated spirits. When his daughter reveals that she is pregnant as a result of her rape and determined to bear the child, he decides to stay on and help where he can. He works at an animal refuge where he helps the woman who runs it, Bev Shaw, to kill and dispose of unwanted strays. He has a brief and joyless but also victimless sexual encounter with Bev. He develops a particular fondness for one young partly crippled dog that befriends him during the brief period of grace before it must be put down. The novel ends with him giving up this animal to its inevitable end and to what has earlier been described as the "disgrace" of dying.

It is easy to see Lurie as an allegorical figure representing, if not the habits and attitudes of the ruling class of the old colonial regime, then at least a certain kind of Eurocentric and cultured cast of mind that sustained the possibility of colonial relations. He is initially disdainful of his daughter's peasant life in the country. He aspires to a higher and more cultured plane of existence. Much of his time is spent preparing to write an opera based on the last days of the life of Byron. Like the rest of his professional life, this project goes nowhere. On this level, his story is one of disempowerment and disgrace: first at the university; then at the hands of the gang who attack him and sexually assault his daughter; then, once again, voluntarily this time, before the family of his young student, Melanie, from whom he asks forgiveness. Despite his apology to the student and her parents, he remains unwilling to change, unrepentant about his rape of the student, and uncomprehending of the social changes taking place around him. He often fails to comprehend the motives of others, especially those of his student, his daughter, and her African neighbour Petrus. At one point, he says to Lucy: "I am not prepared to be reformed. I want to go on being myself" (Coetzee 1999, 77).[3]

Many commentators have been disturbed by the "bleak image" of the "new South Africa" presented in *Disgrace* (Attridge 2004, 164). There is much in the novel besides the character of David Lurie to suggest a gloomy outlook on the possibility of transforming relations between the races. The always tense and sometimes violent interactions between white and black show how deeply the social, linguistic, and psychic structures of the old colonial system are embedded in postapartheid social life. Coetzee points to the enormous difficulty of transforming the inherited structures of temperament and language. At one point, Lurie is represented as becoming more and more "convinced that English is an unfit medium for the truth of South Africa" (Coetzee 1999, 117). The sexual violence inflicted on Lucy during the attack on her farm, the apparent immunity of the perpetrators, along with the transformation of her African neighbour Petrus from gardener and "dog-man" to farmer and landowner, suggest a postapartheid political process in which a rearrangement of positions rather than a genuine transformation of social relations takes place. In these terms, the roles of white and black, oppressor and oppressed, would be simply reversed. While some regard the novel as accurate reportage of attitudes and social relations, others have criticized the novel for its apparent pessimism about the possibility of progress toward a nonracist and nonsexist society.[4] In a widely circulated review, Salman Rushdie takes the mutual incomprehension of the characters in the novel to encapsulate its bleak vision of postapartheid politics: "The whites don't understand the blacks and the blacks aren't interested in understanding the whites . . . Petrus comes closest, but his motives remain enigmatic and his presence grows more menacing as the novel proceeds" (Rushdie 2002, 297–298). On this reading, there is no transformation in either the individual characters or the social relations in which their lives unfold.

By contrast, reading *Disgrace* through the multiple lens of the Deleuzian concepts of life, becoming-minor and becoming-animal brings to light a more affirmative side to the novel. Even if it is only indirectly related to the difficult social and political transitions that provide its historical context, evidence of a capacity for change is portrayed in the lives of the central characters. In Deleuzian terms, there is evidence of minoritarian becoming, both at the level of the micropolitics of social relations and even in the apparently unredeemable character of Lurie. Minoritarian-becoming occurs only if there is movement or transformation in the assemblage concerned. There must be some line of flight or deterritorialization along which this particular majoritarian subject begins to change. In the case of Lurie and his daughter, this transformation takes place by means of a becoming-animal.

Becoming-Minor and Becoming-Animal

In *A Thousand Plateaus*, Deleuze and Guattari develop a version of their ontology of becoming in the form of a theory of multiplicities or machinic assemblages. Ultimately, these assemblages or abstract machines are a kind of open or evolving multiplicity that is itself a process of becoming other. It is not surprising that multiplicities constantly transform into one another, "since becoming and multiplicity are the same thing" (MP 305, 249). The ontological priority of becoming in this machinic metaphysics is reflected in the fact that assemblages are defined not by their forms of conservation but by their forms of modification or metamorphosis, by their "cutting edges of deterritorialization" (MP 112, 88). In these terms, they argue that individuals no less than societies are defined by their lines of flight or deterritorialization. They mean that there is no person and no society that is not conserving or maintaining itself on one level, while simultaneously being transformed into something else on another level. In other words, fundamental shifts in personal and social identity happen all the time. Sometimes these happen by degrees, but sometimes fundamental changes occur through the sudden eruption of events that inaugurate a new field of personal, social, or affective possibilities. These are turning points in individual lives or in history, after which some things will never be the same as before. They are examples, Deleuze suggests, of "a becoming breaking through into history" (P 209, 153: see above, Chapter 4, p. 89; Chapter 5, pp. 109–110).

The sense in which Deleuze and Guattari regard their philosophy as political relates to their concern with the processes of becoming by means of which majoritarian social and political identities are transformed. In *What Is Philosophy?* they distinguish two kinds of becoming. The first, which is common in certain classes of sensible objects, involves "the action by which something or someone continues to become other (while continuing to be what it is)" (QP 168, 177). This kind of becoming is confined to the actual and is more or less what Derrida understands by the process of iteration, namely incremental transformation in the course of repetition of the same. The second kind of becoming involves movement beyond the actual toward the virtual. Philosophy and literature are political in the sense that they are concerned with this kind of becoming, the kind that liberates the individual from the confines of a particular identity and opens up the possibility of transformation. In this sense, to become "is not to attain a form (identification, imitation, Mimesis) but to find a zone of proximity, indiscernibility, or indifferentiation where one can no longer be distinguished from *a* woman, *an* animal, or *a* molecule" (CC xx, 1). Whereas Derrida tends to confine himself to analyses of the structure of iterability in various fields, or to analyses of the "to-come" that remains an immanent condition of the possibility and impossibility of change, Deleuze and Guattari describe a series of more specific ways in which individuals and groups become other.

In Plateau 10, "1730: Becoming-Intense, Becoming-Animal, Becoming-Imperceptible . . . ," they rely on a concept of minority to define a number of different kinds of becoming. These are intimately connected with the processes of deterritorialization that define a given assemblage or multiplicity. Deleuze and Guattari distinguish between minorities and processes of becoming-minor, where the former are conceived as subsystems or determinate elements within a given majority, while the latter are understood as encompassing the myriad ways in which a given element can deviate from the standard or norm that defines the majority in question. In these terms, to become-minor is to embark on a process of deterritorialization or divergence from the standard in terms of which a given majoritarian identity is defined. There is no such thing as becoming-majoritarian: "Majority is never becoming. All becoming is minoritarian" (MP 134, 106). For example, insofar as the subject of rights, duties, and moral obligations in modern European society and political community is human, adult, male, and overwhelmingly white, then animals, children, women, and people of color are minorities. Becoming-animal, becoming-child, becoming-woman, becoming-colored, and so on are potential paths of deterritorialization of the "majority" in this qualitative sense of the term. Taken together, these amount to a series of potential paths beyond existing forms of human sociality toward new Earths and peoples to come.

Consider the case of becoming-animal: Deleuze and Guattari point out that anthropology, myth, and folktales provide evidence of a widespread human propensity for a variety of becomings-animal. From an historical point of view, these processes of becoming-animal are often related to marginal social groups or movements, so that there is "an entire politics of becomings-animal, as well as a politics of sorcery, which is elaborated in assemblages that are neither those of the family nor of religion nor of the State. Instead they express minoritarian groups, or groups that are oppressed, prohibited, in revolt, or always on the fringe of recognised institutions . . ." (MP 302, 247). Literature presents us with many different forms of becoming-animal. These typically involve the one undergoing a becoming standing in a relation to a pack or multiplicity of some kind but also to an anomalous figure located on the border of the multiplicity who represents a limit beyond which everything changes. The white whale in Melville's *Moby-Dick* provides an example of one of these figures with whom an individual enters into a pact to pass beyond a given state of life or being. He is anomalous in the sense that he represents "the unequal, the coarse, the rough, the cutting edge of deterritorialization" (MP 298, 244). Deleuze and Guattari specify that becoming occurs only when there is a certain kind of relationship between two terms or when something passes between them such that both are transformed. Through his relentless pursuit of Moby-Dick, Ahab enters into a becoming-whale while at the same time the object of his pursuit becomes the white wall of human weakness and finitude through which he desires to pass: "How can the prisoner reach outside except by thrusting through the wall? To me, the white whale is that wall, shoved near to me. Sometimes I think there's naught beyond. But 'tis enough" (Melville 1994, 167). Ahab's becoming-whale is a line of flight or deterritorialization that both expresses the extraordinary singularity that he is and takes him beyond the limits of his own individual life.

Becomings-animal are not a matter of imitating the animal, nor do they always imply actual transformation into the animal concerned. When they do, as in Kafka's story of Gregor Samsa's transformation into a gigantic insect, the result is a strange hybrid of human and animal capacities (Kafka 1992). Becoming-animal is always a matter of enhancing or decreasing the powers one has, or acquiring new powers, by entering into a "zone of proximity" with the animal. Moreover, because it is always a human who is the subject of becoming-animal, the metamorphosis can take place on a variety of levels. It can involve the physiological powers of the animal, as in the case of Gregor, or the powers that the animal is merely believed to possess, as in cases of witchcraft and sorcery. Deleuze and Guattari use Spinoza's concept of affect to refer to the different kinds and degrees of power that define an individual body. On this basis, they outline a Spinozist ethology that would define animals not by their species or genus but by the active and passive affects of which the animal is capable: "We know nothing about a body until we know what it can do, in other words, what its affects are, how they can or cannot enter into composition with other affects, with the affects of another body . . . " (MP 314, 257). Understood in this manner, individuals are assemblages defined by their capacities to affect and be affected or, in what amounts to the same thing, by the becomings of which they are capable. The concept of an immanent, nonorganic life underwrites this definition of individuals in terms of their affects or becomings. For Deleuze, all things exist as preindividual singularities on this immanent plane of impersonal life before they are individuated as natural kinds or persons. In turn, this allows for the possibility of "unnatural participation" between assemblages as different as a man and a giant insect. Becoming-animal is always a matter of forming an interindividual assemblage with the real or imagined powers of the animal in question.

In *Disgrace*, both David Lurie and his daughter become entangled in a becoming-animal through their relationships to real and imagined dogs. Their different responses to the attack on them by the young African men are symptomatic of the difficult choices confronting Europeans in this formerly colonial society. Whereas Lurie wants the perpetrators brought to account and his own and his daughter's self-respect restored, his daughter is more concerned about being able to live alongside her

African neighbors. She accepts the transformation in her relations to Petrus, her former helper and "dog man," who now becomes her neighbor and owner of what was formerly her land. In the end, her response is to accept that she will have to rely on Petrus rather than the police or the armed white neighbors for protection against other African men. She even accepts that one of the attackers is a relative of Petrus and as such entitled to the same protection. She agrees to surrender her land in exchange for a place within his extended family and to accept what her father can only perceive as humiliation:

"Perhaps that is what I must learn to accept. To start at ground level. With nothing. Not with nothing but. With nothing. No cards, no weapons, no property, no rights, no dignity."
"Like a dog."
"Yes, like a dog." (Coetzee 1999, 205)[5]

Lucy's becoming-dog must be understood in its specific context. It does not imply her acceptance of all that is associated with dogs in the human imagination. It is explicitly contrasted with the behavior of her attackers, who have marked her out as part of their territory and whom she compares to "dogs in a pack" (Coetzee 1999, 158–159). It does represent an affiliation with the lack of property, rights, and dignity often associated with dogs. Because it implies abandonment of any claim to precedence over her neighbor, it also represents a point of departure for the transformation of psychic and social relations associated with the old regime. While her father cannot see past the injustice done to one of his own by one of Petrus's people, she is personally engaged in bringing into being new social relations and thereby a new people or a "people to come." Throughout the novel, she is far more conscious of the historical changes under way than her father and far more deliberate in her responses to them. It is significant that Petrus describes her as "forward looking" (Coetzee 1999, 136). Lucy's willingness to embark on a becoming-African by transferring her land to Petrus and accepting his protection points toward the possibility of what Deleuze and Guattari would describe as "positive" rather than "negative" deterritorialization of the social and affective structures of the apartheid era.[6]

However, what are we to make of the fact that Coetzee chooses to represent the beginnings of the micropolitical dismantling of apartheid through Lucy's story? As several critics have pointed out, the burden of white guilt in the novel is heavily inscribed on the body of this white woman: "White dominance and the overcoming of white dominance are both figured as involving the subjection of the female body, as part of a long history of female exploitation of which the narrative itself takes note" (Boehmer 2002, 344).[7] If indeed the novel may be supposed to suggest that the acceptance of rape is an inescapable cost of transition toward an effectively postcolonial society, then it is, as Elleke Boehmer suggests, "a disappointing assessment" (Boehmer 2002, 349). But this is already to interpret and to extrapolate beyond anything that is said in the novel. Within the context of the narrative, it is also possible to read Lucy's response to the appalling events over which she has little or no control as evidence of the extraordinary strength of her commitment to a new social order and a people to come. It is her choice not to speak to the police about her rape. She agrees that, in another time and place, this might be a public matter, but she chooses to regard it as her own private business "in this place, at this time," this place being South Africa (Coetzee 1999, 112). She chooses to stay rather than to take up her father's offer to help her leave the country and rejoin her mother in Holland. However implausible this might seem in the light of actual perceptions and affections, she chooses to keep the child that she bears as a result of the attack and to raise it in the difficult context of slowly transforming social relations. Insofar as Lucy appears to move beyond the circumstances of the attack and rape of her body and to become simply a woman with the capacity to bring forth a life, she is embarked on a line of flight or absolute deterritorialization.

As we saw in the example of Melville's Ahab, such becomings typically take place in relation to some particular qualitative multiplicity and are often mediated by an anomalous figure at the border of the multiplicity who represents the threshold of absolute deterritorialization. In relation to Lucy's becoming-African in *Disgrace*, it is Petrus who plays this role. We are only given glimpses of Petrus's own story and then largely through the eyes of his white interlocutors. From their perspective, African people and social relations are mysterious, sometimes threatening, but always other. It is in relation to Petrus's story that Lurie expresses his doubts about the capacity of English to convey the truth of South Africa: "He would not mind hearing Petrus's story one day. But preferably not reduced to English" (Coetzee 1999, 117). At the same time, Petrus is the sole point of ethical contact between Lucy, her father, and the largely undifferentiated indigenous African population. Apart from him, there is only the violence of the young men. It is through her relationship to Petrus and her refusal to dictate the terms of this relation or to give it up after the attack on her that Lucy's becoming-dog is bound up with her becoming-African. Hers is a painful but also a positive micropolitical story of the deterritorialization of the social relations that were both products and supports of the colonial regime. The kind of becoming-African portrayed here is not and cannot be the kind of new beginning that breaks suddenly and completely from the past but is perhaps the only possible form of transition from what South Africa has been toward a truly postcolonial society.

In Lurie's case, too, the beginnings of a shift in his attitudes and sensibility take place by way of a becoming-animal that is also a form of minoritarian-becoming in Deleuze and Guattari's sense of the term. According to their account of the concept, minoritarian-becoming is always complex and tends to occur in combination with other processes that form a "bloc" of becoming. In Lucy's case, her becoming-dog is bound up with her becoming-African. In her father's case, his becoming-dog is bound up with a becoming-woman as he develops an increasingly critical awareness of his masculinity. His identification with the unwanted dogs that are disposed of at the clinic is expressed at one point in the thought that *"we are too menny"* (Coetzee 1999, 146). Over and above the obvious allusion to Thomas Hardy, it is difficult not to read this as referring to maleness.[8] He later becomes aware of the connections between his own sexual behavior and that of the rapists and male dogs. He can inhabit their world, but the question is, he or Coetzee asks, "Does he have it in him to be the woman?" (Coetzee 1999, 160).

Lurie's becoming-dog is of an altogether different kind to that of his daughter. In the course of the novel, he enters into a series of affective alliances with particular animals, including one of the dogs in his daughter's kennel, two sheep destined for slaughter at the hands of Petrus, and the crippled dog at the shelter. Through these encounters and through the attack on himself and his daughter, he acquires new levels of sensitivity toward the feelings of others.[9] He rediscovers within himself a capacity to love and care for others, including the daughter he does not understand. His work with the dogs enables him to cry in a way that he has not been able to before. The experience of putting down the dogs has a profound effect upon him:

He had thought he would get used to it. But that is not what happens. The more killings he assists in, the more jittery he gets. One Sunday evening, driving home in Lucy's kombi, he actually has to stop at the roadside to recover himself. Tears flow down his face that he cannot stop; his hands shake.

He does not understand what is happening to him. Until now, he has been more or less indifferent to animals . . .

His whole being is gripped by what happens in the theatre. He is convinced the dogs know their time has come . . . they flatten their ears, they droop their tails, as if they too feel the disgrace of dying . . . (Coetzee 1999, 142–3)

In the end, despite his repeated protestations that he is too old to learn new tricks, Lurie does become a different person. He learns to accept his daughter's independence and her right to make choices in relation to her own life of which he would be incapable. In some respects, it is true that he remains a figure of the old world, someone who has no place in the new society, slowly and painfully emerging from the ruins of apartheid. Accordingly, at the end of the novel, he spends most of his time with the stray dogs while remaining a spectator to the changes in the lives of his daughter and others actively engaged in the coming to be of the new South Africa. In relation to the historical and political changes occurring around him, his story remains one of negative rather than positive deterritorialization.

Impersonal Life: The Life We Share with Animals

We saw above how Deleuze's preference for Anglo-American literature has to do with the manner in which it traces lines of flight or processes of becoming through which characters, peoples, and worlds are transformed. As Ronald Bogue reminds us, "The line of flight ultimately is the trajectory of a process of becoming-other, the course of a line that always 'passes between'" (Bogue 2003, 6). The different kinds of becoming-dog in *Disgrace* are lines of flight in this sense. They are all associated with a particular kind of disgrace. In normal usage, as Derek Attridge notes, disgrace is opposed to honor rather than grace (Attridge 2004, 178). As well as Lucy's disgrace at the hands of her African attackers and her becoming-dog in response to the danger of continuing to live alone in the country, there is her father's social disgrace at the university. Lurie is disgraced in this sense of the word by his treatment of Melanie and his subsequent refusal to apologize. In this sense, too, he later acknowledges the "state of disgrace" into which he has fallen, immediately before his apology, on his knees and touching his forehead to the floor, to the mother and sister of his former student (Coetzee 1999, 172–173).

However, there is another kind of disgrace that is opposed to grace and that is arguably more important for the central character in the novel. This is "the disgrace of dying" that Lurie is convinced is perceived by the dogs at the refuge and that causes them to "flatten their ears" and "droop their tails" as they are dragged over the threshold (Coetzee 1999, 143). At one point, soon after he has begun assisting Bev Shaw to ease the moment of death for the dogs, she says to him: "I don't think we are ready to die, any of us, not without being escorted" (Coetzee 1999, 84). His role in the refuge of last resort is precisely that of escort and what he shares with the dogs is "the disgrace of dying" (Coetzee 1999, 143). This phrase may be read as an ironic expression of a post-Christian and secular conception of life. For if dying is a disgrace, it is not because we are dishonored by it but because life itself is a state of grace, a gift or a blessing from God. If the animals at Bev's shelter had souls, they too would be forcibly evicted from this state, as indeed we all are eventually.

Early in the novel, Lurie admits to believing that people have souls, but it is also clear that he has never thought of animals in this way. When he first arrives at his daughter's farm, he is convinced that humans are "a different order of creation from the animals" (Coetzee 1999, 74). He invokes approvingly the doctrine of the Church Fathers that we are all souls even before we are born, whereas animals do not have proper souls: "Their souls are tied to their bodies and die with them" (Coetzee 1999, 78). By the end of the novel, he is convinced that the room in which he and Bev administer death to the stray dogs is a place where "the soul is yanked out of the body" before it is "sucked away" (Coetzee 1999, 219). It is apparent that he no longer draws the same sharp distinction between different orders of creation.

Lurie's experience with the dying dogs transforms his attitude to human as well as animal life and death. It is the turning point in his own affective constitution and his relations to others. Through this experience, he comes to accept the mundane and transitory character of his own existence. When he first arrives at the farm, Lucy finds him disapproving of her chosen life and still committed to an intellectualist belief in higher forms of life. She defends her choice of a simple rural life by affirming that "there is no higher life. This is the only life there is. Which we share with animals" (Coetzee 1999, 74). At the end of the novel, Lurie "gives up" his favored dog to death, thereby signaling his own reconciliation to the absence of any higher life and to the finitude of the life that he shares with animals.

For Deleuze, the life that good literature affirms is not the personal life of the individual character but the impersonal and abstract life that is expressed in but irreducible to its particular incarnations. In "Literature and Life," he defines literature as the kind of writing that "discovers beneath apparent persons the power of an impersonal—which is not a generality but a singularity at the highest point: a man, a woman, a beast, a stomach, a child . . . Literature begins only when a third person is born in us that strips us of the power to say 'I'" (CC xx, 3). In an extraordinarily condensed essay published just before his death, "Immanence: A Life . . . ," he outlines the manner in which, as absolute or pure immanence, life is at once impersonal and indeterminate but also singular (DRF 359–363, 388–393). To illustrate this concept, he invokes a passage from *Our Mutual Friend*, in which Dickens describes a near drowning. The character, Riderhood, was a rogue disliked by all who knew him. Nevertheless, when confronted with the sight of him hovering between life and death, those around him cannot help but show a kind of respect and affection for the slightest signs of life: "No one has the least regard for the man: with them all, he has been an object of avoidance, suspicion and aversion; but the spark of life within him is curiously separable from himself now, and they have a deep interest in it, probably because it *is* life, and they are living and must die" (Dickens 1989, 443–445).

Deleuze uses this passage from Dickens to illustrate his concept of an impersonal, indefinite, and singular life that is expressed in the lives of empirical individuals, but not only in these. This is what he calls *a life*, and it is this life that excites the interest of the onlookers: not the everyday life of the individual man but an impersonal and indefinite life that is visible only because it is on the point of withdrawing. Although it becomes visible only in such exceptional moments, this life is present not only at the moment when the individual confronts death but rather persists throughout all the moments that make up his life. This abstract, impersonal life is an instance of what Deleuze calls the virtual or inner realm of being that is actualized in real events and states of affairs: "What I am calling virtual is not something that lacks reality. Rather, the virtual becomes engaged in a process of actualization as it follows the plane which gives it its proper reality. The immanent event is actualized in a state of things and in a state of lived experience, and these states bring the event about" (DRF 363, 392).

The distinction between the actual and the virtual that governs this characterization of a life is one that Deleuze draws in other ways throughout his work. The ontology of events in *The Logic of Sense*, the ontology of pure transcendental Ideas in *Difference and Repetition*, and the machinic ontology of *Anti-Oedipus* and *A Thousand Plateaus* each reproduces in its own terms the concept of an indeterminate, abstract, nonorganic, and intensive life that is prior to its incarnation in fixed and organized forms. For example, he distinguishes between machinic assemblages and the abstract machines that govern their operation or between actual everyday empirical or historical events and the virtual or pure event that is expressed or incarnated in them. The concept of absolute deterritorialization provides yet another name for this abstract life that is expressed in the actual organization of societies, people, things, and historical processes and in their processes of relative deterritorialization. Deleuze and Guattari conceive of it as "identical to the earth itself," or as a "deeper movement for conjugating matter and function" that appears only in the form of "particular territorialities, negative or relative deterritorializations and complementary reterritorializations" (MP 178, 143). This abstract and impersonal life unfolds only in particular forms. These may be biological, technological, cultural, or intellectual, but they are always secondary determinations of an ontologically primary flux of life or becoming: "If everything is alive, it is not because everything is organic or organized but, on the contrary, because the organism is a diversion of life. In short, the life in question is non-organic, germinal and intensive, a powerful life without organs . . . " (MP 623, 499).[10]

At one point in "Immanence: A Life . . . ," Deleuze suggests that the concept of an indeterminate and impersonal but singular life that he finds in Dickens is a concept of life as a pure event. In this passage, he says, "The life of the individual has given way to an impersonal and yet singular life, which foregrounds a pure event that has been liberated from the accidents of internal and external life . . . The singularities or the events which constitute *a life* coexist with the accidents of *the* life that corresponds to it, but they are not arranged and distributed in the same way. They relate to one another in a completely different way than individuals do" (DRF 361–362, 390–391).

Coetzee's *Disgrace* also offers us a conception of pure indeterminate life that is expressed in the everyday existence of humans and animals alike. Despite its reliance on the theological terminology of souls, this is a resolutely secular conception of an immanent life individuated in the form of particular lives, human and animal alike. In effect, it is the perception of a disgrace in dying that forms the zone of indiscernibility in which Lurie becomes-dog. His tearful reaction in the Kombi shows that this is a disgrace more threatening than the one associated with his dismissal from the university and the social death associated with that event. It threatens his sense of himself as a person whose life and whose projects have meaning over and above the life he shares with the animals.

By the end of the novel, Lurie has learned to accept the inevitability of death and the finitude of the life he shares with animals. In his becoming-dog, something passes between the two terms such that both are transformed. He becomes-dog, but the favored dog becomes everything that he is now able to give up, including his honor, his intellectual pride, and his attachment to life itself. He becomes capable of letting go of his social and personal identity. He gives up the state of grace for the disgrace of dying, but only once dying has been revalued to incorporate identification with an impersonal and indeterminate life, the cosmic life that he now sees as passing through himself, his daughter, and her child: "a line of existences in which his share, his gift, will grow inexorably less and less, till it may as well be forgotten" (Coetzee 1999, 217). In the act of giving up his favored dog, Lurie becomes reconciled with his own mortality. He affirms the impersonal life that is expressed in all finite lives, including his own. He is thereby redeemed from what we can only take to be ironically called the "disgrace" of dying.

PART III   NORMATIVE POLITICAL PHILOSOPHY

Philosophy, Politics, and Political Normativity

Deleuzian Political Philosophy?

Deleuze often referred to his work with Guattari as philosophy and sometimes even as political philosophy. For example, he recounts how he began to engage with specific political problems around May 1968 through his contacts with people such as Guattari, Foucault, and Elie Sambar, and suggests that "*Anti-Oedipus* was from beginning to end a work of political philosophy" (P 230, 170).[1] This is a puzzling claim for many political philosophers because normative questions about the justification, nature, and limits of political power, or questions about the principles of a just society, are largely absent from Deleuze and Guattari's collaborative writings. They discuss the institutional forms of political power only in passing and always from the perspective of a global theory of society founded on concepts of desire, desiring-machines, or the different kinds of assemblage described in *A Thousand Plateaus*. They do not employ the language or the methods of contemporary liberal political philosophy. Unlike Habermas, they do not seek to provide clear and unambiguous normative standards for the evaluation of political institutions or social practices. Unlike Rawls, they do not engage in the systematic reconstruction of our considered opinions on the nature of justice, freedom, and political organization. In some respects, I will argue, their approach is closer to a deconstructive rather than a reconstructive political philosophy. Deleuze's remarks about his work with Guattari therefore raise the questions: What kind of political philosophy is this, and what purpose(s) does it serve?

Under the influence of Marxist approaches to politics, Deleuze and Guattari focus on the conditions of revolutionary social change rather than the conditions of maintaining society as a fair system of cooperation among its members. However, they are less interested in the capture of state power than in the qualitative changes in individual and collective identities that occur alongside or beneath the public political domain. In their view, all politics is simultaneously a *macropolitics* that involves social classes and the institutions of political government and a *micropolitics* that involves subterranean movements of individual and collective sensibility, affect, and allegiance. However much they borrow from Marx's analysis of capitalism, their micropolitical focus leads them to abandon key tenets of Marxist social and political theory (Garo 2007, 2008). Their political philosophy incorporates both a recognizably Marxist critique of capitalist society and a post-Marxist critique of revolutionary vanguard politics and the philosophy of history that sustained them. They propose a non-teleological conception of history and a more nuanced appreciation of the deterritorializing as well as the reterritorializing aspects of capitalism. They insist that the impetus for social change is provided by movements of deterritorialization and lines of flight rather than class contradictions. Their rejection of the organizational and tactical forms of traditional Marxist politics is definitively expressed at the end of *Dialogues* when Deleuze and Parnet abandon the goal of revolutionary capture of State power in favor of *revolutionary-becoming* (D 176, 147). This new concept encompasses the multitude of ways in which individuals and groups deviate from the majoritarian norms that ultimately determine the rights and duties of citizens.

What Is Philosophy? further complicates the question by proposing a conception of philosophy as inherently political. Philosophy creates concepts, the function of which is not merely to recognize or reconstruct how things are but to transform existing forms of thought and practice. It is "utopian" in the sense that it carries the criticism of its own time to its highest point and, in doing so, "summons forth" a new Earth and a new people (QP 95, 99). Clearly, this is a stipulative definition that applies to some but not all historical and existing forms of philosophy. Philosophy is distinguished from science and art in a manner that treats these as three different modalities of thought. Each has its own distinct raw materials, methods, and products: Science aims at the representation of objects and states of affairs by means of mathematical or propositional functions. Art aims at the capture and expression of the objective content of particular sensations—affects and percepts—in a given medium. Philosophy does not seek to represent independently existing objects or states of affairs, nor to capture particular affects and percepts, but to produce concepts where these are a different kind of thought object to those produced by the arts or the sciences. Philosophical concepts express pure events such as "to become," "to deterritorialize," "to capture" or "to nomadize." They fulfill their intrinsically political vocation by counter-effectuating existing states of affairs and referring them back to the virtual realm of becoming.

One way to approach the problem what kind of political philosophy Deleuze and Guattari provide is suggested by the tripartite division of thought outlined in *What Is Philosophy?* In some respects, this resembles the division found in Kant's three critiques: science, philosophy, and art as distinct modalities of thought correspond to the Kantian domains of theoretical, practical, and teleological reason. Kant distinguishes theoretical from practical reason by suggesting that theoretical reason is concerned with the knowledge of objects that are given to us by means of the senses, whereas practical reason is concerned with objects that we produce by means of action in accordance with certain principles. When we are concerned with the practical use of reason, Kant argues, we consider it in relation to the determination of the will, which he defines as "a faculty either of producing objects corresponding to representations or of determining itself to effect such objects" (Kant 1996, 148). Deleuze and Guattari do not rely on a concept of the will, much less a concept of human nature as defined by the freedom of the will and the faculty of reason. However, they do rely upon a constructivist conception of philosophy as the creation of concepts, where these are not supposed to represent pregiven objects but rather assist in bringing about new Earths and new peoples. On this basis, we can properly take Deleuze and Guattari's philosophy to be a form of practical reason. The purpose of this comparison is not to undertake a systematic examination of Deleuze's relation to Kant but rather to answer the question raised above about the nature of their political philosophy. In this manner, we can ask whether and if so how far the distinction between science and philosophy corresponds to the Kantian distinction between representation of given objects and the production of objects (or events and states of affairs) not given in experience. We can ask whether the analogy helps us to understand the sense in which Deleuzian philosophical concepts are intended to be action guiding rather than or perhaps as well as descriptive of past or present events.

Treating Deleuze's political philosophy as practical reason points us toward the normative principles implicit in its concepts and analyses, which in turn allows us to explore its relation to liberal democratic institutions and practices and to prepare the way for further comparisons with Rawls's political liberalism (see Chapter 9). Against the background of the resolutely antisubjectivist and antivoluntarist approach of *Anti-Oedipus* and *A Thousand Plateaus*, and in the light of Deleuze and Guattari's preference for minoritarian movements defined in opposition to majoritarian forms of social control, it is surprising to find them referring to "becoming-democratic" as one of the contemporary forms of resistance to the present (QP 108, 113). It is surprising, too, that this feature of Deleuze's later work has attracted so little attention. His analysis of societies of control has attracted considerably more attention than his embrace of some of the political values that inform the institutions and practices of liberal democracy.[2] I argue that while the appearance in *What Is Philosophy?* of the concept of "becoming-democratic" represents a significant inflection in Deleuze's political thought, it does not imply any fundamental rupture in his approach to philosophy or politics. On the contrary, we can make sense of his explicit embrace of democracy and the rule of law in a manner that is not only consistent with but draws on elements of the earlier work. To answer the question posed above and to explain the sense in which Deleuze and Guattari's work can be considered political philosophy, I begin by retracing the development from the formal normativity of the earlier work to their increasing engagement with explicitly political normativity.

Normativity and the Political in *Anti-Oedipus* and *A Thousand Plateaus*

Despite Deleuze's suggestion that *Anti-Oedipus* was a work of political philosophy, this book considers political institutions only from the perspective of a universal theory of society and history. The treatment of the political resembles that of Marx, except that it is founded on a theory of desire rather than the social organization of production:

The truth of the matter is that *social production is purely and simply desiring production itself under determinate conditions*. We maintain that the social field is immediately invested by desire, that it is the historically determined product of desire, and that the libido has no need of any mediation or sublimation, any psychic operation, any transformation, in order to invade and invest the productive forces and the relations of production. *There is only desire and the social, and nothing else.* (AO 36, 31)

The specifically political organization of society plays no independent role in this theory. Rather, it is treated as continuous with the coordination and control of flows of matter and desire in nonstate societies governed by the Territorial machine with its systems of alliance and filiation. Deleuze and Guattari present the state as a new mechanism of alliance rather than as the embodiment of any ideal treaty or contract on the part of its subjects (AO 231, 213). It appeared in human history in the form of the different kinds of Despotic machine, each with its own mechanisms of overcoding the flows of desire, before becoming subordinate to the "civilized machine" that is global capitalism. What they call the Territorial, Despotic, and Civilized social machines are treated only as different regimes of coordination and control of the local machines that constitute individual, familial, and social life. There is no discussion of the norms that regulate modern political life, only the normativity inherent in the typology of desiring machines as embodying either the paranoiac, reactionary, and fascistic pole of desire or the schizoid and revolutionary pole (AO 407, 373). For this reason, their "schizoanalytic" theory and practice of desire proposes neither a political program nor a project for a future form of society. As their alternative to psychoanalysis, schizoanalysis offers a conceptual apparatus within which to pose questions about social investments of desire, including the ways in which it can become complicit in its own repression and the ways in which it might sustain creative or revolutionary social processes. The primary goal is practical, namely to unblock the schizoid processes present in a given social field with a view to the creative transformation of individual and collective life.

A Thousand Plateaus is no more concerned than *Anti-Oedipus* with the nature, justification, or critique of specifically political institutions and practices. It broadens and generalizes Deleuze and Guattari's social ontology so that it becomes a general theory of assemblages and the manner in which these are expressed throughout human history. The last vestiges of Marxist teleology are removed from their universal history so that

Instead of following, as in *Anti-Oedipus*, the traditional succession of Savages, Barbarians, and Civilized Peoples, we now find ourselves before all kinds of co-existing formations: primitive groups, which operate through series and, in a bizarre marginalism, through an evaluation of the 'last' term; despotic communities, which on the contrary constitute groups subjected to processes of centralization (apparatuses of State); nomadic war-machines, which will not take hold of States without these States in turn appropriating a war-machine which they did not originally possess; processes of subjectivation at work in State and warrior apparatuses; the convergence of these processes within capitalism and through the corresponding States; the modalities of revolutionary action; and the comparative factors, in each case, of earth, territory and deterritorialization. (DRF 290, 310–311)

The successive plateaus provide a series of new concepts and associated terminology with which to describe different kinds of assemblages. These include the terminology used to describe social, linguistic, and affective assemblages (strata, content and expression, territories, lines of flight, or deterritorialization); the terminology employed to outline a micro- as opposed to macropolitics (body without organs, intensities, molar and molecular segmentarities, the different kinds of line of which we are composed); and the terminology employed to describe capitalism as a nonterritorially based axiomatic of flows (of materials, labor, and information) as opposed to a territorial system of overcoding. They include a concept of the state as an apparatus of capture that, in the forms of its present actualization, is increasingly subordinated to the requirements of the capitalist axiomatic, and a concept of abstract machines of metamorphosis (nomadic war machines) that are the agents of social and political transformation.

The machinic theory of society is an ontology in the sense that one speaks of Marx's ontology, Rawls's ontology or the ontology of a particular scientific or social theory. It is in this sense that Foucault situates his own practice of genealogy in the lineage of those who have undertaken an "ontology of the present" (Foucault 2007, 95). This is not ontology in the strong philosophical sense of the term but a pragmatic and relativized ontology. Deleuze and Guattari's machinic ontology is normative in a specific and formal sense, namely that the different kinds of assemblage amount to a world in which systematic priority is accorded to certain kinds of movement: to becoming-minor as a process of deviation from a majoritarian standard, to lines of flight or deterritorialization, to nomadic machines of metamorphosis rather than apparatuses of capture, to smooth rather than striated space, and so on. In this sense, their ontology of assemblages is also an ethics or an ethology. This ethics might be characterized in the language of one or other of the plateaus as an ethics of becoming, of flows or lines of flight or, as I argued in *Deleuze and the Political*, as an ethics and a politics of deterritorialization (Patton 2000). It is "political" only in the very broad sense that it enables us to conceptualize and describe transformative forces and movements as well as the forms of "capture" or blockage to which these are subject. Consider how this works in the language of *deterritorialization* and *reterritorialization*.

In the concluding statement of rules governing some of their most important concepts at the end of *A Thousand Plateaus*, deterritorialization is defined as the movement or process by which something escapes or departs from a given territory (MP 634, 508), where a territory can be a system of any kind: conceptual, linguistic, social, or affective. By contrast, reterritorialization refers to the ways in which deterritorialized elements recombine and enter into new relations in the constitution of a new assemblage or the modification of the old. Systems of any kind always include "vectors of deterritorialization," while deterritorialization is always "inseparable from correlative reterritorializations" (MP 635, 509). Deterritorialization can take either a negative or a positive form: It is negative when the deterritorialized element is subjected to reterritorialization that obstructs or limits its line of flight, and it is positive when the line of flight prevails over the forms of reterritorialization and manages to connect with other deterritorialized elements in a manner that extends its trajectory or even leads to reterritorialization in an entirely new assemblage. As well as distinguishing negative and positive deterritorialization, Deleuze and Guattari further distinguish between an absolute and a relative form of each of these processes. Absolute deterritorialization refers to the virtual realm of becoming and pure events, while relative deterritorialization concerns only movements within the actual realm of embodied, historical events and processes. In the terms of their ontology of assemblages, it is the virtual order of becoming that governs the fate of any actual assemblage.

Finally, in accordance with their method of specification of concepts by proliferating distinctions, they distinguish between the *connection* and *conjugation* of deterritorialized elements in the construction of a new assemblage. The effective transformation of a given actuality requires the recombination of deterritorialized elements in mutually supportive and productive ways to form assemblages of connection rather than conjugation. Absolute and relative deterritorialization will both be positive when they involve the construction of *"revolutionary connections* in opposition to the *conjugations of the axiomatic"* (MP 591, 473). Under these conditions, absolute deterritorialization "connects lines of flight, raises them to the power of an abstract vital line or draws a plane of consistency" (MP 636, 510).

Absolute deterritorialization is the underlying condition of all forms of relative deterritorialization. It is the concept of an abstract, nonorganic, and creative life that is expressed both in the deterritorialization of exist-ing assemblages and in the connection of deterritorialized elements and their reconfiguration into new assemblages. It is the immanent source of transformation, the reserve of freedom or movement in reality that is activated whenever relative deterritorialization occurs. For this reason, it expresses the normative ideal at the heart of Deleuze and Guattari's eth-ics. The sense in which absolute deterritorialization amounts to an ethical principle embedded within a conception of the world becomes clear when they describe it as

an Absolute, but one that is neither undifferentiated nor transcendent . . . The deeper movement for conjugating matter and function—absolute deterritorializa-tion, identical to the earth itself—appears only in the form of respective territo-rialities, negative or relative deterritorializations, and complementary reterritori-alizations. (MP 177–178, 142–143)

As such, it is closer to a Bergsonian concept of freedom in the world than a Kantian concept of freedom of the will. It is the freedom expressed in the creative transformation of what is, but at the same time a concept of freedom that is incompatible with liberal concepts predicated upon the continued existence of the stable subject of freedom (Patton 2000, 83–87). The molecular as opposed to the molar line on which individual and col-lective subjects are composed already constitutes a mortal threat to the integrity of such a subject. It is along this line that the subject undergoes "molecular changes, redistributions of desire such that when something occurs, the self that awaited it is already dead, or the one that would await it has not yet arrived" (MP 243, 199). The freedom expressed in Deleuze and Guattari's third line, the line of flight or absolute deterritorialization, threatens the very integrity of the embodied subject. Once embarked on this line, "One has become imperceptible and clandestine in motionless voyage. Nothing can happen, or can have happened, any longer . . . Now one is no more than an abstract line, like an arrow crossing the void. Ab-solute deterritorialization" (MP 244, 199–200).

Paradoxical Normativity

Like all concepts, Deleuze and Guattari's concepts are normative in the sense that they enable some inferences and disable others (Brandom 2001). However, they are also normative in the sense that they provide a framework within which to evaluate the character of particular events and processes. They enable us to pose questions such as: Is this negative or positive reterritorialization? Is this a genuine line of flight? Will it lead to a revolutionary new assemblage in which there is an increase of freedom, or will it lead to a new form of capture or worse (D 172–173, 143–144)? In this sense, as I suggested earlier, they are elements of a form of practical rather than theoretical reason.

Several consequences follow from the normativity of Deleuze and Guattari's concepts. First, we can appreciate why a purely representation-alist reading does not do justice to their analyses. The wealth of empirical material employed in the presentation of their concepts, along with the apparently descriptive character of much of their work, creates a temp-tation to read them as proposing an empirical account of the affective, linguistic, and social world that we inhabit. In this manner, for example, Antonio Negri reads *A Thousand Plateaus* as "a perfectly operational phe-nomenology of the present" (Negri 1995, 108). In the same way, Negri and Michael Hardt take Deleuze and Guattari's account of capitalism as an axiomatic or set of variable relationships between the elements of produc-tion of surplus value as the basis for their understanding of contemporary society. Deleuze's concept of "control society," along with their own ac-count of the real subsumption of labor to capital, also informs their analy-sis of the "material transformation" of the means of production of social reality under late capitalism (Hardt and Negri 2000, 22–25, 325–327). Thus, in relation to their analysis of the biopolitical production of subjec-tivity, they comment that "We are indebted to Deleuze and Guattari and their *A Thousand Plateaus* for the most fully elaborated phenomenological description of this industrial-monetary-world-nature, which constitutes the first level of the world order" (Hardt and Negri 2000, 424 note 23). Hardt and Negri are not alone in assuming that Deleuze and Guattari are engaged in a form of social science. Critics such as Christopher L. Miller rely on this assumption in criticizing the empirical bases of their concepts. Miller argues that their reliance on anthropological sources in their dis-cussion of nomadism commits them to an "anthropological referentiality" that is compromised by the primitivist and colonialist character of those sources (Miller 1998).[3]

Second, even though the basis of the framework of evaluation is assemblages rather than individuals, Deleuze and Guattari's machinic ontology does provide directions for individual actions. Foucault drew attention to this when he famously compared *Anti-Oedipus* to Saint Francis de Sales' *Introduction to the Devout Life*: "I would say that *Anti-Oedipus* (may its authors forgive me) is a book of ethics, the first book of ethics to be written in France in quite a long time" (Foucault 1977, xiii). He went on to suggest that *Anti-Oedipus* could be taken to offer individual guidance in identifying and avoiding all the varieties of "fascism" that entrap our desires and bind us to the forms of power that maintain systems of exploitation and domination. In this sense, Deleuze and Guattari may be taken to provide rules for the conduct of a nonfascist life such as: Pursue thought and action by proliferation, juxtaposition, and disjunction rather than by hierarchization and subdivision; prefer positivity over negativity, difference over uniformity, nomadic or mobile assemblages over sedentary systems; and so on.

While there is no doubt that Deleuze and Guattari sometimes offer guidelines for action, it is important to understand what kind of guidance these provide. At several points in *A Thousand Plateaus*, as though in response to Foucault's provocative characterization, they appear to assume the speaking position of the practical ethicist. For example, they offer guidance in the construction of a "body without organs" (BwO):

You don't do it with a sledgehammer, you use a very fine file. You invent self-destructions that have nothing to do with the death drive. Dismantling the organism has never meant killing yourself, but rather opening the body to connections that presuppose an entire assemblage, circuits, conjunctions, levels and thresholds, passages and distributions of intensity, and territories and deterritorializations measured with the craft of a surveyor . . . You have to keep enough of the organism for it to reform each dawn; and you have to keep small supplies of significance and subjectification, if only to turn them against their own systems when the circumstances demand it, when things, persons, even situations force you to; and you have to keep small rations of subjectivity in sufficient quantity to enable you to respond to the dominant reality. (MP 198, 160)

Immediately after setting out such rules of conduct, however, Deleuze and Guattari go on to caution the reader of the dangers these carry and of the need for further discrimination. In other words, they deny that there are straightforward, unequivocal criteria by which one can lead a nonfascist life or construct one's own body without organs. The reason is that BwOs come in many guises. They exist already in the strata as well as in the destratified planes of consistency on which BwOs are formed, while BwOs formed on a plane of consistency can easily turn cancerous. The problem of evaluation and discrimination reemerges at every stage:

How can we fabricate a BwO for ourselves without its being the cancerous BwO of a fascist inside us, or the empty BwO of a drug addict, paranoiac, or hypochondriac? (MP 202, 163)

This kind of ambivalence inheres in all of Deleuze and Guattari's concepts of life, creativity, and transformation. Consider the lines of flight along which individual or collective assemblages break down or become transformed. On the one hand, insofar as we are interested in bringing about change we cannot avoid experimentation with such lines because "it is always on a line of flight that we create" (D 164, 135). In this sense, lines of flight are potential pathways of mutation in an individual or social fabric and sources of the affect associated with the passage from a lower to a higher state of power, namely joy. On the other hand, lines of flight have their own dangers. Once having broken out of the limits imposed by the molar forms of segmentarity and subjectivity, a line of flight may fail to connect with the necessary conditions of creative development or be incapable of so connecting and turn instead into a line of destruction. When this happens, lines of flight or deterritorialization are a path to the most extreme failure. They can become the source of the affect associated with the passage to a lower state of power: "a strange despair, like an odor of death and immolation, a state of war from which one returns broken" (MP 280, 229).[4]

These features of the normativity implicit in Deleuze and Guattari's practical philosophy enable us to draw a number of conclusions with regard to the kind of evaluation that it sustains. First, evaluation will always be contextual or responsive to the character of the events and processes involved and their relationship to the character of the one judging. It is for this reason that Deleuze and Guattari side with Artaud's hostility to the judgment of God: The judgment of God stratifies the BwO and makes it into an organism. It transforms the BwO of desire into a subject. By contrast, they practice a form of judgment that is not opposed to the organs but to the organism: "The BwO is not opposed to the organs but to that organization of the organs called the organism" (MP 196, 158).[5] In the practical sphere, the judgment of God implies a single unilateral frame of evaluation such as we find in Kant: In the end, actions fall either on the side of good or on the side of evil. For Deleuze and Guattari, following

Nietzsche and Artaud, things are never so simple. Actions take place between finite beings in particular circumstances. They are the outcome of a
specific play of forces rather than universal requirements of rationality or
freedom. They give rise to specific and local forms of obligation, antipathy, or attraction. Evaluation always takes place from somewhere within
such a field of relations of force and power.

Second, the process of evaluation will be endless because it is always
undertaken from the perspective of a particular agent or assemblage. In
this sense, there is no final determination of the character of a given event
or process. Kantian evaluation of the moral character of actions is also
endless, but for a different reason. For Kant, we can never be entirely
sure that we have acted out of duty and not out of self-interest. This is an
epistemological problem rather than a consequence of the equivocal character of the actions as it is for Deleuze and Guattari. The uncertainty and
potential danger associated with lines of flight is the primary reason that
prudence is such an important political virtue for Deleuze and Guattari.
Caution is necessary because we never know in advance which way a line
of flight will turn or whether a given set of heterogeneous elements will
be able to form a consistent and functional multiplicity. In the evaluative
schema of *A Thousand Plateaus*, nothing is unambiguously good or bad:

> Nothing's good in itself, it all depends on a systematic use and prudence. In *A
> Thousand Plateaus* we're trying to say you can never guarantee a good outcome
> (it's not enough just to have a *smooth space*, for example, to overcome striations
> and constraints, or a *body without organs* to overcome organizations). (P 49, 32)

Third, the conditions of evaluation will lead to paradox.[6] I argued
in Chapter 2 that Deleuze and Guattari's practical philosophy resembles
Derrida's deconstructive analysis of all forms of decision. Insofar as absolute deterritorialization is the underlying condition of relative deterritorialization in all its forms, it implies the same kind of paradoxical formula:
Absolute deterritorialization is at once both the condition of possibility of
change and the condition of its impossibility. This affinity with Derridean
aporia is not unrelated to the contextual character of Deleuzian evaluation. They share an ethical orientation toward the event or the emergence
of the new, where this implies a rupture with present actuality and its
possible future forms. As Kant showed in his analysis of genius in art, the
advent of the genuinely new implies the reorganization of rules for the
production and evaluation of the work in question (Kant 2000, 194–196).

By definition, we cannot know in advance what form this will take. This is why Deleuzian principles of evaluation are equivocal and open-ended: They are rules for the creation of the new. If they eschew general prescription, this is because they answer to a pragmatic aim altogether different from that of universalizing judgment: "To bring into existence and not to judge . . . What expert judgment, in art, could ever bear on the work to come?" (CC xx, 135).

Toward a Deleuzian Theory of Right?

Within the domain of practical reason, Kant distinguishes between the ethical, in which the incentive to act in accordance with the moral law is bound up with the very idea of such a law, and the juridical, in which external incentives are attached to publicly promulgated laws. The theory of those laws for which only external incentives such as coercion by force or the threat of punishment are possible is what he calls the Doctrine of Right. It deals with the sum of the conditions under which the actions of individuals can be correlated in accordance with the freedom of each: "Any action is right if it can coexist with everyone's freedom in accordance with a universal law" (Kant 1996, 387). In turn, the theory of right may be divided into private right and public right. The former encompasses the laws regarding the behavior of individuals that apply even in the absence of any public political authority and that are necessary if their actions are to remain consistent with the freedom of others. The latter encompasses the system of laws needed so that a multitude of human beings may live together in a civil condition (Kant 1996, 455).

Anti-Oedipus and *A Thousand Plateaus* do not directly address the political domain of public right. They consider the different forms of modern government only from the Marxist perspective of their subordination to the axioms of capitalist production. From this point of view, authoritarian, socialist, and liberal democratic states are considered equivalent to one another insofar as they function as models of realization of the global axiomatic of capital. Deleuze and Guattari allow that there are important differences among the various modern forms of state but provide little discussion of these differences. Equally, they affirm the importance of changes to the regime of public right that come about through struggles for civil and political rights, for equality of economic condition and

opportunity as well as regional and national autonomy, but offer no normative theory of the basis of such rights nor of the kinds and degrees of
equality or autonomy that should prevail (MP 586–588, 470–471). They
offer no justification for the establishment of differential rights for cultural or national minorities or for particular ways of redistributing wealth.
Instead, they focus on the micropolitical sources of political change such
as the minoritarian becomings that provide the affective impetus for such
struggles. On their view, the sources of political creativity must always be
traced back to subterranean shifts in allegiance, attitude, sensibility, and
belief on the part of individuals and groups. To the extent that such micropolitical movements bring about changes in the majoritarian standards
themselves, along with new forms of right or different status for particular groups, they effectively bring about "new peoples." At the same time,
the significance of such minoritarian becomings for public political right
depends on their being translated into new forms of right and different
statuses for individuals and groups: "Molecular escapes and movements
would be nothing if they did not return to the molar organizations to reshuffle their segments, their binary distributions of sexes, classes and parties" (MP 264, 216–217). In this manner, even though they offer neither
descriptive nor normative accounts of macropolitical institutions and procedures, Deleuze and Guattari do provide a language in which to describe
micropolitical movements and infrapolitical processes that give rise to
new forms of constitutional and legal order. The concepts they invent thus
bear indirectly on the forms of public right. Concepts such as becoming-
minor, nomadism, smooth space, and lines of flight or deterritorialization
are not meant as substitutes for existing concepts of freedom, equality, or
justice; but they are intended to assist the emergence of another justice,
new kinds of equality and freedom, as well as new kinds of political differentiation and constraint.[7]

From the point of view of political judgment, we find in relation
to these movements of becoming, deterritorialization, or the production
of smooth space the same kind of indeterminacy and ambivalence that
arises in relation to the ethical judgment of individual transformations.
Becoming-revolutionary is a matter of finding the lines of flight that undermine the existing order and trace the outlines of the new.[8] It must be
understood in the light of their concern with the emergence of the new or
the advent of the truly Other, as Derrida would say. This Other is irreducible to the possible future forms of the actual present. Similarly, smooth
spaces are like lines of flight or deterritorialization in that, although they

do not amount to spaces of pure freedom, they are nevertheless the kind of space that can lead to the transformation of existing institutions or the displacement of the goals of political conflict. The emergence of smooth spaces is a condition under which "life reconstitutes its stakes, confronts new obstacles, invents new paces, switches adversaries" (MP 625, 500). However, in accordance with the ambivalence that is always present in Deleuzian evaluation, we must always assess what kind of smooth space we are dealing with: Is it one that has been captured by state forces, or one that results from the dissolution of a striated space? Does it allow more or less freedom of movement? Above all, we should never believe "that a smooth space will suffice to save us" (MP 625, 500).[9]

Deleuze's Turn toward Political Normativity

I drew attention above to the manner in which Deleuze and Guattari's political ontology enables us to conceptualize and describe transformative or creative forces and movements, along with the sense in which this ontology has a normative dimension. We saw how this ontology presents a world of interconnected machinic assemblages, the innermost tendency of which is toward the "deterritorialization" of existing assemblages and their "reterritorialization" in new forms. It accords systematic priority to minoritarian becomings over majoritarian being, to lines of flight over forms of capture, to planes of consistency over planes of organization, and so on. Even though Deleuze and Guattari undertook certain kinds of critical engagement with Marxist political thought, all of their conceptual innovations and modifications were carried out within a broadly Marxist perspective that envisaged the emergence of new and better forms of social and political life. However, at no point did they address the normative principles that inform their critical perspective on the present, much less the question how these might be articulated with those principles that are supposed to govern political life in late capitalist societies. Nowhere do they engage directly with the political norms embedded in liberal democratic political institutions and ways of life, such as the equal moral worth of individuals, freedom of conscience, the rule of law, fairness in the distribution of material goods produced by social cooperation, and so on. The principled differences between liberal democratic, totalitarian, and fascist states are mentioned only in passing in the course of their analysis of capitalism and present-day politics as a process of axiomatization of the social and economic field. In this sense, their machinic social ontology remains formal in relation to actual societies and forms of political organization.

Read in the context of Western Marxism during the 1960s and 1970s, Deleuze and Guattari's failure to engage directly with the political values and normative concepts that are supposed to inform the basic institutions of modern liberal democracies is not surprising. Their political philosophy predates widespread understanding and acceptance of the ways in which Marx's critique of capitalist society is bound up with concepts of distributive justice, as it does the efforts to identify the relevant principles of justice that occurred under the impact of so-called analytic Marxism in the course of the 1980s. Since then, there have been numerous attempts to combine Marxist social theory with the normative principles informing varieties of left-liberal political theory.[10] While these developments had little impact in France, there was a similar rediscovery of ethical and political normativity in French political thought during this period. This was expressed, for example, in a renewed interest in human rights, subjectivity, justice, equality, and freedom. We can see evidence of this in the shift in Derrida's concerns that led him to engage directly with concepts of democracy, law, and justice during the course of the 1980s (Patton 2007a; 2007b). Guattari became involved in electoral politics during the latter part of the 1980s, standing as a Green candidate in 1992 regional elections.[11]

Deleuze's writings and comments in interviews from the 1980s mark a significant shift in his thinking about such normative issues. For example, he responds to the renewed interest in human rights during this period by insisting on the importance of jurisprudence as the means to create new rights. While he criticizes the manner in which human rights are represented as "eternal values" and "new forms of transcendence," he makes it clear that he is not opposed to rights as such but only to the idea that there is a definitive and ahistorical list of supposed universal rights.[12] He argues that rights are not the creation of codes or declarations but of jurisprudence, where this implies working with the "singularities" of a particular situation (P 210, 153). He returns to the question of rights and jurisprudence in his *Abécédaire* interviews with Claire Parnet, recorded in 1988–1989, where he affirms the importance of jurisprudence understood as the invention of new rights, along with his own fascination for the law (ABC, *G comme Gauche*). In his 1990 interview with Negri, "Control and Becoming," he reaffirms the importance of jurisprudence as a source of law with reference to the question of what rights should be established in relation to new forms of biotechnology (P 230, 169). Deleuze's endorsement of rights and jurisprudence clearly commits him to the existence of a rule of law and the kind of constitutional state that this implies. The very concept of a legal right implies that certain kinds of action on the part of all citizens will be protected by law and, conversely, the enforcement of limits to the degree to which citizens can interfere with the actions of others. Kant's universal principle of right provides one influential formulation of the underlying idea, namely that actions are right when they are consistent with the freedom of others in accordance with a universal law (Kant 1996, 387).

Deleuze's political writings from the 1980s onward also provide evidence of his commitment to democracy. His 1979 "Open Letter to Negri's Judges" already adopted the speaking position of a democrat committed to certain principles in relation to due process and the rule of law (DRF 156, 169). The preoccupation with democracy becomes more pronounced in *What Is Philosophy?* where there are a series of highly critical remarks about actually existing democracies. Far from dismissing the democratic ideal, these comments imply that other actualizations of the concept or "pure event" of democracy are possible.[13] *What Is Philosophy?* offers no more direct account of principles that are supposed to govern modern democratic societies than *A Thousand Plateaus*. In this sense, it offers no theory of public right. Many of the elements of Deleuze and Guattari's prior commitment to Marxism remain in the diagnosis of the present outlined in *What Is Philosophy?* For example, the analysis of the isomorphic but heterogeneous character of all states with regard to the global capitalist axiomatic is reproduced in identical terms. From this perspective, there are political differences between different kinds of state but also complicity with an increasingly global system of exploitation. They suggest that even the most democratic states are compromised by their role in the production of human misery alongside great wealth (QP 103, 107; P 234, 173). They maintain their commitment to the revolutionary-becoming of people rather than the traditional Marxist concept of revolution, even as they point out that the concept of revolution is itself a philosophical concept par excellence, one that expresses "absolute deterritorialization even to the point where this calls for a new earth, a new people" (QP 97, 101).

The focus of *What Is Philosophy?* is on the inherently political vocation of philosophy. With regard to the present, however, this vocation is aligned with the struggle against capitalism, for example when it is suggested that philosophical concepts are critical of the present to the extent that they "connect up with what is real here and now in the struggle against capitalism" (QP 96, 100). At this point, something new appears in the Deleuzian political lexicon. As the expression of absolute deterritorialization, the concept or pure event of revolution is necessarily further determined in its particular historical incarnations, which always take the form of a particular kind of revolution. In *What Is Philosophy?* the representative case of revolution is not drawn from Lenin but from Kant, in particular from his support for the revolution in the name of a constitutional state that would enshrine the equal rights of men and citizens. Kant's remarks in *The Contest of Faculties* on the "enthusiasm" shown toward the ideals of the French Revolution are presented as evidence of the difference between the pure event and its expression in the bloody events in Paris in 1789.[14] The pure event or concept of revolution is expressed rather in the "enthusiasm" with which it is thought on a plane of immanence. In this form, it is an expression of the infinite in the here and now, an eruption of pure eventness about which there is nothing reasonable or rational (QP 96, 100).

At the same time, *What Is Philosophy?* contrasts the actual universality of the market with the virtual universality of a global democratic state and describes its own political philosophy as reterritorialized on a new Earth and a people to come quite unlike those found in actually existing democracies. In this sense, we can say that in *What Is Philosophy?* Deleuze and Guattari's neo-Marxist support for becoming-revolutionary as the path toward a new Earth and a people to come is modulated by the call for resistance to existing forms of democracy in the name of a "becoming-democratic that is not to be confused with present constitutional states" (QP 108, 113). More generally, the normativity of Deleuze's later political philosophy is defined by the relation between becoming-revolutionary and becoming-democratic.

Becoming-Democratic

But what is meant by "becoming-democratic," and what is the political force of this concept? Given that the term *becoming-democratic* occurs only once in *What Is Philosophy?* it would be an exaggeration to include it among the list of concepts created by Deleuze and Guattari. Nevertheless, I suggest that when combined with the overtly political conception of philosophy outlined in *What Is Philosophy?* some of the elements of their earlier political philosophy do provide the resources needed to develop such a concept.

Recall the definition of philosophy as the creation of concepts, where the creation of concepts calls for "a new earth and people that do not yet exist" (QP 104, 108). On this account, philosophy is a specific kind of thought, defined in terms of its affinity with absolute as opposed to relative deterritorialization. As we saw earlier, relative deterritorialization concerns the historical relationship of things to the territories into which they are organized, including the manner in which these territories break down and are transformed or reconstituted into new forms. Absolute deterritorialization concerns the ahistorical relationship of things and states of affairs to the virtual realm of becoming or pure events that is imperfectly or partially expressed in what happens. It is because it creates concepts that express such pure events—to become, to capture, to deterritorialize, but also to govern democratically, to revolt, and so on—that philosophy is inherently critical of the present in which it takes place. To characterize existing bodies and states of affairs in terms of such philosophical concepts is to re-present them in thought as the expression of "pure events" or "becomings." This re-presentation what Deleuze calls the "countereffectuation" of phenomena. Such philosophical redescription enables us to see things differently or to see them as they might become rather than as they currently are. In this manner, the invention of new concepts can assist the deterritorialization of existing structures and the emergence of new ones without, however, being tied to any positive political program.

Deleuze and Guattari suggest that philosophy is utopian where this means "absolute deterritorialization but always at the critical point at which it is connected with the present relative milieu" (QP 96, 100). In other words, when there is a connection between the absolute deterritorialization expressed in concepts and the forms of relative deterritorialization already at work in the social field, philosophy becomes utopian and achieves its political vocation, taking the criticism of its own time "to its highest point" (QP 95, 99). Deleuze's conception of philosophy is utopian, not in the sense that it posits an ideal society or sets out principles of justice in the light of which we might identify the shortcomings of existing societies but in the sense that it creates concepts that can link up with processes of deterritorialization present in a given historical milieu, informing the perceptions and therefore the actions of those involved. This is an immanent utopianism that can be compared in some respects to Rawls's more cautious and "realistic utopianism" (see Chapter 9, pp. 186–198).

This brief account of Deleuze's utopian and critical conception of the political function of philosophy helps us to see how the concept of "becoming-democratic" might serve that function. Different forms of democratic political society amount to determinate actualizations of the concept or "pure event" of democracy. If we suppose that existing processes of deterritorialization or "lines of flight" in modern societies include the ideals or opinions that motivate or inform particular forms of resistance, it follows that these will draw on elements of existing political normativity to suggest ways in which the unjust or oppressive character of present institutional forms of social life might be removed. "Becoming-democratic" therefore points to ways of criticizing the workings of actually existing democracies in the name of the egalitarian principles that are supposed to inform their institutions and political practices. The philosophical concept of democracy is a means to counter-actualize what passes for democratic society in the present, while "becoming-democratic" is a means to counter-actualize movements or processes of democratization. Philosophy pursues or supports such processes of becoming-democratic, for example, when it challenges existing opinions about what is acceptable, right, or just with the aim of extending the actualization of democracy within contemporary societies.

The complex concept of democracy ties together a number of the political norms at the heart of modern political thought. In principle, there will be as many ways of becoming-democratic as there are elements of the concept of democracy. In practice, philosophy can effectively advance the becoming-democratic of a given political society only when it engages with deterritorializing movements that rely on actualized or actualizable elements of democratic political normativity. Deleuze offers no detailed account of what he understands by "becoming-democratic." Moreover, it is not difficult to imagine forms of populism that would go against the grain of his political sensibility. Like all forms of deterritorialization, this one is not without its dangers. The comments on Heidegger in *What Is Philosophy?* remind us that it is not enough to put one's faith in the people: It depends on what people and how they are constituted as a political community (QP 104–105, 108–109). At the same time, it is not difficult to find elements in his work with Guattari that enable us to fill out the concept of becoming-democratic.

For example, one of the sources of conflict that has been present ever since the introduction of modern democratic government has been the coexistence of formally equal rights alongside enormous disparities of material condition. The history of modern democracies has been in part a history of struggle to reduce material inequality and to ensure that the basic rights of citizens have at least approximately equal value for all. Deleuze alludes to this ongoing problem in his interview with Negri when he contrasts the universality of the market with the manner in which it unequally distributes poverty as well as enormous wealth. He is clearly critical of the way in which modern democratic states fail to live up to the promise of equality of access to the material goods produced by social cooperation: "There is no democratic state that is not compromised to the very core by its part in generating human misery" (P 234, 173). Similarly, in the section *G comme Gauche* of *L'Abécédaire*, he points to the "absolute injustice" of the current unequal global distribution of wealth. Given that the benefits of market economies are not universally shared and inequalities of condition are handed down from generation to generation, in direct contravention of the principle that all are born equal, we can say that achieving a more just distribution of material social goods is one vector of "becoming-democratic."

Another constant source of conflict in democratic nation states ever since their inception has been the struggle to broaden the base of those who count as citizens and thus enjoy full access to the entire range of basic legal and political rights. Democracy has always relied on the principle of majority rule, but the prior question "majority of whom?" has always been settled in advance and usually not by democratic means. This exposes a fault in one of the key components of the concept of democracy, namely the concept of majority. This can mean either the quantitative majority of those counted or the qualitative majority of those among the population at large who are considered fit to be counted. Deleuze and Guattari rely on the latter, qualitative sense of majority in *A Thousand Plateaus* when they point to the existence of a majoritarian "fact" in contemporary European-derived societies, namely the priority of "the average adult-white-heterosexual-European-male-speaking a standard language" (MP 133, 105). The adult, white, etc., male is majoritarian not because he is numerically in the majority but because he forms the standard against which the rights and duties of all citizens are measured. Minoritarian becomings are defined as the variety of ways in which individuals and groups fail to conform to this standard.

The social movements corresponding to these becomings have given rise to a succession of measures to extend the scope of the standard and thereby broaden the subject of democracy: first, by extending the vote to women and other minorities; second, by changing the nature of political institutions and procedures to enable these newly enfranchised members to participate on equal terms. Efforts to change the nature of public institutions in ways that both acknowledge and accommodate many kinds of difference are ongoing in democratic societies, for example in relation to sexual difference, sexual preference, different physical and mental abilities, and cultural and religious affiliations. Deleuze and Guattari affirm the importance of efforts to enlarge the character of the majority, even as they insist that the power of minorities "is not measured by their capacity to enter into and make themselves felt within the majority system, nor even to overturn the necessarily tautological criterion of the majority" (MP 588, 471). By their nature, processes of minoritarian-becoming will always exceed or escape from the confines of any given majority. They carry the potential to transform the affects, beliefs, and political sensibilities of a population in ways that amount to the advent of a new people. In turn, to the extent that a given people or peoples are constituted as a political community, the transformations they undergo will affect citizen's conceptions of what is fair and just and therefore the nature of the rights and duties attributed to the new majority. For this reason, Deleuze and Guattari affirm the importance of the feedback from minoritarian becomings to the character of the majority. As we saw above (p. 150), they insist that the political significance of molecular movements and lines of flight lies in the manner in which these force changes in the molar identities and forms of organization of a given political community (MP 264, 216–217). Minoritarian becomings therefore provide another vector of "becoming-democratic."

A third form of struggle in modern democracies concerns the principle of legitimacy that governs decision making, not only in government but throughout the basic institutions of society. In his "Control and Becoming" interview with Negri, Deleuze comments on the importance of jurisprudence as a source of law and new rights with reference to the question of rights in relation to new forms of biotechnology. He goes on to add that we must not leave decisions on such matters to judges or experts. What is required is not more committees of supposedly well-qualified wise men to determine rights but rather "user groups" (P 230, 169–170). The implicit principle in this recommendation is the democratic idea that decisions ought to be taken in consultation with those most affected by them. This is one of the founding principles of modern democratic governance, and many theorists recommend its extension and application to new contexts such as the workplace (Peffer 1990, 419–420). Ian Shapiro argues that whether someone is entitled to a say in a particular decision depends on whether that person's interests are likely to be affected by the outcome and on the nature of those interests: The more fundamental the interest, the greater his or her entitlement to a voice in the decision-making process (Shapiro 2003, 52). Deleuze's proposed application of the principle in the realm of biotechnologies gives reason to think that the opening-up of decision-making procedures throughout society constitutes a further vector of "becoming-democratic."

Conclusion

Identifying these vectors of becoming-democratic enables us to see how the concept serves the political vocation of philosophy as Deleuze and Guattari define it. Because it is a complex concept with a long history of interpretation and implementation, democracy encompasses many of the political norms at the heart of modern political thought. Different forms of democratic political society will amount to determinate actualizations of this concept or the pure event that it expresses. To the extent that individuals and groups within such societies will draw on elements of this concept to suggest ways in which the injustice of existing institutional forms of social life might be removed, the concept of becoming-democratic will be a means to counter-actualize these forms of resistance to what passes for democratic society in the present. Deleuze and Guattari's call for resistance to the present in the name of becoming-democratic is not unrelated to their conception of philosophy as engaged in an unending struggle against opinion (QP 191, 203). Philosophy pursues or supports processes of becoming-democratic when it challenges existing opinions about what is acceptable, right, or just with the aim of extending the actualization of democracy within contemporary societies. In other words, the political vocation of philosophy calls for critical engagement with existing philosophical opinions about the nature of democratic society.

In his interview with Negri, Deleuze suggests that philosophy provides a way of responding to what is intolerable in the present (P 231, 171). This raises the interesting question: In virtue of what does a particular state of affairs become intolerable? It seems reasonable to think that the contours of the intolerable will be historically determined in part by the mechanisms through which we are governed and by the ideals and opinions expressed in the prevailing political culture. If this is so, it follows that responding to the intolerable in democratic societies will inevitably engage with elements of their prevailing political normativity. It also follows that there will be no reason to suppose that we can ever definitively escape from the intolerable. As Deleuze comments in his discussion of control societies, there is always a conflict within systems of power between the ways in which they free us and the ways in which they enslave us (P 241, 178).

In this as in other respects, Deleuze's conception of the political task of philosophy is close to that of Foucault, who describes the aim of his genealogical criticism as the identification of limits to present ways of thinking, acting, and speaking to find points of difference or exit from the past: "In what is given to us as universal, necessary, obligatory, what place is occupied by whatever is singular, contingent and the product of arbitrary constraints?" (Foucault 1997, 315). Rather than attempt to provide normative justification for such departures from established ways of thinking, acting, and speaking, Foucault prefers to link the limits described in genealogical terms to specific social transformations underway in his present, such as those in relation to prisons and sexual morality. Deleuze expresses a similar view when he links the creation of philosophical concepts to the kinds of relative deterritorialization or minoritarian-becoming available to individuals and groups within a given social milieu. In both cases, a distinction is drawn between present reality, understood as a product of history, and "what we are in the process of becoming—that is to say, the Other, our becoming-other" (QP 107, 112). This becoming-other can be understood only in relation to the virtual or what Deleuze refers to in Foucault's case as the *actuel* (see Chapter 4, p. 93). Particular processes of becoming-other will imply forms of individual and collective self-transformation in response to what is intolerable or shameful in the present. They do not always lead to better or more just social arrangements, but they are the only means to achieve such local improvements in the conditions of a given people.

8

Deleuze and Democracy

Democracy does not play a central role in Deleuze and Guattari's political philosophy. They offer neither descriptive nor normative accounts of democratic political processes. In *A Thousand Plateaus* they consider the different forms of modern government only from the Marxist perspective of their subordination to the axioms of capitalist production. In this light, authoritarian, socialist, and liberal democratic states are all regarded as equivalent to one another insofar as they function as models of realization of the global axiomatic of capital. They point to the combination of isomorphism and heterogeneity between totalitarian and social democratic states whenever these govern societies that are integrated into the world capitalist market. They point to the complementarity between First World democratic states and Third World dictatorships as a consequence of the axioms that have replaced overt colonization (MP 578–582, 463–466). While they allow that there are important differences among the various modern forms of state, they offer little discussion of these differences from a political point of view.

In *What Is Philosophy?* we find the same analysis of the isomorphic but heterogeneous character of all states with regard to the global capitalist market. From this perspective, even the most democratic states are compromised by their role in the production of human misery alongside great wealth (QP 103,107; P 234, 173). At the same time, we find something new. Deleuze and Guattari contrast the actual universality of the market with the virtual universality of a global democratic state. They describe their own political philosophy as reterritorialized on a new Earth and a people to come, unlike those found in actually existing democracies. They call for resistance to the present in the name of a "becoming-democratic that is not to be confused with present constitutional states" (QP 108, 113). Their political philosophy is not so utopian that it is completely disconnected from the normative and conceptual horizons of the present. It incorporates both a recognizably Marxist critique of capitalist society and a post-Marxist critique of revolutionary vanguard politics and the philosophy of history that sustained them. It also criticizes actually existing democracies in the name of the egalitarian principles that are supposed to inform their legal and political institutions. The highly critical remarks about existing democracies in this book imply that other actualizations of this form of political community might be possible. The more nuanced attitude that we find in *What Is Philosophy?* raises a number of questions about Deleuze and Guattari's relationship to democracy and what role this concept plays in their mature political thought.

I argued in Chapter 7 that there is no fundamental incompatibility between Deleuze's political thought and democratic politics. Other commentators take a different view. Arguing from a position of sympathy toward the *Autonomia* tendency within Italian Marxism, Nicholas Thoburn sees Deleuze and Guattari's minoritarian politics as an alternative to Laclau and Mouffe's neo-Gramscian post-Marxism. Whereas Laclau and Mouffe represent a movement "from the politics of *production* to the politics of *democracy* and civil society," Deleuze and Guattari represent an "intensification" of Marx's critical engagement with the entire field of capitalist social relations (Thoburn 2003, 11). For Thoburn, Deleuzian Marxism implies more than just a broader conception of politics: "Inasmuch as it is a critique and problematization of the forms of identity and practice composed in the capitalist *socius*, this politics is an explicit *challenge* to social democratic politics." As such, he suggests, Deleuze's position is "not dissimilar" to the explicitly antidemocratic politics attributed to Marx by some tendencies within Marxism (Thoburn 2003, 142).

Arguing from a position of sympathy toward liberal democratic politics, Philippe Mengue also claims that there is a fundamental antipathy toward democracy in Deleuze's political thought (Mengue 2003). Overlooking the possibility of ambivalence, or indeed of movement toward engagement with the specifically political norms of liberal democratic society, Mengue finds only hostility toward democracy in Deleuze's thought. He argues that Deleuze never explicitly rejects democracy in the way that Nietzsche did but that nevertheless, in his political philosophy, "Democracy is only devalued and rendered secondary, not for its empirical failures but for reasons of principle" (Mengue 2003, 43). In agreement at least with the substance of Thoburn's diagnosis, he attributes this hostility toward democracy to an uncritical acceptance of the Marxist *doxa* common among French intellectuals in the aftermath of May 1968. He suggests that, notwithstanding their abandonment of the language of class struggle and associated concepts, Deleuze and Guattari's account of the relationship between modern forms of state and capital ultimately relies on the thesis of economic determinism. This enables them to reproduce their own version of the classical Marxist denunciation of liberal democracy as little more than a concession or alibi that serves only to maintain the capitalist system of exploitation and repression (Mengue 2003, 107–110).

To whatever extent this is an accurate reading of Deleuze and Guattari's account of the relationship between state and capital, it does not address the issue of their relation to the normative principles of democratic government. Similar problems arise in relation to the interpretation of Marx's own views. Many have argued that his critique of capitalist society ultimately relies on principles of equality that fall within the democratic tradition of political thought.[1] From Rosa Luxembourg to Derrida, Laclau and Mouffe, and beyond, the communist ideal has been defended as an extension of democratic principles to include economic and social as well as political life. From this perspective, there is no inconsistency in criticizing existing forms of liberal democratic government for their complicity with capitalism while remaining committed to liberal and democratic principles. For this reason, I leave aside the question of Deleuze's relation to Marx and that part of his criticism of existing democratic states that is bound up with the analysis of their role within global capitalism to concentrate on the question of his relation to democratic principles.

Thoburn and Mengue's claims of antidemocratic bias in Deleuze's political thought are unconvincing, but they nevertheless raise important questions that help to clarify his approach to politics and his relation to democracy: What is meant by "democracy" in this context? What evidence is there for the claim that Deleuze's philosophy excludes or condemns democratic politics? I explore these questions primarily with reference to Mengue because he presents the more extensive engagement with Deleuze and Guattari's political philosophy. His provocative *Deleuze et la question de la démocratie* takes the relationship to democracy as the focal point for a wide-ranging reflection upon Deleuzian political thought (Mengue 2003). He argues that Deleuze's supposed hostility toward democracy is a

weak point in an otherwise powerful philosophy that exposes the degree
to which its political rhetoric is bound up with the opinions and sensibilities of its time. While the thesis that Deleuze is hostile toward democracy
is ultimately unsustainable, Mengue's important study makes a valuable
contribution to the development of Deleuzian political thought by forcing
us to examine these issues in detail.

What Is Democracy?

Democracy has both wide and narrow senses. In the broad sense, it
refers to a form of society characterized by the absence of class or caste
privilege and by the implementation of the egalitarian principle of the
equal worth of individuals such that no person's life, beliefs, or values are
inherently worth more than those of anyone else. Within a democratic
polity, each citizen is entitled to live according to his or her own conception of the good and to express his or her own ideas on matters of public
policy. Such a political society is an association of equals in which there is
no justification for the exclusion of individuals or groups from the widest
possible system of basic civil and political liberties, nor any justification
for the arbitrary exclusion of particular individuals or groups from the
benefits of social and political cooperation. In the narrow sense, *democracy* refers to a form of government in which the governed exercise control
over governments and their policies, typically through regular and fair
elections. Contemporary liberal democracies purport to be democratic in
both senses of the term. They ensure equal rights to effective participation
in political processes but also set limits to what majorities can decide by
protecting basic civil and political rights and ensuring the maintenance
of a rule of law. These two senses of democracy are not unrelated, and
the connections between them run in both directions. However, it is the
conception of individuals as of equal moral worth that is fundamental.
While this implies a form of government in which individuals have an
equal voice on matters of public concern, it leaves open a range of possible
institutional forms of democratic government.

There is no doubt that Deleuze is not a theorist of democracy in
the narrow sense of the term. Neither the institutions nor the values associated with democratic government features prominently in his work;
and, on the few occasions in which they are mentioned, this is primarily in the context of pointing to the shortcomings of existing democratic

governments. At one point in *What Is Philosophy?* Deleuze offers reasons for skepticism about the importance attached to human rights in contemporary democracies:

> Who but the police and armed forces that coexist with democracies can control and manage poverty and the deterritorialization—reterritorialization of shanty towns? What social democracy has not given the order to fire when the poor come out of their territory or ghetto? Rights can save neither men nor a philosophy that is reterritorialized on the democratic State. Human rights will not make us bless capitalism. (QP 103, 107)[2]

However, it does not follow from this that Deleuze is hostile to democratic government or that his political philosophy implies a rejection of democracy in either the broad or the narrow sense. In fact there is much evidence to suggest that, in his political practice as well as in his theoretical views, he was always committed to egalitarian and democratic values.

Mengue argues that Deleuze's apparent failure to embrace democratic politics is all the more surprising in view of the affinities between his ethicoontological principles and the political domain understood as a field in which conflicting opinions are pitted against one another and resolved according to the principle of majority rule. Because it involves conflicting opinions and radically divergent political orientations, democracy involves a rhizomatic politics rather than a politics of demonstration or deduction. As such, democratic politics is inherently experimental and creative in a way that accords with the Deleuzian ethic of deterritorialization. Because democratic politics is played out in the space in between the orientations or opinions of particular individuals or groups, it is a politics of pure immanence, a politics without foundation: "We are in the middle in all senses, horizontally, between equals, with equal and unprivileged capacities for opinion and choice, and vertically, by virtue of the absence of transcendent values" (Mengue 2003, 47).[3] Although in later writings Deleuze and Guattari argue that philosophy is the enemy of opinion (see below, pp. 178–183), the suggestion that their theory of micropolitics and molecular assemblages has a particular affinity with the mobile and fluctuating character of public opinion is already to be found in *A Thousand Plateaus.* For example, in Plateau 9, "1933: Micropolitics and Segmentarity," they suggest that "Political decision making necessarily descends into a world of microdeterminations, attractions and desires, which it must sound out or evaluate in a different fashion. Beneath linear conceptions and segmentary decisions, an evaluation of flows and their quanta" (MP 270–271, 221).

The issue here, however, is, "What is the relation between such micropolitics and democracy?" Mengue objects that Deleuzian micropolitics is not properly a theory of politics because it does not seek to theorize or render legitimate the institutions required to constitute a properly political society, such as the necessary space for debate and free political action. He insists that

there are institutions that the micro-revolutionary is obliged to want (in order to render his own practice possible) and to endow with full and complete legitimacy, if not superiority. For example, democratic principles must be considered fully and foundationally legitimate insofar as they permit a space for debate which is absolutely necessary for the freedom of political action . . . Power without consent is only violence. (Mengue 2003, 81–82)

In other words, it is only insofar as there are political institutions that subject the exercise of power to the rule of law and the consent of the governed that the concerns of the microrevolutionary can be transformed into political reality. Without these, micropolitics remains no more than the attempt to impose private opinions on others by force. It is undoubtedly true that the space of democratic politics requires more than the unregulated play of conflicting opinions. Without at least some regulation of the constitutional form and procedures within which the play of opinions is resolved, the result would be a populist and unstable form of democracy. Constitutional principles of right are necessary to protect individuals and minorities against majority opinions. In Rawlsian terms, the normative framework of democratic politics is provided by the principles of equality and justice that ultimately rest on the considered moral convictions of those who make up the relevant political community. This is not to say that such principles must be derived from a higher source of authority than the value judgments of the people concerned, or that they are immune to change, but it is to introduce some vertical differentiation into the field in which conflicting opinions and political orientations are played out.

Mengue's objection points to the need for an explicit account of such principles of right in democratic states. If, as he suggests following Rousseau, the goal of political association is to determine a collective will as the basis for laws and public policy, then there is indeed a properly political or "doxological" plane of immanence that forms the space of public debate with a view to collective decision on matters of public policy. What are produced on this plane are not concepts, percepts, or affects but "solidarity and consensus regarding what is to be done here and now" (Mengue

2003, 52). The formation of such consensus or "right opinion" can be understood as the outcome of a specific and rhizomatic play of opinions, expert advice, interests, and values such that it "operates a veritable deterritorialization of opinion" (Mengue 2003, 53). We might add that such collective decision making also involves the reterritorialization of opinion on ideas of the public good, including the ideas that decisions have to be made and that it is appropriate that they respect the wishes of the majority of those concerned.

Mengue is undoubtedly correct to point to the importance of a specifically political reason of this kind for democratic politics. He is also right to point out that it may be characterized in Deleuzian terms, even though Deleuze himself does not provide any such theory of political reason as a specific form of thought irreducible to philosophy, science, or art. However, he is wrong to suggest that this neglect of political reason in Deleuze's thought justifies the charge that he provides an aesthetics or ethics but not properly a theory of politics (Mengue 2003, 56). The neglect of the public political sphere in the elaboration of Deleuzian micropolitics is not sufficient to sustain the stronger charge of antidemocratic bias at the heart of Deleuze's political thought. At most, it might support the claim that, in the absence of an explicit embrace of democratic institutions and processes, micropolitics deprives itself of the institutions necessary to realize its egalitarian ambitions. This amounts to claiming that the Deleuzian theory of micropolitics is only a partial account of the process of political decision making. However, incompleteness is not antipathy, and there is no reason to suppose that Deleuzian theory proposes an alternative rather than a supplement to democratic political theory.

William Connolly presents a compelling case for the latter view of the relationship between Deleuzian theory and democratic politics. He argues for a pluralist and democratic ethos of engagement, "responsive to both the indispensability of justice and the radical insufficiency of justice to itself" (Connolly 1999, 68).[4] He argues that democracy is a unique form of cultural and political practice in that it "enables participation in collective decisions while enabling contestation of sedimented settlements from the past" (Connolly 1995, 103). On this view, a distinctive feature of democratic politics is that even the fundamental convictions expressed in its laws and institutions are open to change; for example, by the extension of basic political rights to include those formerly excluded or by the removal of the priority accorded to certain moral values. Moreover, the efforts of citizens to bring about such changes must be considered a legitimate part of the political process. If we accept that subterranean shifts in the attitudes, sensibilities, and beliefs of individuals and populations are among the conditions of such change, then it follows that the micropolitical sphere of such movements is a no less important dimension of democratic politics. Deleuze and Guattari's micropolitical theory provides a language in which to describe movements of this kind. It thereby supplements liberal democratic conceptions of decision making and challenges these to take into account such micropolitical processes.

Deleuze Critical of Democracy?

Mengue argues that Deleuze's preference for a minoritarian politics of becoming implies both hostility toward and a retreat from the majoritarian politics of the public sphere. He characterizes Deleuze's own political involvements as those of an elite, intellectual minority. He interprets his criticism of the way in which mass media dominate the public sphere as a form of aristocratic disdain for the multitude, mere pretext for a Platonic gesture of retreat from the agora (Mengue 2003, 41–42, 99–101). Such a characterization is difficult to reconcile with the history of Deleuze's interventions on matters of public debate in the form of opinion articles, letters, and petitions. In one of these interventions, an "Open Letter to Negri's Judges," he takes issue with certain questions of legal principle in relation to the charges against Antonio Negri: the lack of consistency in the charges themselves, the failure to follow ordinary logical principles of reasoning in the examination of evidence, and the role of the media in relation to this judicial procedure. Deleuze begins this letter with the claim that there are three principles at stake in this process and suggests that "these three principles implicate [are of importance to] all democrats" (DRF 156, 169).[5] The letter implies that he counts himself among those democrats.

Thoburn draws on Deleuze's *Abécédaire* interview with Claire Parnet, recorded during 1988–1989, for evidence to support his contention that Deleuzian politics pose an explicit challenge to social democratic politics: "For Deleuze, to be 'on the left' is not a matter of democracy" (Thoburn 2003, 9, 142). In the section entitled "*G comme Gauche*," Deleuze responds to Parnet's question "What does it mean to be on the left?" by offering a twofold definition of what it means for him. First, he says it is a matter of perception. Those who are not on the left and who live in the comparative wealth of a relatively privileged First World country perceive problems of inequality and injustice from their own perspective. Sensing that their position is untenable and under threat, they ask "What can we do to make this situation last?" By contrast, those on the left perceive the situation from the perspective of the horizon, the point farthest from their center of privilege. These people "know that it cannot last, that it's not possible, [the fact that] these millions of people are starving to death, it just can't last, it might go on a hundred years, one never knows, but there's no point kidding oneself about this absolute injustice." Those on the left know that such problems must be dealt with, that the problem is not to find ways to maintain the privileges of European-style societies but that of "finding worldwide assemblages" that can address these problems (ABC, *G comme Gauche*).

To the extent that Deleuze here assumes an egalitarian and even cosmopolitan perspective on matters of distributive justice, his position is clearly democratic in the broad sense outlined above. His opposition to existing assemblages is based on the injustice that results from the unequal distribution of wealth and poverty. Similarly, in his 1990 interview with Negri, he juxtaposes the sense in which the market as sphere of exchange of commodities and capital is universal with the sense in which it generates both wealth and misery and distributes these in a manner that is neither universalizing nor homogenizing (P 234, 173). In other words, it is the principle of equality and the idea that such undeserved inequalities of condition are unjust that underpin Deleuze's criticism of both capitalism and the liberal democratic states through which its control of populations is exercised.

The second part of Deleuze's definition of what it means to be on the left is his claim that this is a matter of becoming-minoritarian as opposed to being majoritarian. It is a matter of knowing that the majority is an abstract and empty representation of an ideal identity that is linked to particular systems of power and control and that there are minoritarian becomings in which everyone can be engaged and that have the power to transform these systems. It is for this reason that Deleuze says that being on the left is not a matter of government, indeed that there are no leftist governments. However, while he clearly aligns leftist politics with minoritarian politics, he nowhere says that this has nothing to do with democracy. There is no telling in advance which processes of deterritorialization or becoming-minor might lead to fundamental social, political, or institutional change. There is no privileged minority, such as the proletariat, on which rests the hope for a better future. A legal decision or a sudden imperceptible shift in personal loyalties might set in train processes that lead to the positive deterritorialization of a given system of power and control. Deleuze neither privileges nor excludes democratic political processes from functioning as agents of revolutionary social change. However, the basis of his opposition to the present sociopolitical order is that it is fundamentally inegalitarian and therefore undemocratic in the broader sense of the term.

Mengue advances three primary arguments for Deleuze's supposed hostility toward democracy, each one related to certain key principles of his philosophy: preference for immanence over transcendence, preference for minority over majority, and a conception of philosophy as the creation of new concepts and, as such, resolutely opposed to opinion in all its forms. The remainder of this chapter will examine and respond to each of these arguments in turn before outlining an alternative and more positive account of the relationship of Deleuze's political thought to democracy.

Immanence, Transcendence, and the Creation of Rights

The refusal of transcendence is one of the constant motifs of Deleuze's philosophy. His thought renounces all forms of appeal to transcendent values, concepts of history, or human nature in favor of a radical immanentism. At the same time, it purports to be an untimely philosophy in Nietzsche's sense of the term, opposed to the present in the name of a time and a people to come. This raises a problem: If Deleuzian political philosophical is denied recourse to any kind of transcendence, how does it attain the necessary distance that enables it to be critical of the present? The answer relies on the distinction between virtuality and actuality that runs throughout Deleuze and Guattari's political philosophy. In *A Thousand Plateaus*, they contrast the plane of organization or actuality, on which we encounter real things, real people, and various kinds of becoming (becoming-woman, becoming-animal, and so on), with the plane of immanence or virtuality, on which we encounter abstract machines, pure events, and becoming-imperceptible. On the plane of organization, we encounter processes of deterritorialization and transformation or metamorphosis of what is, as well as processes of reterritorialization, capture, or blockage of such transformative processes. With reference to this dual-aspect ontology, they suggest that every process or event simultaneously inhabits both the historical world of actuality and the ahistorical world of the virtual or pure eventness that is actualized in but irreducible to the former (see Chapter 4, p. 91). It is because the planes of immanence and organization are mutually implicated in one another, and because the plane of immanence is the more profound reality, that this Deleuzian ontology is properly a philosophy of immanence.

The task of philosophy, according to Deleuze and Guattari, is the creation of new concepts or the modification of old ones that give expression to the abstract machines and pure events on the plane of immanence. Indeed, because the concepts that philosophy creates are supposed to express pure events, it follows that philosophy creates many of the events in terms of which we understand and respond to the history that unfolds around us: The social contract, revolution in the name of the rights of human being and citizen, democracy, or the idea of a well-ordered society governed in accordance with an idea of justice are all examples of such concepts. Deleuze and Guattari call the philosophical expression of pure events in concepts the "counter-effectuation" of historical processes and states of affairs. Counter-effectuation may involve concepts of transformative processes, such as becoming-revolutionary and becoming-democratic, or concepts of processes of capture that constrain the forms of actualization of these transformative processes or events, such as the capitalist axiomatic or control-society. Either way, its effect is to restore the connection of the actual to the virtual.

Democracy may be regarded in these terms both as an immanent event or process that is ongoing in the present and as something that has been actualized in particular historical forms. The philosophical concept of democracy would give expression to a pure event or process of democratization that is both incarnated within and betrayed by actually existing democracies. The critical function of the concept is ensured by the fact that, qua expression of a pure event, it is never exhausted by its empirical manifestations. The difference between the pure event or process and its historical forms allows us to reconcile the criticism of actually existing democracies with Deleuze and Guattari's call for resistance to the present in the name of a becoming-democratic not reducible to existing forms of constitutional state.

By contrast, Mengue argues that Deleuze's preference for immanence over transcendence renders him incapable of unequivocally supporting democracy or the idea of a constitutional state governed by law. He draws

on a series of remarks critical of the renewed interest in human rights in
France during the 1980s to support this claim. For example, in conversation with Antoine Dulaure and Claire Parnet in 1985, Deleuze complains
of the resistance to movement in contemporary thought and politics:

[I]n philosophy we're coming back to eternal values, to the idea of the intellectual
as custodian of eternal values. We're back to Benda complaining that Bergson
was a traitor to his own class, the clerical class, in trying to think motion. These
days it's the rights of man that provide our eternal values. It's the constitutional
state (*État de droit*) and other notions that everyone recognizes as very abstract.
And its in the name of all this that thinking is fettered and that any analysis in
terms of movements is blocked. (P 166, 121–122).[6]

Mengue draws from these remarks an argument against human rights
on grounds of principle. Rights of humankind are eternal and abstract.
As such, they are transcendent values. They suppose a universal and abstract subject of rights, identified with no one in particular and irreducible to singular, existent figures. Deleuze's philosophy is resolutely opposed
to transcendence in all its forms. He therefore rejects abstractions such
as human rights on the grounds that these serve to stop movement and
experimentation on the plane of immanence, in thought as much as in
political practice.

    While this argument conforms to Deleuzian principles up to a point,
it is incomplete in that it does not spell out the reasoning behind the claim
that the abstract or the universal stops movement, both at the level of
thought and at the level of action. It concludes that Deleuze is opposed
to any form of abstraction or to the very idea of rights, when in reality his
opposition is only to certain ways of understanding abstraction or rights.
Mengue fails to note that Deleuze's criticisms have to do with a quite specific historical phenomenon, namely the manner in which human rights
were represented as "eternal values," "new forms of transcendence, new
universals," and so on. Nothing in what he says implies rejection of rights,
the rule of law or democratic government as such. The argument attributed
to Deleuze in fact confuses the representation of human rights with human rights themselves and supposes that, just because he refuses the representation of human rights in these terms, Deleuze is opposed to rights in
any form. It is true that existing forms of constitutional state and incipient
forms of constitutional world order increasingly rely on the concept of human rights as the basis for legal rights. It is also true that Deleuze is critical
of the uses made of rights talk in the contemporary world. However, this

does not make him an opponent of rights or even of the idea that some rights should be universal. He is wary of attempts to ground human rights in features of human nature such as human freedom, rationality, or the capacity to communicate. Understood in these terms, human rights presuppose a universal and abstract subject of rights, irreducible to any singular, existent figures. They are eternal, abstract, and transcendent rights belonging to everyone and no one in particular. Human rights understood in this manner "say nothing about the immanent modes of existence of people provided with rights" (QP 103, 107).

Deleuze elaborates on the emptiness of human rights in the abstract in his *Abécédaire* interviews with Claire Parnet, with reference to the situation of an Armenian population subjected to a massacre by Turks and then to a subsequent earthquake (ABC, *G comme Gauche*). He objects firstly that, when people make declarations about human rights in such situations, "these declarations are never made as a function of the people who are directly concerned." In this case, he suggests, the Armenian people concerned have specific needs in the context of a specific and local situation: "Their problem is not 'the rights of man'" (ABC, *G comme Gauche*). Secondly, he argues that all such situations must be considered as *cases* to be decided rather than simply subsumed under existing laws. He explains this idea of a jurisprudence proceeding case by case with reference to French legal decisions relating to the banning of smoking in taxis. A first decision refused to allow such a ban on the grounds that the occupant was considered to be in the position of a tenant renting an apartment. A subsequent decision upheld the ban on the grounds that a taxi was considered to be a public service and the occupant in a public rather than a private space. In other words, the judicial response to such cases is properly creative and not simply the rote application of existing categories. Deleuze's preference for the ongoing process of creating new rights in response to particular situations does not imply hostility toward the rule of law but rather hostility toward a certain conception of law. As he says in the interview with Negri, it is "jurisprudence that truly creates law: this should not be left to judges" (P 230, 169).

Deleuze's understanding of jurisprudence clarifies the sense of his opposition to empty universals such as human rights considered in the abstract. These are useless because they are fixed and ahistorical, unable to evolve in accordance with the requirements of a particular case. Mengue ignores these and other remarks about jurisprudence with good reason because they make it clear that Deleuze is not opposed to rights as such but only to the idea that there exists a definitive set of human rights grounded in some rights-bearing feature of human nature. In the interview with Bellour and Ewald cited in note 6 above, he points out that rights are created by jurisprudence and that this "advances by working from singularities" (P 210, 153). There is nothing nonnatural or idealist about rights understood in this manner, nor any incompatibility between supposing that there are such rights and conceiving of social relations as relations of power and desire. Nietzsche provides a naturalistic framework for thinking about rights in defining them as recognized and guaranteed degrees of power (Nietzsche 1997, 67). Although he discusses the origin of rights primarily in relation to the rights of those in unequal power relations with others, Nietzsche's definition applies equally to the rights of citizens in a democracy where power is exercised over every citizen in the name of all. Rights would then be the "degrees of power" that all citizens are willing to leave to themselves and their cocitizens. Moreover, in the ideal case of a society that is effectively democratic and self-governing, the rights guaranteed for all citizens would not be the result of a simple modus vivendi but would derive from publicly endorsed opinions about what is right and just. These opinions ultimately would be based on what Rawls refers to as the "settled" or "considered convictions" of the people concerned (Rawls 2005, 8). It would be up to the society concerned whether it chose to enshrine those rights in a constitution or other founding legal document. However, some system of basic rights would be required to establish the framework within which democratic decision making and a rule of law could operate. Within this framework, it would be open to the courts to develop jurisprudence in particular ways, in response to circumstances or new social or technological developments. It would even be open to citizens to reconsider the basic rights themselves in the light of changes to the collective view of what was fair or just.[7]

The example of Nietzsche shows that Deleuze's endorsement of jurisprudence and the creation of rights is entirely consistent with his opposition to transcendence. His preference for the elaboration of rights on a case-by-case basis is difficult to reconcile with an antidemocratic disdain for the fate of ordinary people, especially when, as he suggests in the interview with Negri, the ultimate court of appeal in such situations should be the people most directly affected. With reference to a proposal to establish a system of law for modern biology, he comments that what is required is not "an ethical committee of supposedly well-qualified wise men but user groups" (P 230, 170). This appeal to jurisprudence and the need to create new rights that reflect the interests of those affected by biotechnology does not sit well with the picture of Deleuze as antidemocratic.

Finally, it is apparent that his preference for jurisprudence over declarations of human rights or their enshrinement in legal codes is a preference for the ongoing and open-ended creative process that leads to the modification of existing laws and the invention of new rights. As such, it parallels the kind of conceptual abstraction that he endorses in philosophy. Just as philosophy responds to problems by the creation of concepts, so when we respond to particular situations by legal means we are involved in jurisprudence, meaning the creative modification of existing legal principles or the invention of new ones to fit particular cases. In law as in thought, this case-by-case approach is a means to introduce movement into abstractions and thereby to approach more closely the conditions of life:

To act for freedom, becoming revolutionary, is to operate in jurisprudence when one turns to the justice system . . . that's what the invention of law is . . . it's not a question of applying "the rights of man" but rather of inventing new forms of jurisprudence . . . I have always been fascinated by jurisprudence, by law . . . If I hadn't studied philosophy, I would have studied law, but precisely not "the rights of man," rather I'd have studied jurisprudence. That's what life is. There are no "rights of man," only rights of life, and so, life unfolds case by case. (ABC, *G comme Gauche*)[8]

Majority and Minority

Mengue's second argument for the supposed antidemocratic bias of Deleuzian political philosophy relies on the distinction between majority and minority drawn in *A Thousand Plateaus*. Deleuze and Guattari emphasize the difference in kind between the position of majority and minoritarian becoming and, along with this difference, their preference for minoritarian politics. They point to the existence in contemporary societies of a majoritarian "fact," namely the existence of a standard against which the rights and duties of all citizens are measured:

Let us suppose that the constant or standard is the average adult-white-heterosexual-European-male speaking a standard language . . . It is obvious that "man" holds the majority, even if he is less numerous than mosquitoes, children, women, blacks, peasants, homosexuals, etc. That is because he appears twice, once in the constant and again in the variable from which the constant is extracted. Majority assumes a state of power and domination, not the other way around. (MP 133, 105)

At the same time, they point out that this is "the analytic fact of Nobody" and contrast it with the "becoming-minoritarian of everybody" (MP 134, 106). This becoming-minoritarian refers to the potential of individuals or groups to deviate from the standard. It expresses the sense in which individuals and societies never entirely conform to the majoritarian standard but exist in a process of continuous variation. It is from the perspective of their political preference for this creative process of minoritarian becoming that they suggest that "the problem is never to acquire the majority" (MP 134, 106). Mengue relies on this comment to support his strongest version of the claim that Deleuze's political orientation is fundamentally hostile toward democracy. He argues as follows: Democracy is in essence majoritarian. Deleuze supports a conception of minoritarian politics that is never intended to acquire the majority. It follows that, for Deleuze, "democracy is definitively and for reasons of principle excluded and radically condemned" (Mengue 2003, 103).

The difference in kind between majority and minority is fundamental to Deleuze and Guattari's politics of minoritarian becoming. However, difference is not the same as opposition and it is important not to overstate the consequences of this difference. In political terms, it amounts to the difference between the reconfiguration of the majoritarian standard, which is often achieved through democratic and legal means, and the fact and ongoing process of noncoincidence with the standard, however reconfigured. The emptiness of the majoritarian standard corresponds to the emptiness of human rights in the abstract: It represents no one. The emptiness of the majoritarian fact implies a critique of representation that applies to the identity of minorities as much as it does to that of the majority. To the extent that Deleuzian micropolitics refers to a different order of political activity, it represents a departure from representative politics *tout court*. It is not that it proposes an alternative to the politics of majority will formation but rather that it operates alongside or below the realm of democratic deliberation. As Paola Marrati comments: "Its aim is a becoming of the world as a possibility of inventing new forms of life, different modes of existence" (Marrati 2001, 214).

Mengue turns this difference into opposition in suggesting that the position of majority is by nature opposed to the creativity of the minoritarian: Majoritarian democratic politics inevitably "crushes" creative becomings (Mengue 2003, 102). According to this view, to adopt the standpoint of the majority is always to abandon the standpoint of the untimely and the creative in favor of the state and established values. This is a misrepresentation of Deleuze and Guattari's view and an implausible view of democratic politics. Legislative measures introduced in a number of democracies in recent years have served to broaden the standard to include nonwhites and nonmales and even in some cases to allow equal rights to homosexual partners. These measures suggest that, far from "crushing novelty" as Mengue suggests, democratic politics does have its own forms of creativity. No doubt such measures have been implemented in response to micropolitical changes already underway. For this reason, William Connolly reminds us that, to be responsive to new claims for the reconfiguration of the standard, democratic political life needs to be infused with a public ethos of critical engagement (Connolly 1999, 51). For Deleuze and Guattari, the different forms of minority becoming provide the impulse for change at the level of social and political institutions, but this change occurs only to the extent that there is adaptation and incorporation on the side of the majority. When they say that the power of minorities "is not measured by their capacity to enter into and make themselves felt within the majority system, nor even to reverse the necessarily tautological criterion of the majority," they mean that the majorities do not determine the limits of the potential for transformation (MP 588, 471). They do not mean to suggest that minorities do not enter into and produce effects on the majority. On the contrary, they insist on the importance of such piecemeal changes to the form and content of a given majority, arguing that molecular movements and lines of flight would be without political significance if they did not in turn react back upon the molar forms of social organization and "reshuffle their segments, their binary distributions of sexes, classes and parties" (MP 264, 216–217).[9]

Deleuze and Guattari's insistence on the transformative potential of minoritarian becomings does not imply a refusal of democratic politics, much less a rejection of democratic principles. The irreducible character of the difference in kind between majority and minority aligns them firmly with the proponents of democratic pluralism such as Connolly, for whom the key to an open-ended democratic process lies in the "productive tension" between majoritarian governance, rights, and recognition on the one hand, and forms of minoritarian becoming on the other (Connolly 2002, 172). For Deleuze and Guattari, it is precisely those excluded from the majority, as defined by a given set of axioms, who are the potential bearers of the power to transform that set, whether in the direction of a new set of axioms or an altogether new axiomatic. These are the source of minoritarian becomings that carry the potential for new Earths and peoples unlike those found in existing democracies.

Philosophy, Politics, and Opinion

A third stratum of Mengue's argument for the antidemocratic character of Deleuze and Guattari's political philosophy relies on the opposition they establish between philosophy and opinion. Democratic politics, he argues, is a means of reconciling diverse opinions to arrive at collective decisions on public policy. It implies a search for consensus or at least a majority of shared or overlapping opinions. It necessarily proceeds via the exchange of opinions in a variety of forums. By contrast, Deleuzian philosophy has no interest in the exchange of opinions or consensus. He points to remarks such as the following in support of his conclusion that Deleuzian politics cannot possibly be democratic: "The least one can say about discussions is that they do not advance the work at hand, since the participants never talk about the same thing . . . Philosophy has a horror of discussions" (QP 32–33, 28–29).

However, this criticism confuses too many different issues at stake in Deleuze and Guattari's understanding of philosophy, opinion, and the relationship of both of these to the practice of democracy. It is not enough to align democracy and opinion and then to oppose both to philosophy, understood as the creation of concepts. Philosophy is not politics and, while Deleuze and Guattari clearly reject the idea that the exchange of opinions is a means to create concepts, nothing follows from this about the exchange of opinions in the public sphere. Disentangling these issues requires further inquiry into the relationships established by Deleuze and Guattari among democracy, opinion, and philosophy.

To begin, consider the difference between philosophy and opinion from the perspective of the Deleuzian conception of philosophy. Mengue argues that, because democracy is based on public opinion and consensus, while Deleuze's philosophy is resolutely opposed to opinion in all its manifestations, it follows that it rejects democracy. However, much of the criticism of opinion in *What Is Philosophy?* relates to its difference from philosophy rather than its role in politics. Deleuze and Guattari are critical of opinion because of their adherence to a Nietzschean image of thought as creation. All thinking, they argue, whether it takes place in the form of art, philosophy, or science, is a way of bringing order out of chaos. Order is what protects us from chaos. It enables us to recognize ourselves, each other, and the world in which we live. According to Kant, in the absence of the order brought to our perceptions by the pure concepts of human understanding, we would be confronted with nothing more than a disorderly manifold or multiplicity of such perceptions. Order among our percepts and concepts enables us not merely to survive but to conceive and pursue projects that give meaning and purpose to our lives. However, order can also imprison us in fixed and immobile patterns of thought and action, thereby inhibiting creativity or change. Deleuze and Guattari cite a text of D. H. Lawrence on the source of poetry:

People are constantly putting up an umbrella that shelters them and on the underside of which they draw a firmament and write their conventions and opinions. But poets and artists make a slit in the umbrella, they tear open the firmament itself, to let in a bit of free and windy chaos and to frame in a sudden light a vision that appears through the rent—Wordsworth's spring or Cézanne's apple, the silhouettes of Macbeth or Ahab. (QP 191, 203–204).

In these terms, understood as the underside of the umbrella that shields us from chaos, opinions and conventions are the enemies of creativity in all its forms. For this reason, Deleuze and Guattari regard the struggle against chaos as secondary to the more profound struggle against opinion: "We thus come back to a conclusion to which art led us: the struggle against chaos is only the instrument of a more profound struggle against opinion, for it is opinion that gives rise to the misfortune of humankind" (QP 194, 206). It follows that the primary concern of philosophy is to wage war against opinion. Progress in philosophy, art, or science always involves upheavals in thought that allow glimpses of the chaos beyond. Artistic genius, abnormal science, and genuine philosophy all seek to "tear open the firmament and plunge into the chaos" (QP 190, 202).

Mengue relies on this opposition between opinion and philosophy to argue that because democracy implies discussion and public debate, whereas the creation of concepts does not proceed through discussion, Deleuzian politics cannot be democratic: "If thought or philosophy abhors discussion, it is difficult to see how it would not abhor democracy" (Mengue 2003, 43). The flaw in this argument is that it relies on a further unstated premise, namely the equation of Deleuzian politics with a politics of thought. Because Deleuze's criticism of opinion occurs in the context of elaborating a concept of philosophy, this further premise is required to connect his criticism of opinion with any position with regard to politics. In an earlier chapter, Mengue does argue that, for Deleuze, politics is reduced to a politics of thought, indeed to thought as politics. He refers to the brief Exergue to *Negotiations* to support his claim that Deleuze collapses the distinction between intellectual and political activity such that "the thought of the thinker is directly and in essence political." This collapsing of politics into a politics of thought would provide support for the charge that Deleuze is guilty of a "devalorisation of democracy" (Mengue 2003, 41).

The problem, however, is that the text cited supports no such conclusion. In this Exergue, designed to explain the pertinence of the title, "Negotiations (*Pourparlers*)," Deleuze suggests that philosophy is not a power and cannot communicate, or at least that it cannot communicate directly, with the powers that be such as religions, states, capitalism, science, law, television, and opinion. He goes on to suggest that because these powers "are not just external things but permeate each of us, we are all in constant negotiations with and a guerilla campaign against ourselves, thanks to philosophy" (P 7). His argument is that philosophy provides at best an indirect form of resistance to these powers, including the power of opinion. Nothing in this text suggests that philosophy is a substitute for political activity, or that there is no distinction between philosophical and political activity. Philosophy is an aid or a supplement, perhaps a necessary supplement, to political activity in the public sphere. The text provides no support for the claim that Deleuze collapses politics into a politics of thought and therefore no support for the suggestion that he devalues democracy.

What Is Philosophy? devotes several pages to distinguishing opinion from concepts and criticizing the philosophy of communication that "is exhausted in the search for a universal liberal opinion as consensus" (QP 139, 146). In this context, Deleuze outlines a rigorous concept of everyday opinion as a function linking perceptual properties of things to particular perceptions or affections, and both of these to subjects of a certain kind (<faithfulness of dogs, detest: dog-haters>; <foul smell of cheese, love it: bon vivants>; and so on). Considered or embedded opinions in philosophy and politics may be supposed to follow a parallel pattern and to connect particular postulates, doctrines, or beliefs to affects and to sub-jects of certain kinds: <hierarchies of cast, oppose: egalitarian>; <redistri-bution of wealth, endorse: social democrat>; and so on. However, Deleuze insists that philosophical concepts are not functions and therefore irreduc-ible to opinions. He ironizes about "the Western democratic popular con-ception of philosophy" and argues that the exchange of opinions cannot produce concepts, however much it provides for "pleasant or aggressive dinner conversations at Mr Rorty's" (QP 138, 144). He is clearly opposed to the idea that the exchange of opinions is a means to create concepts, although not necessarily opposed to the pleasures of conversation as such. Moreover, from this sharp distinction between philosophical concepts and opinions nothing follows about the exchange of opinions or the need for consensus in the political sphere.

Consider now the relationship between democracy and opinion from the point of view of the political process. As we noted above, Mengue is right to claim that a doxological plane of immanence is necessary for democratic politics. However, it does not follow from this that what passes for public discussion in contemporary liberal democracies is an adequate realization of this plane. As a consequence, when Deleuze criticizes cur-rent political forms of public debate as the "fabrication" of consensus or submission of the masses to the powers in place, he need not be taken to be rejecting the idea of public reason as such, only the forms in which it currently takes place. Mengue claims that, for Deleuze, democracy is the realm of opinion and consensus and as such essentially majoritarian. On this basis, he concludes that Deleuze is opposed to democracy as such. Nothing could be further from the truth.

Democratic politics requires not only a doxological plane of pub-lic reason but also principles on the basis of which to regulate the free play of opinions on this plane. Where do these principles come from? One answer, given by John Rawls, is to say that the ultimate foundation for such principles lies in the considered judgments or settled opinions of the people concerned. This answer is available to any political philosophy committed to the denial of transcendent grounds of political association. It is therefore available to Deleuze. For Rawls, the theory of justice and the conditions of a well-ordered society must be tested against the con-sidered judgments of the society (Rawls 1999b, 17–18; 2005, 8). These judgments are not reducible to the day-to-day opinions of citizens. They are expressed in the institutions and in the constitutional and legal set-tlements of the society. They set limits to the conduct of public debate and provide the normative framework within which disagreements can be settled or at least kept within reasonable bounds so as not to threaten the political order. A liberal conception of democratic politics of this kind therefore implies a distinction between two kinds or levels of opinion: considered judgments about right ways of acting, as embodied in institutions and historical documents, and everyday opinions on matters of current concern or public policy. Political philosophy is primarily concerned with opinion of the former kind. Deleuze's inclusion of opinion among the powers against which philosophy wages a guerilla campaign suggests that he has this kind of opinion in mind.

The important question, however, is: What kind of relationship does philosophy have to opinion understood in this way? Classical Greek philosophy provides one model of critical engagement with *doxa*. Deleuze and Guattari describe this as a dialectic that constructs an ideal or tribunal before which the truth-value of different opinions can be assessed. They suggest that while this dialectic purports to extract a form of knowledge from opinions, opinion continually breaks through so that in the end "philosophy remains a doxography" (QP 77, 80). Rawls's political liberalism provides another model of engagement with opinion that does not seek to gauge the truth or falsity of opinions but rather to reconstruct the considered opinions of a historically specific form of society to render them systematic and coherent. In this way, it produces a concept of a just society, subject to the qualification that this concept might change as the considered opinions of the society change.[10]

Deleuze and Guattari's adherence to a Nietzschean image of thought as experimentation and creation leads them to advocate a more critical relation to opinion. Their conception of the political vocation of philosophy as helping to bring about "new earths and new peoples" suggests more extravagant ambitions than we find in Rawls. It points to their focus on critical engagement with and transformation of considered opinions rather than their systematic reconstruction. Success in this kind of political philosophy is not measured by the test of reflective equilibrium or by the capacity to maintain a well-ordered society but by the capacity of its concepts to engage with and assist movements of deterritorialization in the present. Deleuze's support for minoritarian becomings and his criticisms of the inequalities produced by capitalism should be understood in this light. They challenge existing opinions about what is acceptable with the aim of extending and developing equality of condition within contemporary societies. If this kind of criticism is to open up paths to the invention of new forms of individual and collective life, it will have to engage with actual becomings that are immanent and active in present so- cial and political life. The transformation of existing opinions, especially those that lie behind our conceptions of justice and public reason, will be an important dimension of such becomings. Far from being hostile to democratic politics, philosophy and the guerilla wars it wages will consti- tute an integral part of this process.

Conclusion

In *What Is Philosophy?* Deleuze does say that democracies are majori- ties and that they do not provide optimum conditions for philosophical criticism: "*We lack resistance to the present*" (QP 104,108). However, resis- tance to the present does not imply the rejection of democracy as such but rather resistance to the present state of public opinion, public policy, and the existing institutional forms of democratic politics. His critical remarks about opinion include comments about the conditions under which it is currently produced and circulated. For example, he suggests that all too often we find in the consensus opinions of liberal societies "the cynical perceptions and affections of the capitalist" (QP 139, 146). The implica- tion here is that opinion is fabricated by the powers that be and as such an instrument of domination rather than genuine democracy. However, this is a criticism of the present day reality of public opinion rather than of the idea of public reason as such, and Deleuze is not the first philosopher to advance such views. The circumstances leading up to the 2003 invasion of Iraq are one of many recent indications of the degree to which public opinion can be manipulated by a sustained campaign of disinformation (McClellan 2008). Such criticism implies opposition to the current state of what passes for democratic deliberation in the public sphere of liberal capitalist societies. It points to the perversion of what passes for the con- sensus of an informed majority. But it does not imply rejection of the prin- ciple that government should reflect the opinions of all of the governed.

As we noted at the outset of this chapter, Deleuze's call for resistance to the present is not advanced in the name of some antidemocratic princi- ple of minority rule, as Mengue suggests, but in the name of a "becoming- democratic" that should not be confused with what currently passes for democratic government. Becoming-democratic bears the same relation- ship to actually existing democracy that becoming-revolutionary bears to

actual revolutions. It refers us to a pure event that is both expressed in
and betrayed by its actual historical manifestations. In Deleuzian terms,
this virtual democracy would remain irreducible to its past or present actualizations. We could redescribe it as a democracy to come but only on
the condition that we take this to mean a future form of democracy that
never in fact arrives.[11] The task of philosophy, according to Deleuze and
Guattari, is the counter-effectuation of present historical states of affairs
through the creation of new concepts or the modification of old ones. The
concept of becoming-democratic fulfils this task by giving expression to
efforts underway to enlarge or enforce the application of democratic principles. Deleuze's criticisms of contemporary democracies in the name of
becoming-democratic should not be mistaken for a refusal or a condem-
nation of democracy as such. They amount to resistance to the present in
the name of a virtual democracy or a democracy to come.

9

Utopian Political Philosophy:
Deleuze and Rawls

This chapter explores some further consequences of what I have
called the normative turn in Deleuze's political thought by comparing elements of his conception of philosophy with the liberal normative philosophy of John Rawls. The purpose of this unlikely comparison is not to deny
the real differences that separate these approaches to political philosophy
but rather to use them to bring into focus more sharply some of the un-
examined dimensions of each. It is well known what normative political
philosophy has to offer poststructuralist political thought, namely a more
adequate account of the normative bases of its critique of current social
and political institutions. While the criticisms of poststructuralism's normative inadequacy are often overstated, they are broadly correct in pointing to the need for greater engagement with normative political theory.
In the case of Deleuze, the comparison with Rawls enables us not only
to identify more precisely the normative principles implicit in the critical
stance toward liberal capitalist democracies adopted in *What Is Philosophy?* but also to suggest ways in which these might be further clarified and
defended. In addition, the overtly historical dimension of political liberalism's version of the theory of justice suggests that these principles might be
understood in a manner consistent with Deleuze's broader commitment
to norms that are immanent to particular forms of social and political life.
It is less well known what poststructuralism has to offer normative political philosophy. In the final section of this chapter I propose one relatively
specific answer to this question: Given that Rawls's conception of the purposes of political philosophy includes criticism of present basic institutions of society, then Deleuze's conception of the nature of philosophical
concepts has something useful to contribute. Deleuze's insistence on the
mobility of concepts and on political philosophy's role in the creation of

new forms of life suggests a way of understanding Rawls's principles of justice as open to the ever-present possibility of new forms of becoming-democratic and new expressions of the pure event of democracy.

Extravagant versus Realistic Utopianism

A pretext and focus for comparing Deleuzian and Rawlsian political philosophy is the manner in which both thinkers hold utopian aspirations for their conception of political philosophy, however differently they might understand the aims of this enterprise. At first glance, they appear to be engaged in profoundly different activities: One is primarily critical, while the other is predominantly reconstructive; one is primarily concerned with the dynamics of social and political assemblages, while the other is concerned with elaborating a normative conception of society as a fair system of cooperation. The aim of Rawls's political liberalism is to set out in systematic form principles of justice that plausibly may be supposed to find acceptance among reasonable members of modern democratic society. A "well-ordered" society in his sense of the term is one that is effectively governed in accordance with principles of justice that everyone understands and accepts and knows that everyone understands and accepts. These principles should spell out the terms on which society can operate as a fair system of cooperation. They should determine the structure of the basic political, economic, and social institutions. Most importantly for the comparison with Deleuze, the ideas that form the basis of the conception of justice must be drawn from the public political culture of Western liberal democracy, including its institutions and the historical traditions of their interpretation. In this sense, Rawls insists that the theory of justice is political rather than metaphysical.

In *Justice as Fairness: A Restatement*, he identifies four purposes served by this kind of reconstructive political philosophy:

1. It can help to resolve deeply disputed questions by searching for common philosophical and moral ground between the protagonists. For example, with regard to the conflict within the Western liberal tradition between the values of liberty and equality, political liberalism searches for underlying bases of agreement or higher-order principles in the hope that these might narrow the differences between libertarian and egalitarian concepts of freedom and equality. The aim is to achieve

social cooperation on bases of mutual respect even though irresolvable differences remain.

2. It can serve the task of orientation that seeks to identify reasonable and rational ends, both individual and collective, and to
show "how those ends can cohere within a well-articulated
conception of a just and reasonable society" (Rawls 2001, 3).

3. It can address the task of reconciliation by showing the limits of
what can be achieved within a democratic society characterized
by the existence of "profound and irreconcilable differences in
citizen's reasonable comprehensive religious and philosophical conceptions of the world" (Rawls 2001, 3). In this manner,
political liberalism argues against communitarianism that a political society is not a community in the sense that this implies
shared comprehensive moral views, but also against libertarian-
ism in that it is not simply an association that one can leave at
any time.

4. Finally, political liberalism serves the "realistically utopian" task
of "probing the limits of practicable political possibility." It asks
what a just and democratic society would be like, given the "circumstances of justice" that obtain in the actual historical world
in which we live, but also what it would be like "under reasonably favourable but still possible historical conditions" (Rawls
2001, 4). Rawls recognizes that there is a question about how
we determine the limits of the practicable and what are in fact
the limits of our social world. He notes that these are not simply
given by the actual because we can and do change existing social
and political institutions; however, he does not pursue any further the question of what determines the limits of the practicable
or how we might ascertain what these are (Rawls 2001, 5).

From the perspective of Deleuze's conception of philosophy, which
is concerned above all to challenge the limits of our present social world,
we might say that Rawls lacks a conception of the virtual or of the conditions of the new. *What Is Philosophy?* outlines a conception of philosophy
as the creation of concepts, where the aim is overtly utopian. It presents a
conception of the political vocation of philosophy with far more radical
ambitions than those acknowledged in Rawls's realistic utopianism: "*We
lack resistance to the present. The creation of concepts in itself calls for a future form, for a new earth and people that do not yet exist*" (QP 104, 108).

Success in this kind of political philosophy is not measured by the test of reflective equilibrium or by the requirements of maintaining a well-ordered society but by the capacity of its concepts to engage productively with real movements of social change. At the same time, we should not overestimate the differences between Rawlsian and Deleuzian utopianism. The distance between them is narrower than we might imagine at first glance. On the one hand, Deleuzian political philosophy is not so utopian that it is completely disconnected from the normative and conceptual horizons of the present. It includes a recognizably Marxist critique of the inequalities produced by capitalist society. It also includes a post-Marxist critique of revolutionary vanguard politics and the philosophy of history that sustained them. Deleuze's appeal to the concept of "becoming-democratic" as a means to express resistance to the injustices of liberal capitalist societies provides additional reason to think that the differences between Rawls's political philosophy and his own are neither as profound nor as irreconcilable as they might appear. In effect, "becoming-democratic" points to ways of criticizing the workings of actually existing democracies in the name of the egalitarian principles that are supposed to inform their institutions and political practices. It expresses the will to extend existing forms of relative deterritorialization to the limits of what is possible under present conditions. I will say more about Deleuze's understanding of these limits below.

On the other hand, while it is true that a central concern of Rawls's political liberalism is to provide a systematic rationale for the basic political structure of liberal democratic society, his conception of justice is not so cautious nor so remote from critical engagement with those forces hostile to change as some commentators suggest. For example, in his *Reply to Habermas*, he lists three points on which his theory implies criticism of the current institutional structure of American democracy:

The present system woefully fails in public financing for political elections, leading to a grave imbalance in fair political liberties; it allows a widely disparate distribution of income and wealth that seriously undermines fair opportunities in education and in chances of rewarding employment, all of which undermine economic and social equality; and absent also are provisions for important constitutional essentials such as health care for many who are uninsured. (Rawls 2005, 407)

More generally, his theory of justice implies the need for basic social institutions incompatible with existing liberal forms of welfare-state capitalism, much less neoliberal versions of this regime. The problem with even the most generous welfare states is that they do not provide for equal value of basic political liberties or for real equality of opportunity among all citizens. They allow a relatively small class of citizens to retain control of means of production and, as a result, to exercise disproportionate control over economic and political life. For these reasons, Rawls prefers a form of "property-owning" democracy that would ensure widespread ownership of means of production, including productive assets as well as human capital (Rawls 1999b, 242). Such a society would aim to endow all citizens with the means of being fully participating members of society as a shared system of cooperation. It would aim to provide all with the relevant skills, knowledge, and understanding of institutions necessary for real equality of opportunity from one generation to the next (Rawls 2001, 139). In these and other ways, Rawls's theory of justice is genuinely critical of the basic institutional structure of actually existing democracies. In Deleuze's terms, it provides resources for effective resistance to present forms of liberal capitalist democracy.

It is true that Deleuzian political philosophy is not concerned with setting out the normative principles in terms of which new social arrangements might be qualified as better or more just than those that precede. Rather, it creates concepts that give expression to the forces and processes that produce or inhibit changes to the character of individual and social life: mechanisms of capture, processes of nomadization or the creation of smooth space, minoritarian becomings, deterritorialization, and so on. Of the four functions of political philosophy identified by Rawls, it does not address those of resolution, orientation, or reconciliation. It does address the utopian function, but not by setting out principles against which we might evaluate the justice or fairness of social institutions. It does not offer principles of society as a fair system of cooperation in the light of which we might point out the ways in which present liberal democracies fail to live up to this ideal. Deleuze's suggestion in his interview with Negri that philosophy provides a way of responding to what is intolerable in the present implies that the creation of concepts may assist the emergence of new forms of individual and collective life that, in specific ways, are *better than* existing forms (P 231, 171). But because the contours of the intolerable are themselves historically determined and subject to change, there is no presumption of any end state or perfectly just society. Deleuzian philosophy is utopian by virtue of what it does rather than by virtue of laying out a blueprint for a just society.[1]

Two features of the relationship of philosophy to the social milieu in which it takes place are relevant to the utopianism of Deleuze's political philosophy: the manner in which philosophy is inherently critical of its milieu and the manner in which, when it is effective, this criticism involves processes and tendencies that are immanent to the milieu in question. It is because it creates concepts that express pure events or "becomings" that philosophy is by nature potentially critical of its milieu. However, such criticism is effective only to the extent that it connects with deterritorializing forces already at work within that milieu:

Philosophy takes the relative deterritorialization of capital to the absolute; it makes it pass over the plane of immanence as movement of the infinite and suppresses it as internal limit, *turns it back against itself so as to summon forth a new earth, a new people.* (QP 95, 99)

Let us consider each of these features in turn. *What Is Philosophy?* presents the emergence of philosophy as the result of an entirely synthetic and contingent encounter between the Greek milieu and the plane of immanence of thought. This encounter gave rise to a specific kind of thought defined in terms of its affinity with absolute as opposed to relative deterritorialization. Relative deterritorialization concerns the historical relationship of things to the territories into which they are organized: the manner in which these territories break down and are transformed or reconstituted into new forms. Absolute deterritorialization concerns the ahistorical relationship of things and states of affairs to the virtual realm of becoming or pure events that is imperfectly or partially expressed in what happens. Philosophical concepts express such pure events or becomings, where these are understood as the conditions of change and the emergence of the new:

Actually, *utopia is what links* philosophy with its own epoch, with European capitalism, but also already with the Greek city. Each time it is with utopia that philosophy becomes political and takes the criticism of its own time to its highest point. Utopia does not split off from infinite movement: etymologically it stands for absolute deterritorialization but always at the critical point at which it is connected with the present relative milieu and above all with the forces that are suppressed in this milieu. (QP 95–96, 99)

The sense in which this conception of philosophy is utopian must therefore be understood in terms of the connection between the absolute deterritorialization pursued in philosophy and the relative deterritorializations at work in its social milieu: "There is always a way in which absolute deterritorialization takes over from a relative deterritorialization in a given field" (QP 85, 88). It follows that the utopian vocation of philosophy can be achieved in function only of the kinds of relative deterritorialization at work in a given society. Its concepts must engage with forms of becoming-revolutionary that are active in present social and political life if they are to assist in opening up paths to new forms of individual and collective life. Deleuze's conception of philosophy therefore implies an immanent utopianism in the sense that it does not simply posit an ideal future but rather aims to connect with processes of relative deterritorialization that are present in but stifled by the present milieu, extending these and taking them to extremes. To the extent that these processes or "lines of flight" encompass resistant political forces along with the ideals or opinions that motivate them, it follows that this immanent utopianism will draw on elements of present political normativity to suggest ways in which the injustice or intolerability of existing institutional forms of social life might be removed.

Immanent Utopianism and Becoming-Democratic

In the light of this account of Deleuze's immanent utopianism, it is clear how the concept of "becoming-democratic" serves the task of philosophy. The deterritorializing impulse proper to philosophy and the synthetic relationship between philosophy and its milieu together explain Deleuze's appeal to "becoming-democratic" as one important form of resistance to the present. Because the concept of democracy ties together a number of the values at the heart of contemporary political thought, elements of that concept may be used to counter-actualize certain forms of resistance to the present in public political culture. The appeal to "becoming democratic" as a form of resistance to the present relies on a number of historical claims about the relationship between democracy and modern society. These include: (1) The claim that democracy is the preferred political form of the nation states that sustained the emergence of capitalist economies and now function as the administrative nodes of its global system; (2) The claim that democracy implied certain forms of relative deterritorialization of society, such as the ways in which the idea of fundamental equality of all citizens undermined the hierarchies of pre-capitalist society; (3) The claim that these forms of deterritorialization were reterritorialized on the modern constitutional state and its extension into the international sphere in the form of principles of human rights; (4) The claim that, because there is no universal democratic state, there are only particular democratic states with their own forms of democratic governance and their own institutional implementations of the equal rights of man and citizen; (5) Finally, the claim that processes of democratization remain an important form of relative deterritorialization in modern capitalist societies.

As I argued in Chapter 7, even though Deleuze offers no detailed account of "becoming-democratic," it is possible to fill out the concept with elements of his prior work with Guattari as well as occasional comments in interviews. For example, in his interview with Negri, he invokes the principle that decisions ought to be taken in consultation with those most affected by them. This suggests that the opening-up of decision-making procedures throughout society might constitute a vector of "becoming-democratic" (P 230, 169–170). This is one of the founding principles of modern democratic governance, and Deleuze is not the only theorist to recommend its extension and application to new contexts. Liberal-socialist egalitarians such as Rodney Peffer rely on this principle to argue that democracy should be implemented in the workplace (Peffer 1990, 419–420).

Minoritarian becomings provide another vector of "becoming-democratic." These are defined as the variety of ways in which individuals and groups fail to conform to the majoritarian standard. They have given rise to a succession of measures to extend the scope of the standard and thereby broaden the subject of democracy: first, in purely quantitative terms by extending the vote to women and other minorities; second, in qualitative terms by changing the nature of political institutions and procedures to enable these newly enfranchised members to participate on equal terms. The idea that who are the representatives in a given polity matters as much as the ideas represented has become widely known as "the politics of presence." Anne Phillips sums up the core idea as follows:

When the politics of ideas is taken in isolation from the politics of presence, it does not deal adequately with the experience of those social groups who by virtue of their race or gender have felt themselves excluded from the democratic process. Political exclusion is increasingly—I believe rightly—viewed in terms that can only be met by political presence. (Phillips 2006, 173)

That this remains a difficult struggle is shown by the fact that efforts to achieve political representation of women in proportion to their numbers in the population are ongoing in most democratic societies, despite their having been enfranchised for the better part of a century. Efforts to change the nature of public institutions in ways that both acknowledge and accommodate many kinds of difference are ongoing, for example in relation to sexual orientation and physical and mental abilities, as well as cultural and religious backgrounds. Deleuze and Guattari's support for minoritarian becomings affirms the importance of efforts to enlarge the character of the majority, even as they insist that the power of minorities is not reducible to their capacity to effect change in the nature of the majority (MP 588, 471). By their nature, processes of minoritarian-becoming will always exceed or escape from the confines of any given majority. Nevertheless, they embody the potential to transform the affects, beliefs, and political sensibilities of a population in ways that can lead to the advent of a new people. To the extent that a people is constituted as a political community, the transformations it undergoes will affect its conceptions of what is fair and just. In turn, these will affect the distribution of rights and duties as well as the presence of minority citizens in the public institutions and political functions of the society.

A third vector of "becoming-democratic" involves efforts to achieve a more just distribution of material social goods. Deleuze is often critical of the way in which modern democratic states fail to live up to this aspect of their egalitarian promise. However, his suggestion that democratic states are morally and politically compromised by their role in the perpetuation of this form of injustice implicitly raises the normative question, What principles of distribution should apply in a just democratic society? Should we advocate radically egalitarian principles that would treat any undeserved inequality of condition as unjust, or should we be satisfied with Rawls's difference principle according to which social and economic inequalities are allowed but only when they are attached to positions open to all and when they are "to the greatest benefit of the least advantaged members of society" (Rawls 2005, 6)? Should the principles of distributive justice apply globally or only within the borders of particular democratic states? I am not suggesting that Deleuze provides us with the means to answer these normative questions but only that they are inevitably raised by his criticisms of the existing state of affairs.

Immanent Criticism and Considered Opinion

Deleuze and Rawls both propose an immanent utopianism by virtue of the manner in which their conceptions of the critical function of philosophy rely on normative concepts immanent to the political culture of the society in question. Deleuzian philosophy is utopian insofar as it produces concepts that draw on and connect with processes of relative deterritorialization already underway in the social field. I indicated above how the concept of a "becoming-democratic" points to the role of elements of our existing concept of democracy in historical struggles to implement or expand democratic principles of government. In parallel fashion, Rawls elaborates his theory of justice on the basis of concepts and convictions already present in the public political culture of liberal democracies. Democratic political order requires principles of public reason to set limits to the conduct of public debate and provide the normative framework within which disagreements can be settled, or at least kept within reasonable bounds so as not to threaten stability. Rawls's answer to the question "where do these principles come from?" is to say that their ultimate foundation lies in the settled convictions and considered opinions of the people concerned. The principles of public reason and the political conception of justice on which they are based must be consistent with the settled convictions of the political culture, such as the toleration of religious diversity or the abhorrence of slavery. The ultimate test of an acceptable political conception of justice is the achievement of "reflective equilibrium" between the proposed principles of justice and the firmly held convictions embedded in the institutions and traditions of the political culture: "The most reasonable political conception for us is the one that best fits all our considered convictions on reflection and organises them into a coherent view. At any given time we cannot do better than that" (Rawls 2001, 31).

The overlapping consensus that underpins political liberalism's principles of justice is not reached by means of empirical survey or negotiation between the actual convictions of a particular people. It is nonetheless supposed to be attainable by reasonable persons on the basis of the political convictions that are embedded in liberal democratic institutions, including constitutions, laws, and their traditions of interpretation. The sense in which it appeals to nothing outside the convictions and discourses that form part of a particular political culture justifies the claim that Rawls, like Deleuze, offers an immanent political utopianism. At the same time, the sense in which Deleuzian concepts express pure events that function as vectors of absolute as opposed to relative deterritorialization undermines the possibility of any simple contrast between a "materialist" philosophy of becoming and an "idealist" theory of justice.

Both Rawls and Deleuze define the task of political philosophy in relation to a certain kind of opinion that must be distinguished from the day-to-day opinions of citizens. The role of reflective equilibrium in Rawls's approach explicitly ties the theory of justice to the considered opinions of people on fundamental principles of right, fairness, and justice. Political liberalism therefore implies a distinction between two kinds or levels of opinion: considered opinions about right ways of acting, insofar as these are expressed in the institutions, constitutional settlements, legal decisions, and traditions of interpretation of the society in question, and everyday opinions on matters of current concern or public policy. Deleuze also draws a distinction between everyday opinions on matters of current concern and the opinions embedded in the national characteristics of a people, including their conceptions of right and the practical philosophy that is expressed in their political and legal institutions. He asks at one point whether philosophy in its present critical form is closely aligned with "the modern democratic state and human rights" (QP 98, 102). In reply, he points out that there is no universal democratic state but only particular democratic states, the contours of which are determined in part by philosophical or "nationalitarian" opinions about what is right, fair, and just (QP 99–100, 102–104). The opinions expressed in the political and legal institutions of a given people—their conceptions of right, justice, and equality as opposed to the everyday opinions of people—will determine the national characteristics of their thought. They also condition the institutional and constitutional structure of particular national forms of democracy. Deleuze suggests that, to the extent that modern philosophy is reterritorialized on the idea of the democratic state, this will always be modulated by the features of the "nationalitarian" philosophy concerned:

In each case philosophy finds a way of reterritorializing itself in the modern world in conformity with the spirit of a people and its conception of right. The history of philosophy therefore is marked by national characteristics or rather by *nationalitarianisms which are like philosophical opinions*. (QP 100, 104; emphasis added)

The limits that flow from the manner in which democratic ideals are expressed in accordance with the philosophical opinions of particular peoples amount to one kind of constraint on the institutional and legal actualization of democratic ideals in a given society. Deleuze points to a second kind of constraint on democratization in the present that follows from the requirements of global capitalism. He argues that there is no universal democratic state because "the market is the only thing that is universal in capitalism" (QP 101–102, 106). The account of the relation between contemporary nation states and capitalism in *What Is Philosophy?* remains the same as it was in *A Thousand Plateaus*: National state government and economic systems are "models of realization" of the immanent axiomatic of global capitalism. As such, they will be constrained by their subordination to the requirements of this system. This implies that relations of interdependence compromise even the most democratic nodes of this global economic system insofar as they are direct or indirect beneficiaries of the actions of dictatorial states. It also implies that the extension of the liberal commitment to the fundamental equality and security of citizens in the form of human rights amounts to adding axioms that coexist in the global axiomatic of capital alongside other axioms, "notably those concerning the security of property" (QP 103, 107). These property rules, Deleuze suggests, do not so much contradict the basic rights of individuals as suspend their operation in certain contexts. Thus, when basic political rights coexist alongside private property in large-scale means of production, and in the absence of publicly financed elections, they do not have the same value for all citizens. When private property in means of production exists alongside the absence of mechanisms to provide minimal health care, housing, or education, the basic welfare rights of the poor are effectively suspended. Hence the force of the rhetorical question: "What social democracy has not given the order to fire when the poor come out of their territory or ghetto?" (QP 103, 107). Nor are such extreme situations of poverty and oppression the only manifestations of the subordination of democratic life to the requirements of capital. Deleuze also points to "the meanness and vulgarity of existence that haunts democracies" as this is expressed in the "values, ideals and opinions of our time" (QP 103, 107–108). This is an important part of the reason that "our democracies" do not provide optimum conditions for resistance to the present or the constitution of new Earths and new peoples. The consensus of opinions in these societies all too often reflects "the cynical perceptions and affections of the capitalist" (QP 139, 146).

However, as I suggested above, the day-to-day opinions of citizens must be distinguished from the considered opinions of a given people on fundamental principles of right. Rawls and Deleuze are in agreement that political philosophy should engage with the opinions of the latter kind present in a given social milieu. The difference between a relatively cautious and realistic and a more extravagant and critical utopianism reappears in the difference between their respective relations to philosophical opinion. Rawls's political liberalism seeks to reconstruct the considered opinions of a historically specific form of society to render them systematic and coherent. In this way, it produces a concept of a fair and just society, subject to the qualification that this concept might change as the considered opinions of the society change. By contrast, Deleuze's "utopian" conception of the political vocation of philosophy implies a more critical engagement with considered opinions, aimed at their transformation rather than their systematic reconstruction. That is why, in the brief exergue to *Negotiations*, he presents philosophy as engaged in a "guerilla campaign" against public opinion and other powers that be such as religions and laws (P 7). His criticisms of the inequalities produced by capitalism should be understood in this light. They challenge existing opinions about what is acceptable with the aim of extending and developing equality of condition within contemporary societies.

The second two elements of the concept of becoming-democratic identified above directly confront the two kinds of limitation on the actualization of democracy in the modern world: The struggle against unjust inequality of condition challenges fundamental elements of the capitalist axiomatic, while the struggle against the arbitrary nature of the qualitative majority challenges the weight of nationalitarian political and philosophical opinion in particular cultures. The different kinds of minoritarian-becoming that give rise to movements to reconfigure the subject of democracy, such as the struggle for equal representation of women or for equal rights for homosexual partners, encounter varying degrees and kinds of resistance depending on the details of nationalitarian opinion in each case. Deleuze argues that philosophical concepts are critical of our present to the extent that they "connect up with what is real here and now in the struggle against capitalism" (QP 96, 100). But they are also critical to the extent that they connect up with struggles against the inherited forms of national, social, and sexual culture. The first element in becoming-democratic, the extension of democratic decision making, points to an additional line of flight in contemporary democratic societies that has the potential to connect up with the first two and carry the transformative process forward, even to the point of breaking down the limits imposed by the separation of a private sphere of property relations and a public sphere of deliberation over and regulation of the common good. Like any philosophical concept, becoming-democratic is "the contour, the configuration, the constellation of an event to come" (QP 36, 32–33). In this case, the event to come is the deterritorialization of existing democracies and their reconfiguration in new social and political forms. The specification of these new political territories and peoples requires that we spell out the normative principles governing the basic institutional structure of society. For this reason, the further development of Deleuzian political philosophy along the paths opened up by the concept of "becoming-democratic" implies a need for further engagement with the kind of normative political theory undertaken by Rawls and other egalitarian liberals.

Conceptual and Political Constructivism

A further point at which there is overlap or, as Deleuze might say, a "zone of indiscernability" between himself and Rawls emerges in relation to the constructivism of their approaches to political philosophy. However, it is important to be clear about the sense in which each is constructivist and the ways in which their respective constructivisms apply or do not apply to one another. Deleuze's conception of philosophy is constructivist in the sense that he regards philosophical concepts as the outcome of a certain operation or procedure of construction: "Philosophy is a constructivism, and constructivism has two qualitatively different complementary aspects: the creation of concepts and the laying out of a plane" (QP 38, 35–36). One salient feature of his constructivism is that it implies a conception of political philosophical concepts as essentially open-ended and mobile assemblages, always open to new determinations. This way of understanding concepts stands in marked contrast to that of Rawls, whose constant aim throughout the successive versions of his theory of justice has been to develop a conception of justice that can provide a stable point of reference for public debate and the evaluation of institutions that form part of the basic structure of society. He assumes that the meaning of political concepts must remain relatively immobile if they are to serve fundamental purposes of political theory, such as showing that a well-ordered democratic society is possible, serving as the basis of public reason or narrowing the grounds of disagreement between divergent views.

However, while these are important purposes, they are not the only ones served by political concepts. Because political practices and institutions should be able to, and do, change and adapt in response to changing circumstances, shifts in public opinion and modifications in fundamental moral views, so political concepts also should be able to, and do, undergo change. In some cases, institutional and practical change may even be inspired by new concepts or by shifts in the meaning of old ones. Hence the importance of approaches like that of Deleuze, which assume the inevitability and the value of the mobility of political concepts. Deleuze's conception of concepts as mobile assemblages offers both a normative correction to the unquestioned value placed on stability and a better understanding of the nature of political philosophical concepts, including Rawls's own concept of justice.

Deleuze's description of the procedure of constructing concepts above refers to the concept of a "plane" of immanence or, as he describes it elsewhere, an image of thought in terms of which the production of concepts takes place: The plane of immanence is not a further concept that can be thought, but rather "the image of thought, the image thought gives itself of what it means to think, to make use of thought, to find one's bearings in thought" (QP 39–40, 37). His work repeatedly returns to the idea of an alternative "image of thought" that would allow for the essential mobility of philosophical concepts. Together with the project of a transcendental empiricism put forward in *Difference and Repetition*, the ambition to put movement into thought led him to the conception of thought as an open system and to the idea of concepts as inherently subject to variation (see Chapter 1, p. 23).

In Rawls's case, the plane of immanence on which political philosophy takes place is one on which more or less indeterminate political "ideas" (of justice, freedom, democracy, and so on) are rendered progressively more determined and precise. As he explains in *Political Liberalism*, along with the "opinions" or "settled convictions" of the more or less rational and reasonable individuals who live together in political societies, such ideas provide the raw material that philosophy works up into successively more specific "concepts" and "conceptions." Rawls's "ideas" are relatively indeterminate and often fundamental objects of belief and value, such as the idea of society as a fair system of cooperation over time or the idea of citizens as free and equal persons. "Concepts" then specify the meaning of the general terms employed in elaborating such ideas in particular contexts. For example, the concept of justice as applied to social institutions means the absence of "arbitrary distinctions between persons in assigning basic rights and duties" and the existence of mechanisms for achieving "a proper balance between competing claims." Finally, "conceptions" include, in addition to such meanings, particular principles and criteria for deciding "which distinctions are arbitrary and when a balance between competing claims is proper" (Rawls 2005, 14 fn).

Although he does not say much more than this about the nature of philosophical concepts or the process of creating them, it is apparent that Rawls's procedure in formulating his successive conceptions of justice exemplifies the conditions of concept creation as described by Deleuze. The list of components that make up his conception of justice accords with Deleuze's suggestion that in any concept "there are usually bits or components that come from other concepts, which correspond to other problems and presuppose other planes" (QP 23, 18). This list includes a concept of society as a fair system of cooperation, a concept of the basic structure of a society and of the primary goods that all members are supposed to want. It includes a modified conception of a social contract or "original position" in which free, rational, and mutually disinterested individuals behind a veil of ignorance might agree on fundamental principles of justice. It further includes the concept of a "reflective equilibrium" to be established between those principles and the considered convictions of the parties involved.

This internal complexity of concepts implies the need for something that binds together the components of a given concept. Deleuze suggests that this is provided by means of a certain interaction or "communication" between the components: "Components remain distinct, but something passes from one to the other, something that is undecidable between them . . . These zones, thresholds or becomings, this inseparability, define the internal consistency of the concept" (QP 25, 19–20). So, for example, in the terms of Rawls's original conception of justice, the interest of parties to the original position in leading a life according to their own conception of the good ensures the desire of all to at least a certain minimum of primary social goods. Their rationality then is supposed to lead them to adopt the cautious reasoning strategy that leads to the acceptance of the two principles of justice. However, the consistency of a concept must be maintained not only in relation to its component parts but also in relation to other adjacent concepts and the problems to which they respond. In this sense, every concept relates to "an intersection of problems at which it allies itself with other coexisting concepts" (QP 24, 18). While particular concepts are always invented in response to specific problems, their complex relations both internal and external to other concepts ensure the possibility of change as consistency fails or the terms of their problem change. For Deleuze, these connections to other concepts and other problems are one of the sources of mobility between concepts or between successive versions of the same concept. This is precisely what occurred with Rawls's conception of justice.

The movement from Rawls's earlier to his later conception of justice illustrates the manner in which, according to Deleuze, the relations to other concepts provide pathways along which they may be transformed. Every concept has a *"becoming"* that involves its relationship with other contemporaneous concepts such that "every concept, having a finite number of components, will branch off towards other concepts that are differently composed but that constitute other regions of the same plane, that answer to problems that can be connected to each other and that participate in a co-creation" (QP 23–24, 18). At the beginning of *A Theory of Justice*, Rawls points out that justice is the first but not the only virtue of social institutions. The conception of justice that regulates a well-ordered society is necessarily related to other concepts that respond to other fundamental social problems such as coordination, efficiency, and stability (Rawls 1999b, 5). He devoted particular attention to the concept of stability, in part because he sought to make it a feature of his conception of justice that it could be shown to be more stable than competing conceptions. Thus, one of the advantages of his two principles over utility principles is that they do not require some to accept a lesser share of primary social goods for the sake of others (Rawls 1999b, 155). For a well-ordered society to be stable, "Its principles should be such that when they are embodied in the basic structure of society men tend to acquire the corresponding sense of justice and develop a desire to act in accordance with its principles" (Rawls 1999b, 119).

Rawls's argument that the principles of justice as fairness could serve as the basis of stability depended on a series of further arguments about human psychology and the conditions under which individuals acquire a sense of justice. It also relied on an argument about the good of a well-ordered society and the "congruence" of this public good with the individual conceptions of the good present in the society. In turn, this latter argument relied on assumptions about the moral character of citizens and the good of autonomy that could not be sustained once the fact of reasonable pluralism in relation to individual conceptions of the good was taken into account. As a consequence, once the terms of the original problem were broadened to include plurality of comprehensive moral conceptions, and once due weight was given to the public role of the conception of justice in a well-ordered society, a quite different account of stability had to be provided. This led to a series of modifications of the original concept in the form of new component concepts such as the ideas of overlapping consensus and public justification. In his preface to *Political Liberalism*, Rawls attributes these modifications to the theory of justice to the "serious problem" raised by the manner in which the account of stability presented in *A Theory of Justice* was inconsistent with other elements of justice as fairness. In Deleuzian terms, Rawls's problem of stability proved to be the significant vector of the "becoming" of his conception of justice.

These brief comments about Rawls's changing conception of justice show how he can be considered to exemplify Deleuze's constructivism about philosophical concepts. By contrast, Deleuze does not exemplify Rawls's rather different sense of "constructivism" with regard to the content of fundamental political concepts. By a constructivist approach to the theory of justice, Rawls means that the content of a political conception of justice is not derived from prior moral or political truths but rather may be regarded as the outcome of a procedure that models the character and situation of citizens in a democratic society. This content is provided by the principles that rational agents would accept in an original position suitably devised to model what reasonable individuals would regard as fair conditions (Rawls 2005, 103–104). Deleuze's understanding of the process of constructing concepts bears no resemblance to Rawls's procedure for arriving at principles of justice. He is emphatic that philosophy is not a conversation and that its concepts are not the outcome of any sort of agreement or negotiation. If philosophy has "a horror of discussions," this is not because it requires us to be sure of ourselves but on the contrary because it requires that we invent concepts in order to solve problems the precise outlines of which only become clear in their solutions (QP 23, 29).

Nevertheless, despite these differences between Rawls's constructivism about justice and Deleuze's constructivism about concepts, we can see them as connected at a deeper level once we take into account the fact that both are engaged in philosophy as a kind of practical reason. Deleuze defines philosophical concepts as responses to problems: "All concepts are connected to problems without which they would have no meaning" (QP 22, 16). Rawls similarly conceives of his conception of justice as a response to a particular problem, namely the conditions under which a liberal and democratic society might be well ordered, where this means that it is governed in accordance with a public conception of justice. As Christine Korsgaard suggests, his two principles "simply describe what a liberal society must do in order to *be* a [well-ordered] liberal society . . .

Rawls's principles are derived from the idea of liberalism in itself" (Korsgaard 2003, 115). In other words, the aim of *A Theory of Justice* is to provide a conception of the principles of social justice for a society conceived as an association of individuals in which the benefits and burdens of cooperation are fairly shared and in which everyone regulates his or her behavior in accordance with publicly recognized principles of justice. These principles assign basic rights and duties to individuals and define "the appropriate distribution of the benefits and burdens of social cooperation" (Rawls 1999b, 4).

While societies are often not well ordered in this sense, Rawls suggests that people generally recognize the need for some such principles: "Those who hold different conceptions of justice can, then, still agree that institutions are just when no arbitrary distinctions are made between persons in the assigning of basic rights and duties and when the rules determine a proper balance between competing claims to the advantages of social life" (Rawls 1999b, 5). On this basis, "it seems natural to think of the *concept* of justice as distinct from the various *conceptions* of justice and as being specified by the role which these different sets of principles, these different conceptions, have in common" (Rawls 1999b, 5, emphasis added). Following Korsgaard's suggestion, we can say that the term *concept* here refers to whatever solves the underlying problem, whereas *conception* refers to a particular solution to the problem (Korsgaard 2003, 16). Understood in these terms, political philosophy is the construction of conceptions (of justice, democracy, freedom, and so on) in an effort to address some of the problems posed by the effort to live in democratic societies. As I noted above, Rawls presents a more elaborate statement of the concept–conception distinction in *Political Liberalism*. However, the aim of presenting a fixed conception of justice that can serve as the basis for a well-ordered society remains the same. This approach is helpful in relation to some but not all of the problems to which political philosophy responds.

Utopianism and Conceptual Mobility: Justice as a Mobile Concept

To say that Deleuze and Rawls both see philosophical concepts as responses to problems is of course not to say that, in their political philosophy, they respond to the same problems. Rawls's initial concern was to demonstrate that his two principles of justice provided the strongest defence of the possibility of a stable, well-ordered liberal society. His later work, from his 1980 "Kantian Constructivism in Moral Theory" (1999a, pp. 303–358) onward, focused more on the public role of a conception of justice in societies in which the irreducible plurality of comprehensive moral views is both acknowledged and accepted. *Political Liberalism* defends the possibility of a constitutional regime that citizens with different comprehensive views can acknowledge to be just (Laden 2003, 383). Above all, throughout his work he sought to show that the idea of a just society is not unattainable. By contrast, as we noted above, Deleuze's utopianism consists in the ongoing effort to challenge the limits of our present social world. In Rawlsian terms, he might be described as more concerned to show that our liberal democratic societies can always be more just.

Alongside the plane of immanence on which philosophy constructs its concepts, for Deleuze the most important conditions of philosophical creation are the conceptual personae who speak in and through its statements: In philosophy, "we do not do something by saying it but produce movement by thinking it, through the intermediary of a conceptual persona. Conceptual personae are therefore the true agents of enunciation" (QP 63, 64–65). In Rawls's case, the important political philosophical personae are the rational individuals who deliberate over the appropriate principles for a political conception of justice under the reasonable conditions of the original position, the citizens of a well-ordered society whose conduct is regulated by such principles, and the reasonable individual members of society who deliberate, discuss, and argue over the appropriate elements of a political liberal conception of justice and its applicability to existing social and political institutions (Rawls 1999a, 353). By contrast, the authors of *What Is Philosophy?* appear in the dual role of "friend" of the concept and untimely critic who calls for resistance to the present. The complex concept of the "friend" draws on Nietzsche and Blanchot as well as the Greeks in a manner that already incorporates a critical or agonic relationship. Like the later Derrida, their utopianism does not speak in the name of a particular vision of the future, nor does it speak in the completely empty name of an undetermined future. Rather, it appeals to future transformations of the realities that are counter-actualized by existing political concepts. In these terms, Deleuze's concept of becoming-democratic can be seen to respond to the problem of how a society that purports to be democratic might overcome existing limits to the implementation of democratic ideals.[2]

Deleuze's insistence on philosophy's role in the creation of new forms of life is explicitly bound up with the essential mobility of certain concepts, in particular the two that define the normative orientation of his later political philosophy, becoming-revolutionary and becoming-democratic. Insofar as these are concepts of certain kinds of "becoming," they display the "anexactitude" that is needed to think a world in movement (MP 31, 20).[3] They are intrinsically mobile and subject to variation over time because their components include variables designed to register the impact of forces outside of philosophy: relative deterritorialization, becoming-minoritarian, and so on. The different values assumed by these variables will redefine the contours of the process from one historical context to the next. In this way, the concept of becoming-revolutionary expresses an open-ended series of macro- and micropolitical forms of departure from existing norms and institutionalized behaviors. The concept of "becoming-democratic" is the expression of political or institutional movement toward more democratic forms of social life. As such, it is the name of an open-ended series of solutions to a problem peculiar to modern political life (how to become more democratic), rather than the name of any particular solution. In this sense, like the concept of becoming-revolutionary, it is a mobile concept inherently subject to variation.

Rawls's later conception of justice is also mobile in this sense. The significant changes to the conditions of the problem to which the political conception of justice must provide a solution affect the kinds of solution that are now possible. First, to the extent that the aim is a stable conception of justice for a liberal society that takes into account the fact and the reasonableness of a diversity of reasonable comprehensive views, the political conception of justice is led to accept that this might involve consensus around a family of reasonable conceptions of justice rather than a single conception (Rawls 2005, 450). To this extent, reasonable pluralism affects the central condition of a well-ordered society under justice as fairness. Second, this tension between the goals of stability and remaining open to reasonable disagreement also has consequences along a temporal axis, with the result that the conception of justice becomes unavoidably historical and subject to change over time as the settled convictions of citizens change.

In his early presentation of justice as fairness as a political conception in "Justice as Fairness: Political not Metaphysical," Rawls is careful to make it clear that this conception of justice is worked out for a specific kind of society, namely a modern constitutional democracy in which there is a "plurality of conflicting, and indeed incommensurable, conceptions of the good" (Rawls 1999a, 390). Under these conditions, where there are deep disagreements within the tradition of democratic thought, the most that can be hoped for is an overlapping consensus on the principles that should govern the basic structure. The starting point for any such consensus can only be the "settled convictions" of members of the society about what is just, subject to the acknowledgment that "even firmly held convictions gradually change" (Rawls 1999a, 393; 2005, 8). Examples of particular considered convictions that Rawls considers part of the raw material for his theory of justice include the idea of citizens as free and equal persons because "we start within the tradition of democratic thought" (Rawls 1999a, 397; 2005, 18); and the idea that the fact that we occupy a particular social position is not a good reason for us to propose a conception of justice that favors this position (Rawls 1999a, 401; 2005, 24). As examples of change in such convictions, he points to the now widespread acceptance of religious toleration and the inherent injustice of slavery: In modern liberal democratic societies, no one any longer openly advocates the persecution of heretics or the reinstatement of slavery, "however much the aftermath of slavery may persist in social practices and unavowed attitudes" (Rawls 1999a, 393; 2005, 8). The method of political liberalism is to

> collect such settled convictions as the belief in religious toleration and the rejection of slavery and try to organize the basic ideas and principles implicit in these convictions into a coherent political conception of justice. We can regard these convictions as provisional fixed points which any conception of justice must account for if it is to be reasonable for us. (Rawls 1999a, 393; 2005, 8)

Although this passage appears almost identically in *Political Liberalism*, only the earlier version in "Justice as Fairness: Political not Metaphysical," is explicit that the settled convictions are provisional fixed points that the conception of justice must account for "if it is to *be reasonable for us*" (emphasis added). These settled convictions are "provisional" for at least two reasons. First, the procedure to be followed in achieving reflective equilibrium implies that adjustments may occur on the side of our considered convictions as well as on the side of the proposed principles of justice. The reflective equilibrium test requires that we ask how well the theory articulates our considered convictions of political justice, at all levels of generality, after due examination and "once all adjustments and revisions that seem compelling have been made" (Rawls 2005, 28). Thus, for example, we may feel "coerced" when confronted with certain unanticipated consequences of principles we had supposed we recognized, but neverthe-less decide to accept those consequences. Alternatively, "we may reaffirm our more particular judgments and decide instead to modify the proposed conception of justice with its principles and ideals" (Rawls 2005, 45).

Second, the settled convictions are provisional because even our most firmly held convictions may change. The recognition that this may lead to changes in the political conception of justice is implicit in Rawls's suggestion that the conception of justice the parties to the original posi-tion would adopt "identifies the conception of justice that we regard—here and now—as fair and supported by the best reasons" (Rawls 1999a, 402; 2005, 26). The phrase "here and now" points to the fact that the conception of justice adopted under the restrictions imposed by the veil of ignorance expresses the considered opinions of a historically specific form of society. As those opinions change, so will the details of the conception of justice. The details of the overlapping consensus and the content of the resultant form of public reason will vary according to the particular configuration of comprehensive views present, the historical problems and issues that divide the community in question. As Donald Moon com-ments, the content of public reason "is not invariant, but depends upon the context, upon the specific set of divisive political issues the theory ad-dresses" (Moon 2004, 21).

One source of change in the bases of the conception of justice arises from the unavoidable reliance on "current knowledge and the existing sci-entific consensus" in working out what are the principles of justice. Rawls conceded in *A Theory of Justice* that "as established beliefs change, it is possible that the principles of justice which it seems rational to acknowl-edge may likewise change" (Rawls 1999b, 480 [1971, 548]). By way of ex-ample, he pointed to the manner in which it was once believed that a fixed natural order sanctioned a hierarchical society and suggested that the abandonment of this belief set up a tendency in the direction of his two principles of justice. His later formulations are explicit that the aim is to provide a theory of justice for a modern democratic society in which there are no remaining elements of natural hierarchy. Richard Rorty relied on this concession to describe Rawls's conception of justice as approach as "thoroughly historicist and antiuniversalist" (Rorty 1991b, 180).

However, Rawls was reluctant to embrace this consequence. In "Kantian Constructivism," he stressed the reliance of the principles on a moral idea of the person and an associated ideal of a well-ordered society. He described the possibility that changes in general beliefs ascribed to the parties in the original position might lead to changes in the principles of justice as "a mere possibility noted in order to explain the nature of a constructivist view" (Rawls 1999a, 352). He limited the role of general beliefs about human nature and society to that of saying whether these ideals of person and society are feasible and realizable under "normally favorable conditions of human life":

> It is hard to imagine realistically any new knowledge that should convince us that these ideals are not feasible, given what we know about the general nature of the world, as opposed to our particular social and historical circumstances . . . Thus such advances in our knowledge of human nature and society as may take place do not affect our moral conception, but rather may be used to implement the application of its first principles of justice and suggest to us institutions and policies better designed to realize them in practice. (Rawls 1999a, 352)

In reply, it might be asked: Is it so hard to imagine new knowledge that might convince us of the unattainability of liberal ideals of equality and freedom? It is often suggested, for example in literature and film, that new biological or genetic knowledge might undermine our belief in equality and lead to new forms of social hierarchy. Secondly, we might wonder whether it is true that changes in our understanding of human nature and society do not affect our moral convictions but only our views about their conditions of applicability. At the limit, this view would lead to the denial that there is any change in moral conceptions themselves, which is surely implausible.

This brings me to the second possible source of change in the settled convictions that serve as the bases for the theory of justice, namely changes in the moral beliefs of the people concerned. Even within a recognizably modern conception of persons as citizens, it is clear that real change in moral convictions does take place. Consider Kant's distinction in the *Metaphysics of Morals* (6: 314) between active and passive citizens. He was convinced those such as apprentices, domestic servants, minors, and women whose "preservation in existence" depends on others lacked civil personality because they lacked civil independence (Kant 1996, 458). Was he simply mistaken about the content and applicability of the moral ideal of person or citizen, or did he possess a different ideal?

To the extent that we accept the possibility of change in the conception of justice on either grounds, there will be an element of intrinsic mobility in the conception that is not reflected in the philosophical self-understanding provided by Rawls's comments on ideas, concepts, and conceptions. In this regard, Deleuze's conceptual constructivism provides a useful degree of self-awareness about the nature of the concepts produced. Or, to put the problem more sharply in relation to Rawls, the goal of social stability that is expressed in the idea of a well-ordered society is accompanied by an idea of stability in the conception of justice that is incompatible with the conditions of the problem. His political constructivism would benefit from incorporating elements of Deleuze's conceptual constructivism. In addition, to the extent that we endorse the possibility of certain kinds of change, there is further reason to argue for a transformation in the understanding of such political concepts. To the extent that political liberalism aspires not only to justify existing liberal democratic institutions but also to develop these in ways that accord with elements of their existing normative principles, it might be led not only to countenance a 'family' of reasonable conceptions of justice but also to embrace a core liberal conception that is open ended.

Of course, insofar as Rawls is engaged in the relatively limited task of providing a "defense of the possibility of a just constitutional regime," the fact that the outcome is a static account of the principles that should inform such a regime does not pose any problem (Rawls 2005, 101). As we saw, however, a certain kind of critical aspiration was always present in his work. One of the purposes of the theory of justice was to describe "an ideal arrangement, comparison with which defines a standard for judging actual institutions" (Rawls 1999b, 199). His later writings give more prominence to this utopian aspiration, including it among the functions that political philosophy seeks to fulfil, albeit in a very restrained fashion. Political liberalism serves the "realistically utopian" task of "probing the limits of practicable political possibility," asking what a just and democratic society would be like given the actual circumstances of justice but also what it would be like under reasonably favorable but possible historical conditions (Rawls 2001, 4). He recognizes that the limits of the practicable are not simply given by the actual because we can and do change existing social and political institutions; but he has little to say about what determines those limits or how we ascertain what they are (Rawls 2001, 5).

By contrast, as I suggested earlier, the kinds of resistance to the present that challenge the limits of the practicable are a focus of Deleuze's philosophy. Mobile concepts are a way of taking into account the permanent possibility of changes to what is politically possible.[4] In Deleuze's case, the utopian aspirations of his philosophy are self-consciously bound up with the conception of philosophical concepts as inherently mobile assemblages. Applying Deleuze's conceptual constructivism to Rawls's conceptions of justice enables us not only to see his successive conceptions as different determinations of the same underlying concept of justice as fairness and to point to some of the elements of his later conception that open this up to variation and modification over time but also to see why this might be a valuable corrective to the conception of concepts as fixed and invariant. This way of understanding Rawls's conception of justice would allow us to see it not as definitive and fixed but as open to future modification. In Deleuzian terms, this would amount to a concept of becoming-just that parallels the concept of becoming-democratic outlined above. In this sense, we might understand the political conception of justice as the "contour, configuration or constellation of an event to come" (QP 36, 32–33).

Reference Matter

Notes

INTRODUCTION

1. For example, see Belaval 1974, 1061; Descombes 1980, 136–167; Salanskis 2005, 19–20; Worms 2009, 482–489.

2. See also Derrida's comments about Deleuze in his interview with Richard Kearney (Derrida 1999) and his comments in "The Transcendental 'Stupidity' ('*Bêtise*') of Man and the Becoming-Animal according to Gilles Deleuze" (Derrida 2007b).

3. Among recent comparative discussions of Deleuze and Derrida, see Baross 2000, Baugh 2000, Bearn 2000, Goodchild 2000, Lambert 2000 and 2003, Lawlor 2000 and 2003, Patton and Protevi 2003, Barton 2003, Kuiken 2005, Nancy 2005, and Boundas 2005 and 2006.

4. See the essays in Bignall and Patton (2010). Réda Bensmaïa in particular asks how it is that Deleuze influenced so many postcolonial authors despite his relative lack of engagement with postcolonial literature and theory (Bensmaïa 2010, 119–122).

5. On jurisprudence, see P 209–210, 230, 153; 169–170 and his remarks in *L'Abécédaire, G comme Gauche*. On the philosophical function of shame, see QP 103, 108 and P 231, 172. On becoming-revolutionary, see P 231, 171 and D 176, 147. On becoming-democratic, see QP 108, 113. On societies of control, see "Postscript on Societies of Control," P 240–247, 177–182.

6. On societies of control, see Hardt 1998a,b; Hardt and Negri 2000, 325–350; Surin 2006 and 2007. On law, see Lefebvre 2005, 2006, 2008; along with the papers in the *International Journal for the Semiotics of Law*, 20 (1), March 2007, 1–106, and Braidotti, Colebrook, and Hanafin (2009). See also Sutter (2009).

7. Zourabichvili's *Le vocabulaire de Deleuze* begins with the suggestion that "We do not yet know Deleuze's thought," in part through lack of attention to the rigor of his concepts (Zourabichvili 2003, 3).

8. *L'Abécédaire de Gilles Deleuze avec Claire Parnet* is unpublished in literary form but available on videocassette (1996) and DVD (2004) from Vidéo Editions Montparnasse. I am grateful to Charles J. Stivale for his help in transcribing and translating the remarks cited throughout.

9. On Lacan, see Slavoj Žižek, *Organs without Bodies* (Žižek 2004); Dan Smith, "The Inverse Side of the Structure: Žižek on Deleuze on Lacan" (Smith 2004); and Gregg Lambert 2006, 67–101. On Spinoza, see Thomas Nail, "Expression, Immanence and Constructivism: 'Spinozism' and Gilles Deleuze" (Nail 2008). On Nietzsche, see Craig Lundy, "Deleuze's Untimely: Uses and Abuses in the Appropriation of Nietzsche" (Lundy 2009).

CHAPTER I

1. See also N. Katherine Hayles: "Deleuze and Guattari use metaphors indispensable to their argument and treat them as if they were literally true" (Hayles 2001, 156).

2. This remark does not imply opposition to rights in general but only to a way of understanding these that refers back to an already determined and static set of human rights. His comments on jurisprudence in discussion with Parnet in *L'Abécédaire* (Deleuze 1996) and Negri ("Control and Becoming" in Deleuze 1995, 169–176) make it clear that he prefers a conception of rights as in perpetual transformation in accordance with the requirements of a particular situation (see the discussion of these remarks in Chapter 8, below, pp. 172–173).

3. This eulogy was first published as *"Il me faudra errer tout seul," Libération*, 7 November 1995. Available at www.liberation.fr/culture/0101158943-il-me-faudra-errer-tout-seul

4. This interpretation is suggested by his rhetorical question in *Resistances of Psychoanalysis*, in the context of discussing whether Freud invented a new concept of analysis: "Who besides God, has ever *created*, literally 'created,' a concept? Freud had no choice, if he wished to make himself understood, but to inherit from tradition" (Derrida 1996, 33; 1998, 19). Geoffrey Bennington comments that Derrida's question is evidently aimed at Deleuze (Bennington 2000, 100). I am grateful to Jesper Lohmann for providing these references in his paper "Derrida and the Question of the Creation of Concepts" (Lohmann 2002).

5. John Rajchman also comments on the affinities between the "other logic" that Derrida counter-poses to the classical logic of disjunction and inclusion and the logic of qualitative multiplicities that inform Deleuze and Guattari's practice of conceptual creation (Rajchman 2000, 50–76).

6. Derrida refers here to Fontanier's *Les Figures du Discours*, Paris 1821, reprinted 1968.

7. In this Plateau, it is the initial utterance of such order-words that is dated. Elsewhere, *haeccéities* or abstract machines are dated. For an insightful discussion of Deleuze and Guattari's use of dates to identify pure acts or events, see Lampert 2002 and Lampert 2006, 71–96.

8. For a summary of these criticisms, see Grosz 1994, 163–164 and 173–179. For more recent feminist responses to Deleuze's political and conceptual nomadism, see Buchanan and Colebrook 2000, Braidotti 2002, 65–116, and Colebrook and Weinstein 2008.

9. Curiously, Kaplan notes as a consequence of this implied limitation that it makes Deleuze and Guattari's critical gesture useful only to "Europeans and some North Americans," as though outside of Europe the European colonial imaginary was operative only in North America.

CHAPTER 2

1. See also his comments about Deleuze in "Hospitality, Justice and Responsibility: A Dialogue with Jacques Derrida," where he acknowledges his close proximity to the content of Deleuze's philosophy in many respects while insisting that "the process, the style, the idiom, the strategy are so different, so different in fact that you cannot even locate *a* difference, it's another language . . ." (Derrida 1999, 75).

2. This text was first published as "Le siècle et le pardon" in *Le Monde des Débats*, December 1999, before being reprinted in Derrida 2001a and translated in Derrida 2001b. It is also available at http://hydra.humanities.uci.edu/derrida/siecle.html

3. See also his comments at the beginning of "Pragmatism, Davidson and Truth" (Rorty 1991b, 128).

4. Compare Deleuze's comment about the third synthesis of time in *Difference and Repetition*: "As for the third time in which the future appears, this signifies that the event and the act possess a secret coherence which excludes that of the self; that they turn back against the self which has become their equal and smash it to pieces, as though the bearer of the new world were carried away and dispersed by the shock of the multiplicity to which it gives birth . . . " (DR 121, 89–90).

5. Constantin Boundas notes that the structure of temporality that allows Deleuze to speak of an immemorial past that has never been present and a future that can never become present "can also be found in the writings of Jacques Derrida and Emmanuel Levinas" (Boundas 2007, 492).

6. See Deleuze's comments on the sense in which Nietzsche called for the creation of new values where the new "with its power of beginning and beginning again, remains forever new . . . " (DR 177, 136).

7. See the comments on Deleuze and Derrida and the time of the event in Patton and Protevi 2003 by Lorraine, 30–45, and also by Lawlor, 76–77. Simon Critchley remarks that, with regard to the role of the concept of the here-now (*l'ici-maintenant*) in *Specters of Marx*, "the entire plausibility of SdM rests upon the difficult thought of the *here and maintaining-now without presence as an impossible experience of justice.* If this thought proves absolutely unintelligible, then one can perhaps follow Derrida no further" (Critchley 1999, 153–154).

CHAPTER 3

1. For example, in "Habermas and Lyotard on Postmodernity" (Rorty 1991a, 172–173).

2. In an interview that accompanied the publication of *What Is Philosophy?* Deleuze rejects the idea that philosophy could be understood as a conversation involving the exchange of opinions on the grounds that "Neither 'consensus' nor Rorty's 'rules of democratic conversation' are enough to produce a concept" (DRF 354, 382).

3. Gideon Calder takes "redescription" to encapsulate the central motif of Rorty's conception of philosophy (Calder 2007, 3 and 33).

4. Deleuze endorsed the same conception of "theory," also with reference to Proust's characterization of his book as a pair of glasses through which to view the outside, in his 1972 "Intellectuals and Power" discussion with Foucault (ID 290–291, 208).

5. Similarly, in *Nietzsche and Philosophy*, he argued that, in the terms of this image, thought "seeks truth or that it loves truth 'by right,' that it wants truth 'by right'" (NP 108, 95).

6. François Zourabichvili argued that Deleuze was a critical philosopher for whom philosophy was above all a practice of language. Philosophy has no specific object but rather aims to produce literal statements that express express "differential concepts that enable a clinical deciphering of existence as such" (Zourabichvili 2004a, 10). Statements such as "we are made up of lines" are the expression of beliefs that open up new horizons of intelligibility. In this sense, they are involuntary acts that serve as principles of experience for a given subject or community of subjects.

7. Tim Clark explores a further zone of convergence and divergence between Deleuze and Rorty, on the basis of their common debt to a Humean politics of sympathy. He points to similarities as well as differences between Rorty's limited conception of the aims of sentimental politics and Deleuze and Guattari's theory of minoritarian becoming. Whereas Rorty conceives of the extension of sympathy entirely in terms of existing identities and political institutions, Deleuze and Guattari "carry the Humean principle of maximally extended sympathy to its logical, cosmopolitical end" (Clark 2008, 38).

CHAPTER 4

1. Deleuze and Guattari's text distinguishes between "l'Histoire," meaning the intellectual discipline, and "l'histoire," meaning the course of events. Sometimes his distinction is obscured in the English translation, for example when a sentence begins with "History." To draw attention to the occasions when they are concerned with the difference between the disciplines of History and Philosophy, both terms are capitalized throughout this chapter.

2. In his 1967 essay on structuralism, Deleuze writes: "As regards time, the position of structuralism is thus quite clear: time is always a time of actualization, according to which the elements of virtual coexistence are carried out [*s'effectuent*] at diverse rhythms. Time goes from the virtual to the actual, that is,

from structure to its actualizations, and not from one actual form to another . . ." (ID 251–251, 180).

3. According to Althusser, "For each mode of production there is a peculiar time and history, punctuated in a specific way by the development of the productive forces" (Althusser and Balibar 1970, 99). Because elements of different modes of production can coexist in a given social formation, this implies that different levels of the social formation will develop in their own relatively independent "times." Ted Stolze comments on the "striking affinity" between this aspect of Deleuze's conception of time and that of Althusser and Balibar (Stolze 1998, 60).

4. *Kairos* refers to "a qualitative character of time, to the special position an event or action occupies in a series, to a season when something appropriate happens that cannot happen at 'any' time but only at 'that time,' to a time which marks an opportunity which may not recur" (Smith 1969, 1).

5. This is one of those shifts in Deleuze's thought that calls for interpretative caution. See his "Author's Note for the Italian edition of *Logic of Sense*," where he comments on the relation of this book to *Difference and Repetition* and suggests that, although the concepts remained the same, they were reorganized in relation to the problem of surfaces: "The concepts changed and so did the method, a type of serial method peculiar to surfaces; and the language changed" (DRF 60, 65).

6. James Williams provides a helpful discussion of Bousquet and the concept of freedom that is implied in Deleuze's comments about him and his work (Williams 2008, 153–158).

7. This last phrase is a direct quotation from Nietzsche's "On the Uses and Disadvantages of History for Life" (Nietzsche 1983, 60). See also "Overturning Platonism" (LS 306, 265).

8. See also the description of the May events in *A Thousand Plateaus* as a molecular flow or "line of flight" (MP 264, 216); in *Dialogues* as the "explosion of . . . a molecular line" (D 159, 132); and in *Negotiations* as "pure reality breaking through" (P 198, 144–145).

9. In *The Gay Science*, Paragraph 343 "*The meaning of our cheerfulness*," he describes the death of God as an event "far too great, distant, and out of the way even for its tidings to be thought of as having *arrived* as yet. Even less may one suppose many to know at all *what* this event really means—and, now that this faith has been undermined, how much must collapse because it was built on this faith, leaned on it, had grown into it—for example, our entire European morality" (Nietzsche 2001, 199).

10. Foucault's text actually contrasts this border region with "our actuality" (Foucault 1969, 172; 1972, 130). Deleuze offers a more extended commentary on this passage from *The Archaeology of Knowledge* in "What Is a Dispositif?" where he writes: "The novelty of a *dispositif* in relation to those that precede it is what we call its actuality, our actuality. The new is the *actuel*. The *actuel* is not what we are but rather what we are becoming, what we are in the process of becoming,

that is to say the Other, our becoming-other. In every *dispositif* we must distinguish what we are (what we are already no longer) and what we are becoming: the part of history and the part of the actual." The original text reads: "*La nouveauté d'un dispositif par rapport aux précédents, nous l'appelons son actualité, notre actualité. Le nouveau, c'est l'actuel. L'actuel n'est pas ce que nous sommes, mais plutôt ce que nous devenons, ce que nous sommes en train de devenir, c'est-à-dire l'Autre, notre devenir-autre. Dans tout dispositif, il faut distinguer ce que nous sommes (ce que nous ne sommes déjà plus), et ce que nous sommes en train de devenir: la part de l'histoire, et la part de l'actuel*" (DRF 322, 350).

11. See DR 244–245,189; LS 68, 53; QP 106–107, 111; and P 230, 170.

12. Compare the same account in Deleuze's interview with Negri:

> In a major philosophical work, *Clio*, Péguy explained that there are two ways of considering events, one being to follow the course of the event, gathering how it comes about historically, how it's prepared and then decomposes in history, while the other way is to go back into the event, to take one's place in it as in a becoming, to grow both young and old in it at once, going through all its components or singularities. Becoming isn't part of history; history amounts only to the set of preconditions, however recent, that one leaves behind in order to "become," that is, to create something new. This is precisely what Nietzsche calls the Untimely. (P 231, 170–171)

See also James Williams's commentary on this passage and the differences between Péguy and Deleuze (Williams 2009, 142–149).

13. Deleuze sometimes appears to suggest that Foucault's genealogical method is not historical (P 130, 94). However, what he means is what he says more clearly in "What Is a *Dispositif*?" namely that Foucault, like Nietzsche, used history but for the ahistorical purpose of diagnosing and reinforcing certain kinds of becoming-other in contemporary societies (DRF 323–325, 350–352). In *Foucault*, he suggests that what interests Foucault are the historical conditions of particular forms of knowledge, power, and relation to the self: "This is why he calls his work historical research and not the work of a historian" (F 124, 1116).

14. This analysis appears initially in Plateau 8: "1874: Three Novellas, or 'What Happened?'" but reappears in Plateau 9: "1933: Micropolitics and Segmentarity" and in Chapter 4 ("Many Politics") of *Dialogues*. My discussion of these lines draws on all three of these presentations.

15. Guillaume Sibertin-Blanc, in an excellent discussion of this plateau in the course of an account of Deleuze's antihistoricism, describes the question raised by events of this molecular kind—"What happened?"—as the "form of expression of historicity as a pure form of thought" (*forme d'expression de l'historicité comme forme pure de la pensée*) (Sibertin-Blanc 2003, 137).

16. This phrase roughly translates Deleuze and Guattari's deliberately paradoxical formula in relation to "becoming-imperceptible": "One has become like everybody else but in a way that nobody else can become like everybody else"

(MP 244, 200). Sibertin-Blanc describes the rupture effected on this line as a pure event, abstracted from any notion of the past. As such, it provides "the unconditioned Idea which abolishes history, but the superior experience of which gives history to thought as a problem" (*Idée inconditionée qui abolit l'histoire mais dont l'expérience supérieure donne à la pensée l'histoire comme problème*) (Sibertin-Blanc 2003, 141). Note that in Deleuze's earlier discussion of Fitzgerald's *The Crack-Up* in *The Logic of Sense*, Series 22 "Porcelain and Volcano," the third line is not mentioned. There is only a two level distinction in which Fitzgerald's crack is identified with the incorporeal pure event (LS 181, 155).

17. The translation of this passage is modified. The English text goes on to say that becoming is "the opposite" of history, thereby eliminating all the nuance of Deleuze's use of the verb *s'opposer*.

CHAPTER 5

1. He published a series of articles on the plight of the Palestinian people including "Les gêneurs" in *Le Monde,* April 7, 1978, translated as "Spoilers of Peace," (DRF 147–149, 161–163); "Les Indiens de Palestine" in *Libération*, May 8–9, 1982, translated as "The Indians of Palestine" (DRF 179–184, 194–200); "Grandeur de Yasser Arafat" in the *Revue d'Études Palestiniennes*, 10, 1984, translated as "The Importance of Being Arafat" (DRF 221–225, 241–245); and "Les Pierres" in *Al-Karmel*, 29, 1988, translated as "Stones" (DRF 311–312, 338–339). Guillaume Sibertin-Blanc discusses Deleuze's friendship with Elias Sanbar and his involvement with the *Revue d'Études Palestiniennes* (Sibertin-Blanc, in press). See also Dosse 2007, 308–311. Sibertin-Blanc also points to Deleuze's long-standing interest in the question of national minorities, stemming from his study of Kafka in 1975 and reflected in the brief remarks about minorities at the end of Plateau 13 "7000 B.C.: Apparatus of Capture."

2. See also "The Grandeur of Yassar Arafat," where he comments that "Israel never once hid its aims: to empty the Palestinian territory. Even better, to act as if the land was already empty, since it had always been destined for the Zionists. It was indeed a question of colonization, but not in the nineteenth century European sense: instead of exploiting the country's inhabitants, they would be forced out . . ." (DRF 222, 242).

3. See the essays in Bignall and Patton 2010.

4. In a letter originally published as a preface to Jean-Clet Martin's *Variations* (Martin 1993), Deleuze offers the following advice: "In the analysis of concepts, it is always better to begin with extremely simple, concrete situations, not with philosophical antecedents, *not even with problems as such* (the one and the multiple, etc) . . . I have only one thing to tell you: stick to the concrete and always return to it" (DRF 339, 366–367).

5. The concept of the untimely is drawn from Nietzsche, while the concept of the "aternal" is drawn from Péguy (see Chapter 4, pp. 93–96).

6. I owe this example to Eugene Holland.

7. These are the terms in which Justice Burton described Aboriginal law in the 1836 New South Wales case of *R v Murrell* (Reynolds 1996, 62).

8. *Mabo v Queensland* (1992) 175 *CLR* 1; 66 *ALJR* 408; 107 *ALR* 1. Future references are to Bartlett 1993.

9. *Delgamuukw v British Columbia* (1997) 3 SCR 1010. Future references are to Persky 1998. As in the Australian case above, the Canadian judges characterized Aboriginal title as a form of property that arose in the encounter between two legal orders. Chief Justice Lamer suggested that the characteristics of Aboriginal title "cannot be completely explained by reference either to the common law rules of real property or to the rules of property found in aboriginal legal systems. As with other aboriginal rights, it must be understood by reference to both common law and aboriginal perspectives" (Persky 1998, 86). Alexandre Lefebvre discusses *Delgamuukw* as evidence for the Deleuzian view of legal concepts as created and composite and as evidence for the view that adjudication, like thought, is at its best when it involves the creation of problems (Lefebvre 2008, 207–238).

10. See *Thus Spoke Zarathustra*, Book II, "On Great Events": "The greatest events—those are not our loudest but our stillest hours. Not around the inventors of new noise, but around the inventors of new values does the world revolve; *inaudibly* it revolves" (Nietzsche 2005, 114).

11. Deleuze uses another form of this geographically specific image in *The Logic of Sense* when he refers to incorporeal events as understood by the Stoics as like "a mist over the prairie" (LS 14–15, 5).

12. Deleuze here alludes to Nietzsche's characterization of untimely thought as "acting counter to our time and thereby acting on our time and, let us hope, for the benefit of a time to come" (Nietzsche 1983, 60). See Chapter 4, pp. 88–89.

13. Marcelo Svirsky provides a compelling argument to show that the Zionist colonization of Palestine involved a novel form of *Terra Nullius*: a unique collective assemblage of desire that sought to produce "the effective incremental disappearance of the Other" ("The Production of *Terra Nullius* and the Zionist-Palestinian Conflict," in Bignall and Patton 2010, 220–250).

14. *Calder et al v Attorney-General of British Columbia* 1973 SCR 313. For this and other key Canadian cases, see Kulchyski 1984.

15. See Asch 1999; Patton 2001.

16. *Wik Peoples v Queensland (1996) 187 CLR 1; Yorta Yorta Aboriginal Community v Victoria (2002) 194 ALR 538*. For an account of these and other key Australian native title cases, see Strelein 2006.

CHAPTER 6

1. Affinities between Deleuze and Coetzee, particularly those arising from their shared interest in Kafka, have been noted by a number of French critics. See Engélibert 2003, 2007a; Brezault 2007; Coqio 2007; and Gabaude 2007. See also Hamilton 2010.

2. Derek Attridge identifies explicit points of connection between the lives of the characters and "the times" in which they live, which he locates in South Africa around 1997 or 1998 (Attridge 2004, 165–172).

3. Grant Farred comments that, through Lurie's intransigence, "Coetzee takes us away from the heart of the country to the hard core of the dilemma: How does one reform the recalcitrant?" (Farred 2002, 17).

4. In April 2000, the ANC used *Disgrace* as evidence of persistent racism among white South Africans in a submission to a Human Rights Commission inquiry into racism in the media. For discussion of this episode and its implied reading of the novel, see McDonald 2002 and Attwell 2002.

5. Lucy's affirmation of these words, which are also the last words of K in Kafka's *The Trial*, amounts to her acceptance of a form of humiliation that Catherine Coquio describes in the following terms: "The humiliation of the descendants of colonizers is the new form of shame in a world in which the innocent has become *really* guilty, in which a *crime* has indeed occurred and for which reparation must be made with her person. Disgrace is the form assumed in Coetzee's novel by the bitter survival (*survivance*) with which Kafka quits his readers at the end of *The Trial*" (Coquio 2007, 97–98).

6. Relative (as opposed to absolute) deterritorialization is negative when the deterritorialized element is immediately subjected to forms of reterritorialization that enclose or obstruct its line of flight. It is positive when the line of flight prevails over secondary reterritorializations, even though it may still fail to connect with other deterritorialized elements or enter into a new assemblage (MP 634–635, 508–510). See also Patton 2000, 106–107.

7. Georgina Horrell argues that the conditions of white people remaining in the new South Africa are "negotiated through the body of the (white) woman in the text . . . an inscription of guilt is performed upon gendered flesh. The implications of this observation demand interrogation" (Horrell 2002, 31, 32). See also Louise Bethlehem 2002.

8. This phrase recalls the note left by little Jude in Thomas Hardy's *Jude The Obscure*: "*Done because we are too menny*" (Hardy 1998, 336)

9. Elleke Boehmer comments on the role of animals in *Disgrace* as "the essential third term in the reconciliation of human self and human other" (Boehmer 2002, 346). She also points to Lurie's abjection in the course of the attack and suggests that it is "from this point on that Lurie begins to work out that breakthrough into feeling the self of another, rather than rationalizing its experiences in terms of his own needs" (Boehmer 2002, 348). She goes on to point out problematic aspects of this apparent "atonement" on Lurie's part.

10. Giorgio Agamben distinguishes Deleuze's concept of life from Aristotle's concept of the bare biological life common to all living things. For Aristotle, the condition or ground on which a thing is said to be living is what he calls the "nutritive faculty." This is "the movement implied in nutrition and decay or growth. This is why all plants seem to us to live. It is clear that they have in themselves

a principle and a capacity by means of which they grow and decay in opposite directions . . ." (Aristotle, *De anima*, cited Agamben 1999: 231). Aristotle's characterization of the nutritive faculty describes the most basic, vegetative form of life, thereby providing a principle on the basis of which other things can be called living. By contrast, Deleuze's concept of life functions in the opposite way. It is not the lowest common form of life shared by all living things but rather "a principle of virtual indetermination, in which the vegetative and the animal, the inside and the outside and even the organic and the inorganic . . . cannot be told apart" (Agamben 1999, 233). It is because this virtual is not a transcendent plane of existence but a more profound dimension of the actual world that Deleuze's ontology is a philosophy of immanence.

CHAPTER 7

1. In an interview after the publication of *Mille Plateaux* (1980), Deleuze described this book as "philosophy, nothing but philosophy, in the traditional sense of the word" (DRF 163, 176). In an interview in 1988, he suggested that "A philosophy is what Félix and I tried to produce in *Anti-Oedipus* and *A Thousand Plateaus*, especially in *A Thousand Plateaus*, which is a long book putting forward many concepts" (P 187, 136).

2. Deleuze, "Postscript on Control Societies" (P 240–247, 177–182). For commentary see: Hardt 1998a,b; Hardt and Negri 2000; Razac 2008; and Surin, 2006, 2007.

3. This chapter is a slightly revised version of Miller 1993. See also the exchange between Miller and Eugene Holland over the question of the referential status of Deleuze and Guattari's concepts in *Research in African Literatures*, 34, 2003 (Holland 2003a, b and Miller 2003). Unlike Miller, Hardt and Negri do recognize that the concept of nomads is a primarily normative rather than an empirical concept, the purpose of which is to express forces of resistance to the mechanisms of control. They specify that these must be forces that are "capable of not only organizing the destructive power of the multitude, but also constituting through the desires of the multitude an alternative" (Hardt and Negri 2000, 214).

4. Todd May draws attention to the dangers of the different kinds of line, and to the contextual and experimental character of Deleuze and Guattari's ethico-political injunctions. He describes these as "ways to conceive ourselves and our being together that allow us to begin to experiment with alternatives. But there is no general prescription. There are only analyses and experiments in a world that offers us no guarantees, because it is always other and more than we can imagine" (May 2005, 152).

5. Alexandre Lefebvre points out that the real enemy of the BwO is not simply the organism but the principle of reflective judgment that "takes the organism as a purposive whole and assigns to its parts functions within that organization" (Lefebvre 2008, 150). The normativity implicit in Deleuze and Guattari's concepts therefore opposes a very particular kind of judgment, namely reflective

teleological judgment that views nature and its parts as purposive: "The *judgment of God*, the system of the judgment of God, the theological system, is precisely the operation of He who makes an organism, an organization of organs called the organism, because He cannot bear the BwO" (MP 196–197, 158–159).

6. At one point, they refer to the "paradox" of fascism understood in terms of the ambiguity of the line of flight, although without spelling out precisely what is the paradox: that of a suicidal state perhaps (MP 281, 230)?

7. May contrasts Deleuze's post-Nietzschean concern with the question of how we might live in the absence of any transcendent grounds of conduct with the Kantian concern with how we should act (May 2005, 1–25). While Deleuze does not suppose a universal framework of judgment in the manner of Kant, there is no reason to think that he would deny the importance of historical and contingent principles of public right that govern our ways of living together.

8. Kenneth Surin elaborates on the difference between the question of revolution posed in terms of the actual and the question of becoming-revolutionary posed in terms of the virtual in commenting on Deleuze's "Immanence: A Life" (Surin 2005). He suggests that the question of whether revolution is possible is uninteresting when posed in terms of the actual because it cannot encompass the truly revolutionary break with the actual. Only the question posed in terms of the virtual can encompass the conditions under which absolute deterritorialization is manifest in positive form, leading to new kinds of social assemblage, new Earths, and new peoples.

9. Eyal Weizman provides a striking example of the political polyvalence of the concept of smooth space in "Walking through Walls" (Weizman 2006, 11). He describes the Israeli military tactic of literally walking through walls and presents evidence in the form of interviews with Israeli Defence Force officers to show that they drew on Deleuze and Guattari's concepts of smooth and striated space to theorize this tactic. See also Weizman 2007, 200–201.

10. For example, Mandle 2000; Peffer 1990 and 2001. For an introduction to some of the varieties of "analytic" Marxism, see Kymlicka 2002, 166–207. For a comprehensive survey of the debate over Marx and justice, see Geras 1985.

11. See Genosko 2009, chapter 3, and Dosse 2007, 454–463.

12. See his conversations with Antonin Dulaure and Claire Parnet, published in *L'Autre Journal*, 8, October 1985, and with Raymond Bellour and François Ewald, published in the *Magazine Littéraire*, 257, September 1988 (P 165–212, 121–155). For comments on Deleuze's remarks, see Daniel Smith 2003, 314–315, and Chapter 8, pp. 172–175.

13. Philippe Mengue's provocative argument that Deleuze is fundamentally antithetical to democracy provided an important stimulus to my thinking about this question (Mengue 2003). For further discussion of his argument, see Chapter 8.

14. See also the commentaries on this text by Foucault, Habermas, and Lyotard mentioned here by Deleuze (QP 96, 100 n.13).

CHAPTER 8

1. See, for example, Cunningham 2001; Derrida 1993, 1994b; Laclau and Mouffe 1985; Peffer 2001; Smith 1998.

2. Similarly, in a short text originally published in Arabic in 1988, he comments: "They say the Israeli secret service are admired throughout the world. But what sort of a democracy is it whose politics are indistinguishable from the actions of its secret service?" (DRF 312, 334).

3. Mengue refers to Claude Lefort's idea that democracy is the sole political regime to function without foundations. See Lefort 1988, chapter 1.

4. See also the discussions of the "politics of becoming" and the "ethos of critical responsiveness" in Connolly 1995 and 2002.

5. This letter was first published in *La Repubblica*, May 10, 1979.

6. Similarly, in conversation with Raymond Bellour and François Ewald in 1988, when asked why, unlike Foucault, he took no part in the human rights movement, Deleuze replied: "If you are talking about establishing new forms of transcendence, new universals, restoring a reflective subject as the bearer of rights, or setting up a communicative intersubjectivity, then it's not much of a philosophical advance" (P 208, 152).

7. For a related approach to an immanent historical understanding of the origin of rights, see Patton 2004, 43–61.

8. I discuss Deleuze's interest in jurisprudence with reference to the role of law in colonization in Patton 2000, 120–131. Daniel Smith comments on this discussion and on these passages from *L'Abécédaire* (Smith 2003, 312–317). Alexandre Lefebvre also comments on these passages in discussing Deleuze's concept of jurisprudence (Lefebvre 2008, 53–59).

9. Elsewhere, after redescribing the noncoincidence of minority and majority in the language of axiomatic set theory, they write, "this is not to say that the struggle on the level of the axioms is without importance; on the contrary, it is determining (at the most diverse levels): women's struggle for the vote, for abortion, for jobs; the struggle of the regions for autonomy; the struggle of the Third World" (MP 588, 470–471).

10. Rawls admits this dependency of the principles of justice on current knowledge and the existing scientific consensus and concedes that "as established beliefs change, it is possible that the principles of justice which it seems rational to choose may likewise change" (Rawls 1999b, 480; 1971, 548). For this reason, Rorty describes his approach as "thoroughly historicist and antiuniversalist" (Rorty 1991b, 180). This feature of Rawls's political liberalism, along with the sense in which it seeks to elaborate a conception of justice on the basis of values immanent to the political culture of modern liberal democratic societies, allows the comparison with Deleuze's political philosophy in Chapter 9.

11. Although this expression is widely used by Derrida, Deleuze and Guattari also describe the kind of concept that philosophy creates as "the contour, the

configuration, the constellation of an event to come" (QP 36, 32–33). I argue for the partial convergence between the philosophical vocabularies of Deleuze and Derrida with respect to their orientation toward an open future in Chapter 2 above, p. 57.

CHAPTER 9

1. Eugene Holland draws a useful distinction between utopianisms that elaborate an ideal blueprint and utopianism as process to suggest that Deleuze's utopianism is of the latter kind (Holland 2006, 218).

2. The weakness of Deleuze's concept is that it remains at the level of naming the problem when what is required are conceptions of what becoming-democratic might mean in the present. My attempt to elaborate some of the forms that becoming-democratic might take in the present are gestures towards such a conception (see above, pp. 192–193; Chapter 8, pp. 156–159).

3. See Chapter 1, p. 23. In *A Thousand Plateaus*, Deleuze and Guattari define what they call "minoritarian becoming" as the variety of ways in which individuals or groups differ or differentiate themselves from the standards or norms of behavior, in particular domains of social life: becoming-animal, becoming-woman, becoming-child, and so on. In its most general sense, however, the "becoming" of empirical objects and states of affairs must be understood in the light of their concern with the emergence of the new alongside or at the same time as maintenance of what is. In these terms, becoming in the realm of the sensible is defined in *What Is Philosophy?* as "the action by which something or someone continues to become other (while continuing to be what it is)" (QP 168, 177).

4. William Connolly points to a further problem with respect to political liberalism's understanding of the concepts of justice, personhood, and the reasonable, on which it relies. Given the possibility of ongoing changes to what it is possible to say, to do, or to be and therefore changes to what is practically politically possible, the (static) conception of justice that provides the standard of critical evaluation of existing institutions will inevitably lag behind newly emerging forms of reasonable criticism of existing limits: "Rawls is pulled by the demand that things be still at bottom. He wants—after the historical becoming of secularism—persons and the generic facts about them to remain stationary so that liberal justice can be (nearly) sufficient unto itself . . . But it is even more important to remember that things don't stay still. Even the dense, unconscious coding of personhood shifts over time" (Connolly 1999, 69).

Bibliography

Agamben, G. (1999). "Absolute Immanence," in *Potentialities: Collected Essays in Philosophy*, pp. 220–239. Stanford, CA: Stanford University Press. Reprinted in Jean Khalfa, ed., *An Introduction to the Philosophy of Gilles Deleuze*, 151–169. London: Continuum, 2003.

Althusser, L., and Balibar, E. (1970). *Reading Capital*. London: New Left Books.

Anscombe, E. (1959). *Intention*. Oxford, UK: Blackwell.

Asch, M. (1999). "From *Calder* to *Van der Peet*: Aboriginal Rights and Canadian Law, 1973–96," in P. Havemann, ed., *Indigenous Peoples' Rights in Australia, Canada & New Zealand*, 428–446. Auckland, NZ: Oxford University Press.

Attridge, D. (2004). *J. M. Coetzee and the Ethics of Reading: Literature in the Event*. Chicago and London: The University of Chicago Press.

Attwell, D. (2002). "Race in *Disgrace*." *Interventions*, 4:3, 331–341.

Austin, J. L. (1975). *How to Do Things with Words*, edited by J. O. Urmson and Marina Sbisà. Oxford, UK: Oxford University Press.

Baross, Z. (2000). "Deleuze and Derrida, by Way of Blanchot: An Interview." *Angelaki*, 5:2, 17–41.

Bartlett, Richard H., ed. (1993). *The Mabo Decision*. Sydney, Australia: Butterworths.

Barton, John C. (2003). "Iterability and the Order-Word Plateau: 'A Politics of the Performative' in Derrida and Deleuze/Guattari." *Critical Horizons*, 4:2, 227–264.

Battersby, C. (2003). "Terror, Terrorism and the Sublime: Rethinking the Sublime after 1789 and 2001." *Postcolonial Studies*, 6:1, 67–89.

Baudrillard, J. (1995). *The Gulf War Did Not Take Place*, Paul Patton, trans. Sydney, Australia: Power Institute Publications.

Baugh, B. (2000). "Death and Temporality in Deleuze and Derrida." *Angelaki*, 5:2, 73–83.

Bearn, Gordon C. F. (2000). "Differentiating Derrida and Deleuze." *Continental Philosophy Review* 33: 441–465.

Belaval, Y. (1974). "*La philosophie de langue française depuis la second guerre mondiale,*" *Encyclopédie de la Pléiade, Histoire de la Philosophie*, III, 1046–1063. Paris: Éditions Gallimard.

Bell, J., and Colebrook, C., eds. (2009). *Nietzsche and History*. Edinburgh, UK: Edinburgh University Press.

Bennington, G. (2000). *Interrupting Derrida*. London and New York: Routledge.

Bensmaïa, R. (2010). "Postcolonial Haecceities," in Bignall and Patton, eds. (2010), 119–162.

Bethlehem, L. (2002). "Pliant/compliant; grace/Disgrace; plaint/complaint." *scrutiny2*, 7:1, 20–24.

Bignall, S., and Patton, P., eds. (2010). *Deleuze and the Postcolonial*. Edinburgh, UK: Edinburgh University Press.

Blanchot, M. (1992) *The Infinite Conversation*, Susan Hanson, trans. Minneapolis: University of Minnesota Press.

Boehmer, E. (2002). "Not Saying Sorry, Not Speaking Pain: Gender Implications in *Disgrace*." *Interventions* 4:3, 342–351.

Bogue, R. (2003). *Deleuze on Literature*. London and New York: Routledge.

Borrows, J. (2001). "Questioning Canada's Title to Land: The Rule of Law, Aboriginal Peoples and Colonialism," in *Speaking Truth to Power: A Treaty Forum*, 35–72. Ottawa: Law Commission of Canada/ Vancouver: British Columbia Treaty Commission.

Boundas, C. V. (2005). "Review Essay: Between Deleuze and Derrida." *Symposium*, 9:1, 99–114.

———. (2006). "What Difference Does Deleuze's Difference Make?" *Symposium*, 10:1 (Spring), 397–423. Reprinted in Boundas, ed., *Deleuze and Philosophy*, 3–30. Edinburgh, UK: Edinburgh University Press, 2006.

———. (2007). "Different/ciations: The Case of Gilles Deleuze," in Boundas, ed., *The Edinburgh Companion to Twentieth-Century Philosophies*, 489–503. Edinburgh, UK: Edinburgh University Press.

Braidotti, R. (2002). *Metamorphoses: Towards a Materialist Theory of Becoming*. Cambridge, UK: Polity.

Braidotti, R., Colebrook, C., and Hanafin, P. (2009). *Deleuze and Law: Forensic Futures*. Houndmills, Basingstoke, UK: Palgrave Macmillan.

Brandom, R. (2001). "Reason, Expression and the Philosophic Enterprise," in C. P. Ragland and S. Heidt, eds., *What Is Philosophy?* 74–95. New Haven and London: Yale University Press.

Brezault, Éloïse. (2007). "*L'artiste en jeune homme: un autre fiction*." In Engélibert, ed. (2007), 167–179.

Buchanan, I., and Colebrook, C., eds. (2000). *Deleuze and Feminist Theory*. Edinburgh, UK: Edinburgh University Press.

Buchanan, I., and Thoburn, N., eds. *Deleuze and Politics*. Edinburgh, UK: Edinburgh University Press.

Calder, G. (2007). *Rorty's Politics of Redescription*. Cardiff, UK: University of Wales Press.

Caputo, J. D. (1997). *Deconstruction in a Nutshell*. New York: Fordham University Press.

Chesterman, J., and Galligan, B. (1997). *Citizens without Rights: Aborigines and Australian Citizenship*. Melbourne, Australia: Cambridge University Press.

Clark, T. (2008). "Becoming Everyone: The Politics of Sympathy in Deleuze and Rorty." *Radical Philosophy*, 147 (January/February), 33–44.

Coetzee, J. M. (1999). *Disgrace*. London: Secker & Warburg.

Connolly, W. E. (1995). *The Ethos of Pluralization*. Minneapolis and London: University of Minnesota Press.

———. (1999). *Why I Am Not a Secularist*. Minneapolis and London: University of Minnesota Press.

———. (2002) *Neuropolitics: Thinking, Culture, Speed*. Minneapolis and London: University of Minnesota Press.

Colebrook, C., and Weinstein, J., eds. (2008). *Deleuze and Gender. Deleuze Studies*, Volume 2, Supplement. Edinburgh, UK: Edinburgh University Press.

Coquio, C. (2007). "'Comme un chien,' Coetzee et Kafka," in Engélibert, ed. (2007), 89–106.

Critchley, S. (1999). *Ethics-Politics-Subjectivity*. London and New York: Verso.

Cunningham, F. (2001). "Whose Socialism? Which Democracy?" in M. Howard, ed., *Socialism*. Amherst, NY: Humanity Books.

Day, D. (1996). *Claiming a Continent: A History of Australia*. Sydney, Australia: Angus & Robertson.

Deleuze, G. (1953). *Empirisme et subjectivité. Essai sur la nature humaine selon Hume*. Paris: Presses Universitaires de France.

———. (1962). *Nietzsche et la philosophie*. Paris: Presses Universitaires de France.

———. (1963). *La Philosophie critique de Kant*. Paris: Presses Universitaires de France.

———. (1966). *Le Bergsonisme*. Paris: Presses Universitaires de France.

———. (1968a). *Différence et répétition*. Paris: Presses Universitaires de France.

———. (1968b). *Spinoza et le problème de l'expression*. Paris: Éditions de Minuit.

———. (1969). *Logique du sens*. Paris: Éditions de Minuit.

———. (1983). *Nietzsche and Philosophy*, Hugh Tomlinson, trans. Minneapolis: University of Minnesota Press.

———. (1986a). *Foucault*. Paris: Éditions de Minuit.

———. (1986b). *Kafka: For a Minor Literature*, Dana Polan, trans. Minneapolis: University of Minnesota Press.

———. (1988a). *Foucault*, Seán Hand, trans. Minneapolis: University of Minnesota Press.

———. (1988b). *Le Pli: Leibniz et le Baroque*. Paris: Éditions de Minuit.

———. (1990a). *The Logic of Sense*, Mark Lester with Charles Stivale, trans.; Constantin Boundas, ed. New York: Columbia University Press.

———. (1990b). *Pourparlers*. Paris: Éditions de Minuit.

———. (1993a). *Critique et clinique*. Paris: Éditions de Minuit.

———. (1993b). *The Fold: Leibniz and the Baroque*, Tom Conley, trans. Minneapolis and London: University of Minnesota Press.

————. (1994). *Difference and Repetition*, Paul Patton, trans. London: Athlone; New York: Columbia University Press.

————. (1995). *Negotiations 1972–1990*, Martin Joughin, trans. New York: Columbia University Press.

————. (1996). *L'Abécédaire de Gilles Deleuze avec Claire Parnet*, available on videocassette and DVD (2004) from Vidéo Editions Montaparnasse.

————. (1997). *Essays Critical and Clinical*. Daniel W. Smith and Michael A. Greco, trans. Minneapolis: University of Minnesota Press.

————. (2002). *L'Île Désert et Autres Textes. Textes et Entretiens 1953–1974*, David Lapoujade, ed. Paris: Éditions de Minuit.

————. (2003). *Deux Régimes de Fous. Textes et Entretiens 1975–1995*, David Lapoujade, ed. Paris: Éditions de Minuit.

————. (2004). *Desert Islands and Other Texts 1953–1974*, David Lapoujade, ed.; Mike Taormina, trans. New York: Semiotext(e).

————. (2007). *Two Regimes of Madness: Texts and Interviews 1975–1995*, Ames Hodges and Mike Taormina, trans. New York: Semiotext(e) [Revised Edition].

Deleuze, G., and Guattari, F. (1972). *L'Anti-Oedipe*. Paris: Éditions de Minuit.

————. (1975). *Kafka: pour une littérature mineure*. Paris: Éditions de Minuit.

————. (1976). *Rhizome*. Paris: Éditions de Minuit.

————. (1980). *Mille plateaux*. Paris: Éditions de Minuit.

————. (1981). "Rhizome," Paul Foss and Paul Patton, trans. *Ideology & Consciousness*, 8, 49–71.

————. (1987). *A Thousand Plateaus: Capitalism and Schizophrenia*, Brian Massumi, trans. Minneapolis: University of Minnesota Press.

————. (1991). *Qu'est-ce que la philosophie?* Paris: Éditions de Minuit.

————. (1994). *What Is Philosophy?*, Hugh Tomlinson and Graham Burchell, trans. New York: Columbia University Press.

————. (2004). *Anti-Oedipus*, R. Hurley, M. Seem, and H. R. Lane, trans. London: Continuum.

Deleuze, G., and Parnet, C. (1996). *Dialogues* (avec Claire Parnet). Paris: Flammarion; new edition, Collection Champs, 1996.

————. (2002). *Dialogues II*, Hugh Tomlinson and Barbara Habberjam, trans.; "The Actual and the Virtual," Eliot Ross Albert, trans. London: Athlone Press.

Derrida, J. (1967). *De la grammatologie*. Paris: Éditions de Minuit.

————. (1972). *Marges—de la philosophie*. Paris: Éditions de Minuit.

————. (1974). *Of Grammatology*, Gayatry Chakravorty Spivak, trans. Baltimore: Johns Hopkins University Press.

————. (1982). *Margins of Philosophy*, Alan Bass, trans. Chicago: University of Chicago Press.

————. (1987). *Psyché. Inventions de l'autre*. Paris: Éditions Galilée.

————. (1988). *Limited Inc.* Evanston, IL: Northwestern University Press.

————. (1990). *Limited Inc.* Paris: Éditions Galilée.

———— . (1992a). "Force of Law: The 'Mystical Foundation of Authority,'" in Drucilla Cornell et al., eds., *Deconstruction and the Possibility of Justice*, 3–67. London and New York: Routledge.

———— . (1992b). *Points de suspension*. Paris: Éditions Galilée.

———— . (1993). *Spectres de Marx*. Paris: Éditions Galilée.

———— . (1994a). *Force de loi*. Paris: Éditions Galilée.

———— . (1994b). *Specters of Marx*, P. Kamuf, trans. London and New York: Routledge.

———— . (1995). *Points: Interviews 1974–1994*, Peggy Kamuf, trans. Stanford, CA: Stanford University Press.

———— . (1996). *Résistances à la psychanalyse*. Paris: Éditions Galilée.

———— . (1997a). *Cosmopolites de tous les pays, encore un effort!* Paris: Éditions Galilée.

———— . (1997b). *De l'hospitalité: Anne Dufourmantelle invite Jacques Derrida à répondre*. Paris: Éditions Calmann-Lévy.

———— . (1998). *Resistances of Psychoanalysis*, Peggy Kamuf, Pascale-Ann Brault, and Michael Naas, trans. Stanford, CA: Stanford University Press.

———— . (1999). "Hospitality, Justice. and Responsibility: A Dialogue with Jacques Derrida," in R. Kearney and M. Dooley, eds. (1999), 65–83. London and New York: Routledge.

———— . (2000). *Of Hospitality: Anne Dufourmantelle Invites Jacques Derrida to Respond*, Rachel Bowlby, trans. Stanford, CA: Stanford University Press.

———— . (2001a). *Foi et savoir*, suivi de *Le siècle et le pardon*. Paris: Éditions du Seuil.

———— . (2001b). *On Cosmopolitanism and Forgiveness*, Mark Dooley and Michael Hughes, trans., with a preface by Simon Critchley and Richard Kearney. London and New York: Routledge.

———— . (2001c). "Affirmative Deconstruction," in Paul Patton and Terry Smith, eds., *Jacques Derrida: Deconstruction Engaged—The Sydney Seminars*. Sydney: Power Publications, 55–104.

———— . (2001d). "I'm Going to Have to Wander All Alone," in Pascale-Ann Brault and Michael Naas, trans. and eds., *The Work of Mourning*, 189–196. Chicago: University of Chicago Press.

———— . (2002a). *Negotiations: Interventions and Interviews 1971–2001*. Edited, translated, and with an introduction by Elizabeth Rottenberg. Stanford, CA: Stanford University Press.

———— . (2002b). *Without Alibi*. Edited, translated, and with an introduction by Peggy Kamuf. Stanford, CA: Stanford University Press.

———— . (2003). "Autoimmunity: Real and Symbolic Suicides," in G. Borradori, ed., *Philosophy in a Time of Terror*, 85–172. Chicago and London: University of Chicago Press.

———— . (2007a). *Psyche: Inventions of the Other, Volume I*, Peggy Kamuf and Elizabeth Rottenberg, eds. Stanford, CA: Stanford University Press.

————. (2007b). "The Transcendental 'Stupidity' ('*Bêtise*') of Man and the Becoming-Animal according to Gilles Deleuze," in G. Schwab, ed., 2007, 35–60.

Descombes, V. (1980). *Modern French Philosophy*, L. Scott-Fox and J. M. Harding, trans. Cambridge, UK, and New York: Cambridge University Press.

Dickens, C. (1989). *Our Mutual Friend*. Oxford, UK: Oxford University Press.

Dosse, F. (2007). *Gilles Deleuze et Félix Guattari: Biographie Croisée*. Paris: Éditions de la Découverte.

Eco, U. (1992). *Interpretation and overinterpretation*, with Richard Rorty, Jonathan Culler, and Christine Brooke-Rose; Stefan Collini, ed. Cambridge, UK: Cambridge University Press.

Engélibert, Jean-Paul. (2003). *Aux Avant-postes du progrès: essai sur l'oeuvre de J. M. Coetzee*. Limoges: Presses Universitaires de Limoges.

————, ed. (2007). *J. M.Coetzee et la littérature européenne: écrire contre la barbarie*. Rennes: Presses Universitaires de Rennes.

————. (2007a). "L'oeuvre dans l'histoire J. M. Coetzee et le classique," in Engélibert, ed. (2007), 11–24.

Farred, G. (2002). "Back to the Borderlines: Thinking Race *Disgrace*fully." *scrutiny2*, 7:1, 16–19.

Foucault, M. (1969). *L'Archéologie du savoir*. Paris: Éditions Gallimard.

————. (1972). *The Archaeology of Knowledge*, A. M. Sheridan, trans. London: Tavistock.

————. (1977). Preface to Deleuze and Guattari, *Anti-Oedipus: Capitalism and Schizophrenia*, Robert Hurley, Mark Seem, and Helen R. Lane, trans., xiii–xvi. New York: Viking Press. Reprinted London: Continuum, 2004.

————. (1984). *The Foucault Reader*, P. Rabinow, ed. New York: Pantheon Books.

————. (1997). *Essential Works of Foucault 1954–1984, Volume 1, Ethics*, Paul Rabinow, ed., Robert Hurley and others, trans. New York: The New Press.

————. (2000). *Essential Works of Foucault 1954–1984, Volume 3: Power*, James D. Faubion, ed., Robert Hurley et al., trans. New York: New Press.

————. (2007). *The Politics of Truth*, Sylvère Lotringer, ed. New York: Semiotext(e).

Gabaude, F. (2007). "*Ecce Animot: Coetzee, Kafka, Rilke et les animaux dénaturés*," in Engélibert, ed. (2007), 107–122.

Garo, I. (2007). "Deleuze, Marx and Revolution: What It Means to 'Remain Marxist,'" in J. Bidet and S. Kouvelakis, eds., *Critical Companion to Contemporary Marxism*, 605–624. Leiden and Boston, MA: Brill.

————. (2008). "Molecular Revolutions: The Paradox of Politics in the Work of Gilles Deleuze," in Buchanan and Thoburn, eds. (2008), 54–73.

Genosko, G. (2009). *Félix Guattari: A Critical Introduction*. London and New York: Pluto Press.

Geras, N. (1985). "The Controversy about Marx and Justice." *New Left Review*, 150, 47–85. Reprinted in A. Callinicos, ed., *Marxist Theory*. Oxford, UK: Oxford University Press, 1989.

Goodchild, P. (2000). "Spirit of Philosophy: Derrida and Deleuze." *Angelaki*, 5:2, 43–587.

Grosz, E. (1994). *Volatile Bodies: Towards a Corporeal Feminism*. Bloomington: Indiana University Press; Sydney, Australia: Allen and Unwin.

Hacking, I. (1995). *Rewriting the Soul, Multiple Personality and the Sciences of Memory*. Princeton, NJ: Princeton University Press.

Hallward, P. (2006). *Out of This World: Deleuze and the Philosophy of Creation*. London and New York: Verso.

Hamilton, G. (2010). "Becoming-Nomad: Territorialisation and Resistance in J. M. Coetzee's *Waiting for the Barbarians*," in Bignall and Patton, eds. (2010), 183–200.

Hardt, M. (1998a). "The Withering of Civil Society," in Eleanor Kaufman and Kevin Jon Heller, eds., *Deleuze & Guattari: New Mappings in Politics, Philosophy, and Culture*, 23–39. Minneapolis: University of Minnesota Press.

———. (1998b). "The Global Society of Control." *Discourse*, 20:3, 139–152.

Hardt, M., and Negri, A. (2000). *Empire*. Cambridge, MA: Harvard University Press.

Hardy, Thomas. (1998). *Jude the Obscure*. London: Penguin Classic.

Hayles, Katherine N. (2001) "Desiring Agency: Limiting Metaphors and Enabling Constraints in Dawkins and Deleuze/Guattari." *SubStance* 94/95, 144–159.

Holland, E. (2003a). "Representation and Misrepresentation in Postcolonial Literature and Theory." *Research in African Literatures*, 34:1, Spring, 159–172.

———. (2003b). "To The Editor." *Research in African Literatures*, 34:4, Winter, 187–190.

———. (2006). "The Utopian Dimension of Thought in Deleuze and Guattari," in A. Milner, M. Ryan, and R. Savage, eds., *Imagining The Future: Utopia and Dystopia*, 217–242. (*Arena* Journal New Series No. 25/26). Melbourne, Australia: Arena Publications Association.

Horrell, G. (2002). "J. M. Coetzee's *Disgrace*: One Settler, One Bullet and the 'New South Africa.'" *scrutiny2*, 7:1, 25–32.

International Journal for the Semiotics of Law. (2007). "Deleuze and the Semiotics of Law," 20:1, 1–106.

Kafka, Franz. (1992). "The Transformation," in *The Transformation and Other Stories* (1915), 76–126. M. Pasley, ed. and trans. London: Penguin.

Kant, I. (1996). *Practical Philosophy. Cambridge Edition of the Works of Immanuel Kant*, Mary J. Gregor, ed. and trans. Cambridge, UK: Cambridge University Press.

———. (2000). *Critique of the Power of Judgment. Cambridge Edition of the Works of Immanuel Kant*, Paul Guyer, ed.; Eric Matthews, trans. Cambridge, UK: Cambridge University Press.

Kaplan, C. (1996). *Questions of Travel: Postmodern Discourses of Displacement*. Durham, NC, and London: Duke University Press.

Kearney, R. (2003). "Terror, Philosophy and the Sublime: Some Philosophical Reflections on 11 September." *Philosophy and Social Criticism*, 29:1, 23–51.

Kearney, R., and Dooley, M., eds. (1999). *Questioning Ethics: Contemporary Debates in Philosophy*. London and New York: Routledge.

Korsgaard, C. M. (2003). "Realism and Constructivism in Twentieth-Century Moral Philosophy," in *Philosophy in America at the Turn of the Century*, APA Centennial Supplement to *The Journal of Philosophical Research*. Charlottesville, VA: The Philosophy Documentation Center. Available at: www.pdcnet.org /pdf/8Korsgaard.pdf

Kuiken, Kir. (2005). "Deleuze/Derrida: Towards an Almost Imperceptible Difference." *Research in Phenomenology*, 35: 1, 290–310.

Kulchyski, P., ed. (1984). *Unjust Relations: Aboriginal Rights in Canadian Courts*. Toronto, Ontario: Oxford University Press.

Kymlicka, W. (2002). *Contemporary Political Philosophy*. Oxford, UK: Oxford University Press.

Laclau, E., and Mouffe, C. (1985). *Hegemony and Socialist Strategy: Towards a Radical Democratic Politics*. London and New York: Verso.

Laden, A. S. (2003). "The House that Jack Built: Thirty Years of Reading Rawls." *Ethics*, 113, 367–390.

Lambert, G. (2000). "The Subject of Literature between Derrida and Deleuze: Law or Life?" *Angelaki*, 5:2, 177–190.

———. (2003). *"Une Grande politique*, or the New Philosophy of Right?" *Critical Horizons*, 4:2, 177–197.

———. (2006). *Who's Afraid of Deleuze and Guattari?* London: Continuum.

Lampert, J. (2002) "Dates and Destiny: Deleuze and Hegel." *Journal of the British Society for Phenomenology*, 33:2, 206–220.

———. (2006). *Deleuze and Guattari's Philosophy of History*. London and New York: Continuum.

Lawlor, Len. (2000). "A Nearly Total Affinity: The Deleuzian Virtual Image Versus the Derridean Trace." *Angelaki*, 5:2, 59–71.

———. (2003). *Thinking through French Philosophy: The Being of the Question*. Bloomington: Indiana University Press.

Lefebvre, A. (2005). "A New Image of Law: Deleuze and Jurisprudence." *Telos*, 130, 103–126.

———. (2006). "Habermas and Deleuze on Law and Adjudication." *Law and Critique*, 17:3, 389–414.

———. (2008). *The Image of Law: Deleuze, Bergson, Spinoza*. Stanford, CA: Stanford University Press.

Lefort, C. (1988). *Democracy and Political Theory*, David Macey, trans. Cambridge, UK: Polity Press.

Lohmann, J. (2002). "Derrida and the Question of the Creation of Concepts," delivered at "Derrida/Deleuze: Politics, Psychoanalysis, Territoriality," Critical Theory Institute, University of California at Irvine, April 12–13.

Lundy, C. (2009). "Deleuze's Untimely: Uses and Abuses in the Appropriation of Nietzsche," in Bell and Colebrook, eds. (2009), 188–205.

Mandle, J. (2000). *What's Left of Liberalism? An Interpretation and Defense of Justice as Fairness*. Lanham, MD: Lexington Books.

Marrati, P. (2001). "Against the Doxa: Politics of Immanence and Becoming-Minoritarian," in Patricia Pisters, ed., *Micropolitics of Media Culture: Reading the Rhizomes of Deleuze and Guattari*, 205–220. Amsterdam: Amsterdam University Press.

Martin, J-C. (1993). *Variations: La Philosophie de Gilles Deleuze*. Paris: Éditions Payot.

May, T. (2005). *Gilles Deleuze: An Introduction*. Cambridge, UK: Cambridge University Press.

McDonald, P. D. (2002). "Disgrace Effects." *Interventions*, 4:3, 321–330.

McClellan, S. (2008). *What Happened: Inside the Bush White House and Washington's Culture of Deception*. New York: Public Affairs.

Melville, H. (1994). *Moby Dick*. Harmondsworth, Middlesex, UK: Penguin Popular Classics.

Mengue, P. (2003). *Deleuze et la question de la démocratie*. Paris: L'Harmattan.

Miller, C. L. (1993). "The Postidentitarian Predicament in the Footnotes of *A Thousand Plateaus*: Nomadology, Anthropology, and Authority." *Diacritics*, 23:3, 6–35.

———. (1998). "Beyond Identity: The Postidentitarian Predicament in *A Thousand Plateaus*," in *Nationalists and Nomads: Essays on Francophone African Literature and Culture*, 171–244. Chicago and London: University of Chicago Press.

———. (2003). " 'We Shouldn't Judge Deleuze and Guattari': A Response to Eugene Holland." *Research in African Literatures*, 34:3, Fall, 129–141.

Moon, J. D. (2004). "The Current State of Political Theory: Pluralism and Reconciliation," in Stephen K. White and J. Donald Moon, eds., *What Is Political Theory?* 12–29. London: Sage.

Nail, T. (2008). "Expression, Immanence and Constructivism: 'Spinozism' and Gilles Deleuze." *Deleuze Studies* 2:2, 201–219.

Nancy, J-L. (2005). "Les différences parallèles. Deleuze et Derrida," in A. Bernold and R. Pinhas, eds., *Deleuze épars*, 7–30. Paris: Hermann Éditeurs.

Negri, A. (1995). "On Gilles Deleuze and Félix Guattari, *A Thousand Plateaus*," Charles T. Wolfe, trans. *Graduate Faculty Philosophy Journal*, 18:1, 93–109.

Nietzsche, F. (1983). "On the Uses and Disadvantages of History for Life," in *Untimely Meditations*, Reginald J. Hollingdale, trans. Cambridge, UK: Cambridge University Press, 59–123.

———. (1994). *On the Genealogy of Morality*, Keith Ansell-Pearson, ed.; Carol Diethe, trans. Cambridge, UK: Cambridge University Press.

———. (1997). *Daybreak: Thoughts on the Prejudices of Morality*, Maudemarie Clark and Brian Leiter, eds.; R. J. Hollingdale, trans. Cambridge, UK: Cambridge University Press.

————. (2001). *The Gay Science*, Bernard Williams, ed.; Josefine Nauckhoff, trans. Cambridge, UK: Cambridge University Press.

————. (2005). *Thus Spoke Zarathustra*, Graham Parkes, trans. Oxford, UK: Oxford University Press.

Patton, P. (2000). *Deleuze and the Political*. London and New York: Routledge.

————. (2001). "Reconciliation, Aboriginal Rights and Constitutional Paradox in Australia." *The Australian Feminist Law Journal*, 15, 25–40.

————. (2004). "Power and Right in Nietzsche and Foucault." *International Studies in Philosophy*, 36:3, 43–61.

————. (2007a). "Derrida, Politics and Democracy to Come." *Philosophy Compass*, 2. Available at: www.blackwell-compass.com/subject/philosophy /section_home?section=phco-continental

————. (2007b). "Derrida's Engagement with Political Philosophy," in Mark Bevir, Jill Hargis, and Sara Rushing, eds., *Histories of Postmodernism*, 149–169. New York and London: Routledge.

Patton, P., and Protevi, J., eds. (2003). *Between Deleuze and Derrida*. London and New York: Continuum.

Peffer, R. (1990). *Marxism, Morality and Social Justice*. Princeton, NJ: Princeton University Press.

————. (2001). "Rawlsian Theory, Contemporary Marxism and the Differ-ence Principle," in M. Evans, ed., *The Edinburgh Companion to Contemporary Liberalism*, 113–132. Edinburgh, UK: Edinburgh University Press.

Péguy, C. *Clio*. Paris: Éditions Gallimard, 2002.

Persky, S., ed. (1998). *The Supreme Court Decision on Aboriginal Title: Delga-muukw*. Vancouver and Toronto: Greystone Books.

Phillips, A. (2006). "Dealing with Difference: A Politics of Ideas or a Politics of Presence?" in R. E. Goodin and P. Pettit, eds., *Contemporary Political Phi-losophy*, second edition, 171–181. Oxford, UK, and Malden, MA: Blackwell. Originally published in *Constellations*, 1, 1994, 74–91.

Protevi, J. (2007). "Out of This World: Deleuze and the Philosophy of Creation." *Notre Dame Philosophy Reviews*, 2007.08.03. Available at: http://ndpr.nd.edu/

Rajchman, J. (2000). *The Deleuze Connections*. Cambridge, MA: MIT Press.

Rawls, J. (1971). *A Theory of Justice*. Cambridge, MA: Harvard University Press.

————. (1999a). *John Rawls: Collected Papers*, S. Freeman, ed. Cambridge, MA: Harvard University Press.

————. (1999b). *A Theory of Justice*, revised edition. Cambridge, MA: Harvard University Press.

————. (2001). *Justice as Fairness: A Restatement*. Cambridge, MA: Harvard University Press.

————. (2005). *Political Liberalism: Expanded Edition*. New York: Columbia University Press.

Razac, O. (2008). *Avec Foucault/Après Foucault: Disséquer la société de contrôle*. Paris: L'Harmattan.

Reynolds, H. (1996). *Aboriginal Sovereignty*. Sydney, Australia: Allen & Unwin.

Rorty, R. (1979). *Philosophy and the Mirror of Nature*. Princeton, NJ: Princeton University Press.

———. (1982). *Consequences of Pragmatism*. Minneapolis: University of Minnesota Press.

———. (1983). "Unsoundness in Perspective." *Times Literary Supplement*, June 17, 619–620.

———. (1989). *Contingency, Irony, and Solidarity*. Cambridge, UK: Cambridge University Press.

———. (1991a). *Essays on Heidegger and Others: Philosophical Papers Volume 2*. Cambridge, UK: Cambridge University Press.

———. (1991b). *Objectivity, Relativism, Truth: Philosophical Papers Volume 1*. Cambridge, UK: Cambridge University Press.

———. (1995). *Rorty and Pragmatism: The Philosopher Responds to His Critics*, H. J. Saatkamp Jr., ed. Nashville and London: Vanderbilt University Press.

———. (1998a). *Achieving Our Country: Leftist Thought in Twentieth Century America*. Cambridge, MA: Harvard University Press.

———. (1998b). *Truth and Progress: Philosophical Papers Volume 3*, Cambridge, UK: Cambridge University Press.

———. (2000). "Universality and Truth," in R. Brandom, ed., *Rorty and His Critics*, 1–30. Oxford, UK, and Malden, MA: Blackwell.

Rushdie, S. (2002). "Light on Coetzee," in *Step across This Line: Collected Nonfiction 1992–2002*, 297–298. New York: Random House.

Salanskis, J-M. (2005). *"La philosophie de Jacques Derrida et la spécificité de la déconstruction au sein des philosophies du linguistic turn,"* in Charles Ramond, ed., *Derrida: La déconstruction*, 13–51. Paris: Presses Universitaires de France.

Schwab, G., ed. (2007). *Derrida, Deleuze, Psychoanalysis*. New York: Columbia University Press.

Shapiro, I. (2003). *The State of Democratic Theory*. Princeton, NJ: Princeton University Press.

Sibertin-Blanc, G. (2003). "Les impensables de l'histoire: Pour une problématisation vitaliste, noétique et politique de l'anti-historicisme chez Gilles Deleuze." *Le Philosophoire*, 19, 119–154.

———. (in press). "Peuple et territoire: Deleuze lecteur de la *Revue d'Études Palestiniennes*." To appear in Catherine Mayaux, ed., *Écrivains et intellectuels français face au monde arabe*, Actes du Colloque de l'Université de Cergy-Pontoise, January 31–February 2. Available online at: www.europhilosophie .eu/recherche/IMG/pdf/Deleuze_et_Palestine.pdf

Smith, A. M. (1998). *Laclau and Mouffe: The Radical Democratic Imaginary*. London: Routledge.

Smith, Daniel W. (2003) "Deleuze and the Liberal Tradition: Normativity, Freedom and Judgment." *Economy and Society*, 32: 2, 312–317.

———. (2004). "The Inverse Side of the Structure: Žižek on Deleuze on Lacan." *Criticism*, 46:4, 635–650.

Smith, J. E. (1969). "Time, Times and the 'Right Time': *Chronos* and *Kairos*." *The Monist*, 53 (1), 1–13.

Stolze, T. (1998). "Deleuze and Althusser." *Rethinking Marxism*, 10: 3, 51–63.

Strelein, L. (2006). *Compromised Jurisprudence: Native Title Cases Since Mabo*. Canberra, Australia: Aboriginal Studies Press.

Surin, K. (2005). "The Socius and Life." Paper presented at *The Living Thought of Gilles Deleuze*, International Conference, Copenhagen, November 3–5.

———. (2006). "Control Society and State Theory," in A. Parr, ed., *The Deleuze Dictionary*, 54–57. New York: Columbia University Press, 2006.

———. (2007). "The Society of Control and the Managed Citizen." *Junctures*, 8, 11–25.

Sutter, L de. (2009). *Deleuze: La pratique du droit*. Paris: Éditions Michalon.

Thoburn, N. (2003). *Deleuze, Marx and Politics*. London: Routledge.

Tully, J. (1994). "Aboriginal Property and Western Theory: Recovering a Middle Ground." *Social Philosophy and Policy*, 11:2, 153–180.

———. (1995). *Strange Multiplicity: Constitutionalism in an Age of Diversity*. Cambridge, UK: Cambridge University Press.

———. (1998) "A Fair and Just Relationship." *Meanjin*, 57:1, 146–167.

Weizman, E. (2006). "Walking through Walls: Soldiers as Architects in the Palestinian–Israeli Conflict." *Radical Philosophy*, 136, March–April 2006, 8–22.

———. (2007). *Hollow Land: Israel's Architecture of Occupation*. London and New York: Verso.

Williams, J. (2008). *Gilles Deleuze's* Logic of Sense: *A Critical Introduction and Guide*. Edinburgh, UK: Edinburgh University Press.

———. (2009) "Ageing, Perpetual Perishing and the Event as Pure Novelty: Péguy, Whitehead and Deleuze on Time and History," in Bell and Colebrook, eds., 142–160.

Worms, F. (2009). *La philosophie en France au xxᵉ siècle. Moments*. Paris: Gallimard.

Žižek, S. (2004). *Organs without Bodies: Deleuze and Consequences*. New York and London: Routledge.

Zourabichvili, F. (2003). *Le vocabulaire de Deleuze*. Paris: Éditions ellipses.

———. (2004a). "Are Philosophical Concepts Metaphors? Deleuze and His Problematic of Literality." Paper delivered at the International Association for Philosophy and Literature, 28th Annual Conference. Syracuse, NY, May 23.

———. (2004b) *Deleuze. Une philosophie de l'événement*, séconde édition, *La Philosophie de Deleuze*, 5–116. Paris: Presses Universitaires de France.

Index

Cultural Memory | *in the Present*

Jacques Derrida, *Paper Machine*

Renaud Barbaras, *Desire and Distance: Introduction to a Phenomenology of Perception*

Jill Bennett, *Empathic Vision: Affect, Trauma, and Contemporary Art*

Ban Wang, *Illuminations from the Past: Trauma, Memory, and History in Modern China*

James Phillips, *Heidegger's Volk: Between National Socialism and Poetry*

Frank Ankersmit, *Sublime Historical Experience*

István Rév, *Retroactive Justice: Prehistory of Post-Communism*

Paola Marrati, *Genesis and Trace: Derrida Reading Husserl and Heidegger*

Krzysztof Ziarek, *The Force of Art*

Marie-José Mondzain, *Image, Icon, Economy: The Byzantine Origins of the Contemporary Imaginary*

Cecilia Sjöholm, *The Antigone Complex: Ethics and the Invention of Feminine Desire*

Jacques Derrida and Elisabeth Roudinesco, *For What Tomorrow . . . : A Dialogue*

Elisabeth Weber, *Questioning Judaism: Interviews by Elisabeth Weber*

Jacques Derrida and Catherine Malabou, *Counterpath: Traveling with Jacques Derrida*

Martin Seel, *Aesthetics of Appearing*

Nanette Salomon, *Shifting Priorities: Gender and Genre in Seventeenth-Century Dutch Painting*

Jacob Taubes, *The Political Theology of Paul*

Jean-Luc Marion, *The Crossing of the Visible*

Eric Michaud, *The Cult of Art in Nazi Germany*

Anne Freadman, *The Machinery of Talk: Charles Peirce and the Sign Hypothesis*

Stanley Cavell, *Emerson's Transcendental Etudes*

Stuart McLean, *The Event and Its Terrors: Ireland, Famine, Modernity*

Beate Rössler, ed., *Privacies: Philosophical Evaluations*

Bernard Faure, *Double Exposure: Cutting Across Buddhist and Western Discourses*

Alessia Ricciardi, *The Ends of Mourning: Psychoanalysis, Literature, Film*

Alain Badiou, *Saint Paul: The Foundation of Universalism*

Gil Anidjar, *The Jew, the Arab: A History of the Enemy*

Jonathan Culler and Kevin Lamb, eds., *Just Being Difficult? Academic Writing in the Public Arena*

Jean-Luc Nancy, *A Finite Thinking*, edited by Simon Sparks

Theodor W. Adorno, *Can One Live after Auschwitz? A Philosophical Reader*, edited by Rolf Tiedemann

Patricia Pisters, *The Matrix of Visual Culture: Working with Deleuze in Film Theory*

Andreas Huyssen, *Present Pasts: Urban Palimpsests and the Politics of Memory*

Talal Asad, *Formations of the Secular: Christianity, Islam, Modernity*

Dorothea von Mücke, *The Rise of the Fantastic Tale*

Marc Redfield, *The Politics of Aesthetics: Nationalism, Gender, Romanticism*
Emmanuel Levinas, *On Escape*
Dan Zahavi, *Husserl's Phenomenology*
Rodolphe Gasché, *The Idea of Form: Rethinking Kant's Aesthetics*
Michael Naas, *Taking on the Tradition: Jacques Derrida and the Legacies of Deconstruction*
Herlinde Pauer-Studer, ed., *Constructions of Practical Reason: Interviews on Moral and Political Philosophy*
Jean-Luc Marion, *Being Given That: Toward a Phenomenology of Givenness*
Theodor W. Adorno and Max Horkheimer, *Dialectic of Enlightenment*
Ian Balfour, *The Rhetoric of Romantic Prophecy*
Martin Stokhof, *World and Life as One: Ethics and Ontology in Wittgenstein's Early Thought*
Gianni Vattimo, *Nietzsche: An Introduction*
Jacques Derrida, *Negotiations: Interventions and Interviews, 1971-1998*, ed. Elizabeth Rottenberg
Brett Levinson, *The Ends of Literature: The Latin American "Boom" in the Neoliberal Marketplace*
Timothy J. Reiss, *Against Autonomy: Cultural Instruments, Mutualities, and the Fictive Imagination*
Hent de Vries and Samuel Weber, eds., *Religion and Media*
Niklas Luhmann, *Theories of Distinction: Re-Describing the Descriptions of Modernity*, ed. and introd. William Rasch
Johannes Fabian, *Anthropology with an Attitude: Critical Essays*
Michel Henry, *I Am the Truth: Toward a Philosophy of Christianity*
Gil Anidjar, *"Our Place in Al-Andalus": Kabbalah, Philosophy, Literature in Arab-Jewish Letters*
Hélène Cixous and Jacques Derrida, *Veils*
F. R. Ankersmit, *Historical Representation*
F. R. Ankersmit, *Political Representation*
Elissa Marder, *Dead Time: Temporal Disorders in the Wake of Modernity (Baudelaire and Flaubert)*
Reinhart Koselleck, *The Practice of Conceptual History: Timing History, Spacing Concepts*
Niklas Luhmann, *The Reality of the Mass Media*
Hubert Damisch, *A Theory of /Cloud/: Toward a History of Painting*
Jean-Luc Nancy, *The Speculative Remark: (One of Hegel's bon mots)*
Jean-François Lyotard, *Soundproof Room: Malraux's Anti-Aesthetics*
Jan Patočka, *Plato and Europe*
Hubert Damisch, *Skyline: The Narcissistic City*
Isabel Hoving, *In Praise of New Travelers: Reading Caribbean Migrant Women Writers*
Richard Rand, ed., *Futures: Of Jacques Derrida*